Reading STREET

Grade 6

Scott Foresman
ELL Teaching Guide

Editorial Offices: Glenview, Illinois • Parsippany, New Jersey • New York, New York
Sales Offices: Needham, Massachusetts • Duluth, Georgia • Glenview, Illinois
Coppell, Texas • Sacramento, California • Mesa, Arizona

ISBN: 0-328-14604-8

1 2 3 4 5 6 7 8 9 10 V031 14 13 12 11 10 09 08 07 06 05

Contents

Unit 4:   Explorers, Pioneers, and Discoverers

Unit 5:   Resources

Unit 6:   Exploring Cultures

The ELL Teaching Guide provides weekly lesson materials to support English language learners with scaffolded comprehension instruction and vocabulary development. It builds on the Student Edition and on literacy instruction in the Teacher's Edition. Support for English language learners and teachers is based on the Three Pillars, developed by Dr. Jim Cummins:

Activate Prior Knowledge/Build Background

Access Content

Extend Language

Scott Foresman Reading Street provides these resources:

- **Student Edition** that builds every student's reading and language skills
- **Decodable Readers** for practicing emergent literacy skills (grades K–3)
- **Leveled Readers** for differentiated instruction
- **Teacher's Edition** with ELL instructional strategies built into the lesson plans
- **ELL Readers** that develop English language learners' vocabulary and comprehension skills
- **ELL Posters** with high-quality illustrations and five days of activities supporting key vocabulary and concepts
- **Ten Important Sentences** to focus on comprehension while expanding English
- **ELL and Transition Handbook** that supports teachers' professional development and students' transition to advanced levels of English proficiency
- **ELL Teaching Guide** see below

E L L Teaching Guide Features

"Week at a Glance" Lesson Planners offer a quick reference to the ELL support materials for each lesson of the year.

"Picture It!" Comprehension Lessons provide teaching strategies for each comprehension skill. A reproducible "Picture It!" student practice page helps students learn the key comprehension skill through illustrations, graphic organizers, sheltered text, and ELL-friendly activities.

Vocabulary Activities and Word Cards stimulate language production and reinforce target vocabulary. Small-group and partner activities use reproducible Word Cards to practice listening, speaking, reading, and writing. Home-language activities allow students to connect their prior knowledge to key vocabulary and concepts in English.

Multilingual Summaries of each main reading selection provide a brief, accessible summary in English and translations of the summary in the next most common five languages among the U.S. school population: Spanish, Chinese, Vietnamese, Korean, and Hmong. Students and parents can use the summaries to prepare for reading, build comprehension, support retellings, and strengthen school-home connections.

ELL Reader Lessons and Study Guides support every ELL Reader with scaffolded instruction to help students understand and respond to literature. The reproducible Study Guides support students' comprehension and provide writing and take-home activities for learners at various English proficiency levels.

Multilingual Lesson Vocabulary provides translations of the target vocabulary in Spanish, Chinese, Vietnamese, Korean, and Hmong.

Old Yeller   Student Edition pages 22–35

Week at a Glance	Customize instruction every day for your English Language Learners.				
	Day 17	**Day 2**	**Day 3**	**Day 4**	**Day 5**
Teacher's Edition	Use the ELL Notes that appear throughout each day of the lesson to support instruction and reading.				
ELL Poster 1	• Assess Prior Knowledge • Develop Concepts and Vocabulary	• Preteach Tested Vocabulary	• Public Service Announcement	• Helpful Pets	• Monitor Progress
ELL Teaching Guide	• Picture It! Lesson, pp. 1–2 • Multilingual Summaries, pp. 5–7	• ELL Reader Lesson, pp. 212–213	• Vocabulary Activities and Word Cards, pp. 3–4 • Multilingual Summaries, pp. 5–7		
ELL Readers		• Teach *Ranches of the American West*	• Reread *Ranches of the American West* and other texts to build fluency		
ELL and Transition Handbook	Use the following as needed to support this week's instruction and to conduct alternative assessments: • Phonics Transition Lessons • Grammar Transition Lessons • Assessment				

Picture It! Comprehension Lesson
Setting

Use this lesson to supplement or replace the skill lesson on pages 18–19 of the Teacher's Edition.

Teach

Distribute copies of the Picture It! blackline master on page 2.
- Have students name and describe the animals and scenery in the picture. Then read the paragraph aloud.
- Ask: *What kind of setting does this picture show?* (the country)
- Share the Skill Points (at right) with students.
- Ask students whether they think the boy in the picture is happy living in the country.

Practice

Read aloud the directions on page 2. Have students fill in the graphic organizer. Have students keep their organizers for later reteaching.

Answers for page 2: *Setting:* The country. *Effect on Characters:* Possible response: The boy is happy and comfortable in the country. He likes doing things outdoors.

> ## Skill Points
> ✓ The **setting** is the time and place in which a story occurs. Sometimes the author tells you the setting. Sometimes you must determine the setting using clues in the story.
>
> ✓ The setting can determine what happens in a story.
>
> ✓ It can also affect how the characters feel and what they do.

Name _____

Look at the picture. **Read** the paragraph.

- What kind of setting do you see in the picture? **Write** the word in the oval labeled *Setting*.
- How does the setting affect what the boy does? **Write** your answer in the oval labeled *Effect on Characters*.

Life in the Country

This boy lives in the country. He likes being outdoors. He plays with small animals, such as frogs and lizards. He fishes in the stream. He hikes in the mountains. Sometimes he and his friends sleep outdoors under the stars.

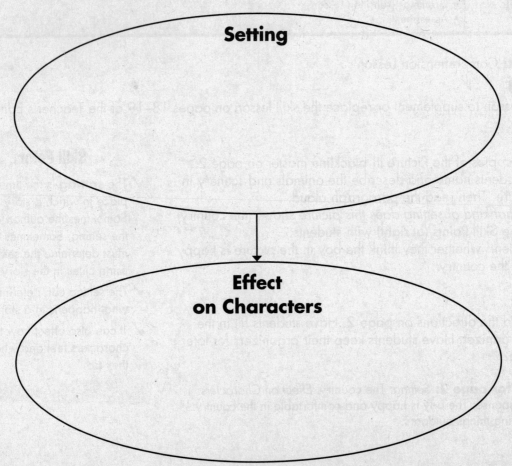

Setting

Effect on Characters

Vocabulary Activities and Word Cards

Copy the Word Cards on page 4 as needed for the following activities.
Use the blank cards for additional words that you want to teach.
Also see suggestions for teaching vocabulary in the ELL and Transition Handbook.

Fill in the Blanks	Can You Guess?	Home Language Clues
• Give each student a complete set of Word Cards. Have students place the cards face up on their desks or tables. • Choose one vocabulary word and think of a context in which it can be used. Describe the context, omitting the word. For example: *The children are playing a _____ game in the backyard. They are running, yelling, and laughing together.* • Have students examine their Word Cards and choose the word that best fits the context. • Repeat the context clue several times as students search for the correct word.	• Place one set of Word Cards face down in a pile. • Have one student choose a card and give verbal, visual, or oral clues that will help the rest of the group guess the word. • Repeat the process until all students have had a chance to provide clues.	• Pair students who have writing proficiency in the same home language, and give each student a set of Word Cards. • Have students work together to write translations of the vocabulary words in their home language on the back of each card. (See the Multilingual Lesson Vocabulary beginning on page 272 for suggested translations.) • Have partners lay out the cards with the home language sides facing up. • Have each student choose a card, read the home language translation, and then say the vocabulary word in English.

lunging

nub

romping

rowdy

slung

speckled

Multilingual Summaries

Old Yeller

Little Arliss is Travis's little brother. Little Arliss likes to bring animals home. His pockets are always full of bugs or snakes. The family adopts a stray yellow dog named Old Yeller. Little Arliss begins bringing home bigger animals that Old Yeller has caught.

Old Yeller catches a big catfish in the river. Arliss claims that he caught it himself. Travis knows that Arliss likes to tell big stories.

One evening Travis is fixing the fence. He hears Little Arliss scream. Travis knows Arliss is in trouble. Travis runs towards the scream. Travis finds Arliss. He is holding onto a bear cub. The mother bear comes after Arliss. She wants her cub back. Arliss does not let go of the cub. Then Old Yeller jumps on the mother bear. He saves Arliss. The family is grateful.

Old Yeller

El pequeño Arliss es el hermano menor de Travis. Al pequeño Arliss le gusta llevar animales a la casa. Sus bolsillos siempre están llenos de insectos o serpientes. La familia adopta un perro callejero y amarillo al que llaman Old Yeller. El pequeño Arliss comienza a traer a la casa animales más grandes de los que Old Yeller ha cazado.

Un día Old Yeller agarra un bagre grande en el río. Arliss afirma que él lo cazó. Travis sabe que a Arliss le gusta agrandar las historias.

Una tarde, Travis está arreglando la cerca. Escucha gritar al pequeño Arliss. Travis se da cuenta que Arliss tiene un problema. Travis sale corriendo hacia donde había escuchado el grito. Travis encuentra a Arliss. Él está cargando un cachorro de oso. La madre osa se está acercando hacia Arliss. Ella quiere recuperar a su cachorro. Arliss no deja ir al cachorro. Entonces Old Yeller salta sobre la madre osa. Él salva a Arliss. La familia está agradecida.

Multilingual Summaries

老黃狗

小阿里斯是崔維斯的弟弟，他喜歡把外面的動物帶回家，口袋裡總是裝滿了小蟲或蛇。這家人收留了一隻流浪的黃狗，他們幫狗狗取了一個名字叫「老黃狗」。因為老黃狗會捉動物，所以小阿里斯帶回家的動物也比以前要來得大。

有一次，老黃狗從河裡捉到一隻大鯰魚，阿里斯卻跟大家說那是他捉的，崔維斯不相信，因為他知道阿里斯喜歡吹牛。

有一天傍晚，崔維斯在修理籬笆的時候，突然聽見小阿里斯的尖叫聲，崔維斯知道阿里斯有麻煩了，他趕緊往傳出尖叫聲的方向跑過去，他看到阿里斯了，他手上正抱著一隻熊寶寶，母熊在後面追著他們，想把寶寶要回來，可是阿里斯卻不肯放開熊寶寶。老黃狗為了救阿里斯竟然跳到母熊背上，結果救了小主人一命，崔維斯一家人都很感激老黃狗。

Chú Chó Old Yeller

Bé Arliss là đứa em trai của Travis. Arliss thích mang những con thú về nhà. Túi áo của bé lúc nào cũng đầy côn trùng hoặc rắn. Gia đình nuôi một con chó hoang màu vàng tên Old Yeller. Bé Arliss bắt đầu mang về nhà những con thú lớn hơn mà Old Yeller bắt được.

Old Yeller bắt được một con cá trê dưới sông. Arliss nói là bé tự mình bắt được. Travis biết là Arliss thích đặt chuyện.

Một buổi tối nọ Travis đang sửa hàng rào. Cậu nghe Bé Arliss thét lên. Travis biết là Arliss đang gặp nạn. Travis chạy về hướng có tiếng thét. Travis tìm gặp Arliss. Bé đang ôm giữ một con gấu con. Gấu mẹ tấn công Arliss. Gấu mẹ muốn lấy lại con của mình. Arliss không muốn thả gấu con. Rồi chú chó Old Yeller nhảy chồm lên gấu mẹ. Nó cứu Arliss. Gia đình mang ơn chú chó.

Multilingual Summaries

Korean

올드 옐러

어린 알리스는 트래비스의 남동생이다. 동물들을 집에 데려오는 걸 좋아하는 알리스의 주머니에는 항상 벌레나 뱀이 가득 들어 있다. 가족은 올드 옐러라는 길 잃은 노란색 개를 데려온다. 알리스는 올드 옐러가 잡은 더 큰 동물들을 집에 데려오기 시작한다.

올드 옐러가 강에서 큰 메기를 잡았다. 알리스는 자기가 스스로 잡은 것이라고 주장하지만 트래비스는 알고 있다. 알리스가 부풀려 얘기하는 것을 좋아하는 것을...

어느 날 저녁 트래비스가 울타리를 고치고 있는데 알리스의 비명소리가 들려온다. 알리스가 곤경에 처했음을 알고 트래비스는 비명소리가 나는 쪽으로 달려간다. 트래비스는 새끼곰을 데리고 있는 알리스를 찾아낸다. 그리고 엄마곰이 새끼곰을 찾으러 알리스를 따라오고 있지만 알리스는 새끼곰을 놔주지 않는다. 그러자 올드 옐러가 엄마곰 위에 몸을 날려 알리스를 구한다. 가족은 올드 옐러에게 고마워한다.

Hmong

Old Yeller

Arliss Me Me yog Travis tus nus. Arliss Me Me nyiam nqa tsiaj txhu los tsev. Nws ris hnab yeej meem muaj kab muaj nab puv npo. Nws tsev neeg nrhiav tau ib tug aub qus hu ua Old Yeller. Arliss Me Me pib nqa tsiaj txhu loj dua los tsev uas Old Yeller tau ntes.

Old Yeller ntes ib tug ntses miv (catfish) hauv tus dej. Arliss hais tias nws nuv ntses ntawd tab sis Travis paub tias Arliss nyiam tso dag xwb.

Muaj ib hmo Travis xov laj kab. Nws hnov Arliss Me Me quaj ho nws thiaj paub Arliss muaj teeb meem. Travis khiav mus rau tom lub suab quaj ntawd. Travis nrhiav tau Arliss. Nws khaws ib tug me nyuam dais. Tus niam dais khiav lawv qab Arliss vim nws xav rov qab tau nws tus me nyuam dais. Arliss tsis tso tus me nyuam dais ntawd tseg. Ua ciav, Old Yeller dhia mus rau saum tus niam dais. Nws pab cawm Arliss ces nws tsev neeg ris txiaj heev.

Mother Fletcher's Gift Student Edition pages 46–61

<div>**Week at a Glance**</div>	**Customize instruction every day for your English Language Learners.**				
	Day 1	**Day 2**	**Day 3**	**Day 4**	**Day 5**
Teacher's Edition	Use the ELL Notes that appear throughout each day of the lesson to support instruction and reading.				
ELL Poster 2	• Assess Prior Knowledge • Develop Concepts and Vocabulary	• Preteach Tested Vocabulary	• Review Character	• Defining Community	• Monitor Progress
ELL Teaching Guide	• Picture It! Lesson, pp. 8–9 • Multilingual Summaries, pp. 12–14	• ELL Reader Lesson, pp. 214–215	• Vocabulary Activities and Word Cards, pp. 10–11 • Multilingual Summaries, pp. 12–14		
ELL Readers	• Reread *Ranches of the American West*	• Teach *Birds of a Feather*	• Reread *Birds of a Feather* and other texts to build fluency		
ELL and Transition Handbook	Use the following as needed to support this week's instruction and to conduct alternative assessments: • Phonics Transition Lessons • Grammar Transition Lessons • Assessment				

Picture It! Comprehension Lesson
Character

Use this lesson to supplement or replace the skill lesson on pages 42–43 of the Teacher's Edition.

Teach

Distribute copies of the Picture It! blackline master on page 9.
• Have students describe the picture. Then read the paragraph aloud.
• Ask: *What kind of person do you think Mrs. Fletcher is?* Have students tell what Mrs. Fletcher does that shows what kind of person she is.
• Have students tell the things that other characters do that show what kind of person Mrs. Fletcher is.
• Share the Skill Points (at right) with students.

Practice

Read aloud the directions on page 9. Have students fill in the graphic organizer. Have them keep their organizers for later reteaching.

Answers for page 9: *Description of Character:* Mrs. Fletcher is a kind and gentle woman. *Actions of Character:* She likes to cook meals for people. She makes special gifts for them. *Actions of Other Characters:* When Mrs. Fletcher gets sick, her neighbors help to take care of her.

Skill Points

✓ **Characters** are the people or animals in a story.

✓ You can understand the characters by thinking about their words and actions. You can also understand characters by thinking about the way other people speak about them and act toward them.

8 *Mother Fletcher's Gift* Unit 1, Week 2

© Scott Foresman 6

Look at the picture. **Read** the paragraph.

- Which sentence tells you what kind of person Mrs. Fletcher is? **Write** the sentence in the area labeled *Description of Character*.

- What actions by Mrs. Fletcher show what kind of person she is? **Write** the sentences in the area labeled *Actions of Character*.

- What action by other characters shows what kind of person Mrs. Fletcher is? **Write** the sentence in the area labeled *Actions of Other Characters*.

Making Everyone Happy

Mrs. Fletcher is a kind and gentle woman. She likes to cook meals for people. She makes special gifts for them. When Mrs. Fletcher is sick, her neighbors help to take care of her.

Description of Character

Actions of Character

Actions of Other Characters

Vocabulary Activities and Word Cards

Copy the Word Cards on page 11 as needed for the following activities.
Use the blank cards for additional words that you want to teach.
Also see suggestions for teaching vocabulary in the ELL and Transition Handbook.

Secret Word	Fishing Game	Poster Game
• Divide students into pairs, and give each pair of students a complete set of Word Cards. • Have each pair of students place the Word Cards face up on a desk or table so that both students can see them. • Have one student choose one of the words and give verbal and visual clues that will help the other student guess the word. Have the student pause after each clue so that his or her partner can guess the word. • Have students take turns giving clues and guessing words.	• Make one or more sets of Word Cards. Attach a metal paper clip to each card, and put the cards in a bucket. Tie a string to a short stick, and fasten a magnet to the loose end of the string. • Students take turns "fishing" for words. When they "catch" a word, ask them to read it and use it correctly in a sentence. If they do so, they keep their "catch." • Students take turns playing until all have had a turn, or until there are no more "fish" left.	• Reproduce one set of Word Cards for students to use in a poster game. • Have students take turns choosing a Word Card without letting others see it. • Ask one student to point to a scene or detail on the ELL Poster, and then give clues about the word without saying it until other students guess the word. • Repeat the process until all students have participated in the activity.

© Scott Foresman 6

apparently

fixtures

flimsy

incident

subscribe

survive

Multilingual Summaries

Mother Fletcher's Gift

Officer O'Brien works in Harlem. That is where he first hears about old Mother Fletcher. Everyone there knows who she is. O'Brien helps Mother Fletcher. She makes him a sweater to say "thank you."

O'Brien gets to know Mother Fletcher. He sees her in the neighborhood. He talks to her. She invites him to Christmas dinner. O'Brien does not want to go. He thinks Mother Fletcher's neighborhood might be dangerous. He argues with his wife Kathy. She wants to go. His daughter Meaghan wants to go.

On Christmas morning, Kathy and Meaghan put on their coats. They tell O'Brien that they are going to Mother Fletcher's. He is worried, but he goes with them. Mother Fletcher is happy to have visitors. Everyone has a nice dinner.

Spanish

El regalo de Mamá Fletcher

El teniente O'Brien trabaja en Harlem. Allí es donde escuchó hablar por primera vez de Mamá Fletcher. Todos por ahí saben quién es ella. O'Brien ayuda a Mamá Fletcher. Ella le teje un suéter para darle las gracias.

O'Brien tiene la oportunidad de conocer más a Mamá Fletcher. Él la ve en el barrio. Habla con ella. Ella lo invita a la cena de Navidad. O'Brien no quiere ir. Piensa que el barrio de Mamá Fletcher puede ser peligroso. Él discute con su esposa Kathy. Ella quiere ir. Su hija Meaghan también quiere ir.

En la mañana de Navidad, Kathy y Meaghan se ponen sus abrigos. Ellas le dicen a O'Brien que van a casa de Mamá Fletcher. Él está preocupado pero va con ellas. Mamá Fletcher está feliz de tener invitados. Todos tienen una comida agradable.

Multilingual Summaries

弗勒契修女的禮物

　　歐布萊恩警官在哈萊姆工作，他在那裡第一次聽到弗勒契修女的名字。那裡的人都認識弗勒契修女。有一次，歐布萊恩幫了弗勒契修女一個忙，修女幫他做了一件毛衣跟他說「謝謝」。

　　那次以後，歐布萊恩便開始認識弗勒契修女這個人。有一回，歐布萊恩在修道院附近遇到弗勒契修女，他上前跟她打招呼，修女邀請他一起吃耶誕節晚餐。歐布萊恩不想去，因為他覺得修道院附近可能會有危險。為了這件事，歐布萊恩跟他太太吵了一架，因為他太太凱西想跟弗勒契修女吃耶誕節晚餐，他女兒米根也想去。

　　耶誕節早晨，凱西和米根穿上外套跟歐布萊恩說她們要去弗勒契修女那裡。歐布萊恩擔心她們有危險，所以也跟著去了。弗勒契修女看到他們一家人都來了覺得非常高興，那一頓耶誕節晚餐大家都吃得很開心。

Món Qùa Của Mẹ Fletcher

　　Viên cảnh sát O'Brien làm việc ở Harlem. Cũng ở nơi đó mà lần đầu tiên ông nghe về Bà Mẹ Già Fletcher. Mọi người ở đó ai cũng biết bà. O'Brien giúp Mẹ Fletcher. Mẹ đan cho ông chiếc áo ấm để tỏ lòng "cám ơn".

　　O'Brien dần dần quen biết với Mẹ Fletcher. Ông ta gặp mẹ trong khu phố. Ông trò chuyện với mẹ. Mẹ mời ông đến ăn tối mừng Giáng Sinh. O'Brien không muốn đi. Ông nghĩ là khu phố của Mẹ Fletcher có thể nguy hiểm. Ông cãi vã với vợ của mình là Kathy vì bà ấy muốn đi. Con gái của ông là Meaghan muốn đi.

　　Sáng Lễ Giáng Sinh, Kathy và Meaghan mặc áo khoác vào. Họ nói với O'Brien là họ đi đến nhà của Mẹ Fletcher. Ông ấy lo lắng, nhưng ông cũng đi với họ. Mẹ Fletcher vui mừng có khách đến. Mọi người có một bữa ăn tối vui vẻ.

Multilingual Summaries

플레처 아주머니의 선물

오브라이언 경관은 할렘에서 일한다. 그는 이곳에서 플레처 아주머니에 대한 얘기를 처음 듣는데 이곳의 모든 사람들이 그 아주머니를 알고 있었다. 오브라이언이 플레처 아주머니를 도와주자 아주머니는 스웨터를 만들어주며 고맙다고 말한다.

오브라이언이 플레처 아주머니에 대해 알게 된다. 그는 동네에서 아주머니를 보고 말을 건다. 아주머니는 그를 크리스마스 저녁식사에 초대하지만 오브라이언은 가고 싶지 않아 한다. 아주머니가 사는 동네가 위험할 지도 모른다는 생각 때문이다. 그는 아주머니의 집에 가고 싶어하는 아내 캐시와 말다툼을 한다. 딸 메건도 가고 싶어한다.

크리스마스 아침에 캐시와 메건은 코트를 입고 오브라이언에게 플레처 아주머니의 집에 간다고 말한다. 그는 고민하다가 이들과 함께 간다. 플레처 아주머니는 손님들을 맞아 행복해하고 모두 다 즐겁게 저녁식사를 한다.

Niam Fletcher Khoom Plig

Tub ceev xwm O'Brien ua hauj lwm nyob Harlem. Nyob ntawd nws xub thawj hnov txog Niam Fletcher laus. Sawv daws nyob ntawd paub nws tas. O'Brien pab Niam Fletcher. Nws thiaj li xaws ib lub tsho ntev pub rau nws.

O'Brien nrog Niam Fletcher pib ua phooj ua ywg. Nws pom Niam Fletcher nyob hauv zej zos lawv thiaj sib tham ces Niam Fletcher caw nws los noj ib rooj mov Christmas. O'Brien tsis xav mus vim tias nws xav Niam Fletcher lub zej zos tsis ruaj ntseg li. Nws nrog nws tus poj niam Kathy sib cav sib cem vim Kathy thiab nws tus ntxhais Meaghan xav mus.

Sawv ntxov, hnub ua koob tsheej Christmas, Kathy thiab Meaghan lawv hnav tsho ntev tiv no. Lawv hais rau O'Brien tias lawv yuav mus xyuas Niam Fletcher. Nws nyuaj siab, tab sis nws nrog nkawd mus thiab. Niam Fletcher zoo siab lawv tuaj ces sawv daws noj hmo nyob kaj siab lug.

Viva New Jersey

Week at a Glance	Customize instruction every day for your English Language Learners.				
	Day 1	**Day 2**	**Day 3**	**Day 4**	**Day 5**
Teacher's Edition	Use the ELL Notes that appear throughout each day of the lesson to support instruction and reading.				
ELL Poster 3	• Assess Prior Knowledge • Develop Concepts and Vocabulary	• Preteach Tested Vocabulary	• Review Compare and Contrast	• Talk Show	• Monitor Progress
ELL Teaching Guide	• Picture It! Lesson, pp. 15–16 • Multilingual Summaries, pp. 19–21	• ELL Reader Lesson, pp. 216–217	• Vocabulary Activities and Word Cards, pp. 17–18 • Multilingual Summaries, pp. 19–21		
ELL Readers	• Reread *Birds of a Feather*	• Teach *American Immigrants*	• Reread *American Immigrants* and other texts to build fluency		
ELL and Transition Handbook	Use the following as needed to support this week's instruction and to conduct alternative assessments: • Phonics Transition Lessons • Grammar Transition Lessons • Assessment				

Picture It! Comprehension Lesson
Compare and Contrast

Use this lesson to supplement or replace the skill lesson on pages 66–67 of the Teacher's Edition.

Teach

Distribute copies of the Picture It! blackline master on page 16.
- Have students identify ways in which Alicia's life in Mexico was different from her life in America.
- Ask: *In what ways is Alicia's life the same in Mexico and America?*
- Share the Skill Points (at right) with students.
- Ask students to compare and contrast Alicia's life in Mexico with her life in America.

Skill Points

✓ **Comparing** is telling how things are alike.

✓ **Contrasting** is telling how things are different.

Practice

Read aloud the directions on page 16. Have students fill in the graphic organizer. Have them keep their organizers for later reteaching.

Answers for page 16: *Mexico:* sees relatives, shares meals with family, never eats in restaurants; *America:* eats in restaurants, speaks English; *Both:* plays with friends, goes to school

Look at the picture. **Read** the paragraph.

• What things did Alicia do in Mexico that she doesn't do in America?
  Write them in the circle labeled *Mexico*.

• What things does Alicia do in America that she didn't do in Mexico?
  Write them in the circle labeled *America*.

• What are some things that Alicia does in America and also did in Mexico?
  Write them in the middle section.

Living in America

In Mexico, Alicia saw her aunts and uncles every week. Her whole family ate big meals together. They never ate in restaurants. In America, Alicia misses her relatives, but she likes eating in restaurants. She also likes speaking English. In Mexico, Alicia liked playing with friends and going to school. In America, she likes playing and going to school, too.

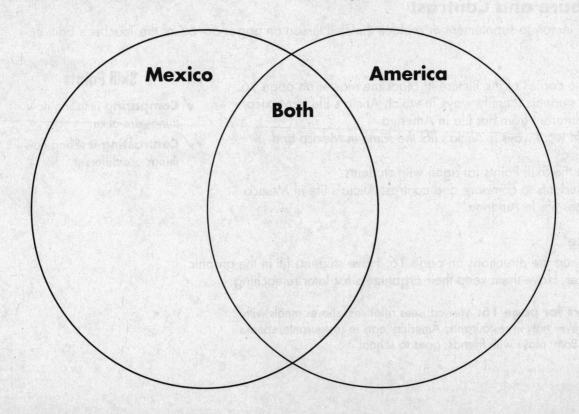

Vocabulary Activities and Word Cards

Copy the Word Cards on page 18 as needed for the following activities.
Use the blank card for an additional word that you want to teach.
Also see suggestions for teaching vocabulary in the ELL and Transition Handbook.

Charades	Clue Game	Newcomer's Story
• Reproduce two sets of Word Cards. Place one set face up so that all students can see them. • Divide students into pairs or small groups. Give each group one Word Card. • Have each group discuss how to act out its vocabulary word. • Have the groups take turns acting out scenes while the others try to guess the words, using the displayed set of Word Cards as clues.	• Reproduce one set of Word Cards. Write the definition of each vocabulary word on the back of its card. • Have one student read the definition and ask the others to try to guess the word. • Once the students correctly identify the word, have several students create sentences using the word.	• Form small groups of students, and give each group a set of Word Cards. • Tell groups to use at least five of the Word Cards in a story about a character who has just moved to a new community. • Give each group a sheet of chart paper. Tell them to write the story on the paper, taping the Word Cards at the appropriate places. • When they are finished, invite groups to read their stories aloud to the class.

corridors

destination

groping

menacing

mongrel

persisted

pleas

Multilingual Summaries

Viva New Jersey

Lucinda's family moves from Cuba to New Jersey. The family lives in an apartment building. Lucinda is lonely and misses Cuba. On her way to school, she passes a dog that is tied to a tree. The dog is dirty.

Lucinda unties the dog and takes him home. She gives him food and a bath. She finds a paper in the dog's collar. It says the dog's name is Chauncey. She hides the dog in the basement. The building's electric switches are in the basement.

The lights in the building go out. Lucinda thinks Chauncey hit an electric switch. Lucinda runs to find him. She finds a girl from school that she knows. They look for the dog together. But Lucinda cannot find Chauncey. She goes home. The lights go out again. This time Lucinda finds the dog. She takes him to her new friend's house.

Viva Nueva Jersey

La familia de Lucinda salió de Cuba y se fue a vivir en Nueva Jersey. La familia vive en un edificio de apartamentos. Lucinda está sola y extraña Cuba. En el camino a la escuela, ella ve un perro que está atado a un árbol. El perro está sucio.

Lucinda desata al perro y lo lleva a la casa. Ella le da comida y lo baña. En el collar del perro encuentra un papel que dice que su nombre es Chauncey. Ella esconde al perro en el sótano. Los interruptores eléctricos están en el sótano.

Las luces del edificio se apagan. Lucinda piensa que Chauncey le pegó a un interruptor eléctrico. Lucinda corre para buscarlo. Ella encuentra a una niña de la escuela que ella conoce. Las dos van a buscar al perro. Pero Lucinda no puede encontrar a Chauncey. Ella regresa a la casa. Las luces se apagan otra vez. Esta vez, Lucinda encuentra al perro. Ella lo lleva a casa de su nueva amiga.

Multilingual Summaries

紐澤西萬歲

　　露辛達和家人從古巴搬到紐澤西，住在一棟公寓裡。露辛達覺得很孤獨，很想念古巴的一切。有一天在上學途中，她看到一隻狗被綁在樹下，狗狗身上很髒。

　　露辛達把狗狗的繩子解開，帶牠回家，給牠東西吃，還幫牠洗澡。露辛達在狗狗的項圈裡發現一張小字條，上面寫著，這隻狗狗的名字叫昌西。露辛達把昌西藏在地下室，公寓的電源開關也在地下室裡。

　　有一天，公寓裡的電燈突然熄滅了，露辛達想，一定是昌西碰到電源開關了，她趕緊去找昌西。在找昌西的時候，露辛達碰到學校的同學，她們兩個於是一起找狗狗。找了好久還是找不到，露辛達只好回家，這個時候公寓裡的電燈又熄滅了，這次終於找到昌西了。露辛達決定把昌西送到新朋友家，讓朋友代她照顧昌西。

New Jersey Muôn Năm

　　Gia đình của Lucinda dọn đến New Jersey từ Cuba. Gia đình sống trong một khu nhà chung cư. Lucinda thấy cô đơn và nhớ Cuba. Trên đường đi học, cô bé đi ngang qua một con chó bị cột vào cái cây. Con chó trông dơ bẩn.

　　Lucinda mở dây cho chó và đem chó về nhà. Cô cho chó ăn và tắm cho nó. Cô tìm thấy một mảnh giấy bên trong dây đeo cổ của con chó. Trên giấy ghi tên chó là Chauncey. Cô bé đem chó đi giấu dưới hầm nhà. Những nút tắt mở điện của tòa nhà nằm dưới hầm nhà.

　　Đèn trong tòa nhà bị tắt. Lucinda nghĩ là Chauncey đã đụng phải một nút tắt mở điện. Lucinda chạy đi tìm chó. Cô bé gặp một cô bạn học chung trường. Cả hai cô cùng đi tìm con chó. Nhưng Lucinda không tìm được Chauncey. Cô đi về nhà. Đèn lại bị tắt lần nữa. Lần này Lucinda tìm ra con chó. Cô dẫn chó đến nhà người bạn mới của mình.

Multilingual Summaries

뉴저지 만세

　루신다의 가족은 쿠바에서 뉴저지로 이사와 아파트에서 산다. 루신다는 외로워하며 쿠바를 그리워한다. 루신다는 학교 가는 길에 나무에 묶인 더러운 개 옆을 지나간다.

　루신다는 그 개를 풀어주고 집에 데려와 먹이도 주고 목욕도 시켜준다. 그녀는 개 목걸이에서 쪽지를 하나 발견하는데 거기에는 개의 이름이 촌시라고 적혀 있다. 그녀는 개를 건물의 전기 스위치가 있는 지하실에 숨겨놓는다.

　건물의 불이 나가자 루신다는 촌시가 전기 스위치를 건드려서 불이 나갔다고 생각한다. 루신다는 촌시를 찾으러 가다가 같은 학교에 다니는 친구를 만나 함께 개를 찾기로 한다. 하지만 촌시를 찾지 못하고 집으로 돌아가고 만다. 그 후에 불이 다시 나가고 이번에는 개를 찾아낸 루신다는 촌시를 새 친구의 집으로 데려간다.

Viva New Jersey

Lucinda tsev neeg tsiv tsev los ntawm Cuba teb los txog lub xeev New Jersey. Lawv nyob rau hauv ib lub tsev kem. Lucinda kho kho siab nco txog teb chaws Cuba. Muaj ib hnub nws mus kev mus tom tsev kawm ntawv dhau ib tug aub uas raug khi lawm rau ib tsob ntoo. Tus aub ntawd qias heev.

Lucinda daws pob caus thiab muab tus aub ntawd coj los tsev. Nws pub nws noj thiab ntxuav nws lub cev. Nws nrhiav tau ib daig ntawv nyob rau hauv tus aub dab tsho aub. Nws hais tias tus aub ntawd lub npe hu ua Chauncey. Nws muab tus aub nkaum rau hauv chav hauv qab lawj. Lub tsev ntawd lub tshuab tawm cov hluav taws xob nyob rau hauv chav hauv qab lawj.

Ua cas teeb tua lawm. Lucinda xav tias Chauncey ntaus ib qhov kav hluav taws xob ntawd. Lucinda khiav mus nrhiav nws. Nws nrhiav tau ib tug ntxhais hluas nws paub uas mus kawm ntawv tom nws tsev kawm ntawv. Nkawd nrhiav tus aub ua ke. Tab sis Lucinda nrhiav tsis tau Chauncey. Nws rov mus tsev. Cov teeb rov tua dua. Ziag no Lucinda nrhiav tau nws tus aub. Nws coj nws mus xyuas nws tus phooj ywg lub tsev tshiab.

Saving the Rain Forests
Student Edition pages 92–105

Week at a Glance	Customize instruction every day for your English Language Learners.				
	Day 1	**Day 2**	**Day 3**	**Day 4**	**Day 5**
Teacher's Edition	Use the ELL Notes that appear throughout each day of the lesson to support instruction and reading.				
ELL Poster 4	• Assess Prior Knowledge • Develop Concepts and Vocabulary	• Preteach Tested Vocabulary	• Rain Forest Editorial	• Building an Ecosystem	• Monitor Progress
ELL Teaching Guide	• Picture It! Lesson, pp. 22–23 • Multilingual Summaries, pp. 26–28	• ELL Reader Lesson, pp. 218–219	• Vocabulary Activities and Word Cards, pp. 24–25 • Multilingual Summaries, pp. 26–28		
ELL Readers	• Reread *American Immigrants*	• Teach *A Visit to El Yunque*	• Reread *A Visit to El Yunque* and other texts to build fluency		
ELL and Transition Handbook	Use the following as needed to support this week's instruction and to conduct alternative assessments: • Phonics Transition Lessons • Grammar Transition Lessons • Assessment				

Picture It! Comprehension Lesson

Fact and Opinion

Use this lesson to supplement or replace the skill lesson on pages 88–89 of the Teacher's Edition.

Teach

Distribute copies of the Picture It! blackline master on page 23.
• Have students describe the picture. Then read the paragraph aloud.
• Share the Skill Points (at right) with students.
• Have students identify the facts and opinions in the story.

Practice

Read aloud the directions on page 23. Have students fill in the graphic organizer. Have them keep their organizers for later reteaching.

Answers for page 23: *Facts:* During the summer, the water is about 68 degrees. People can swim in the ocean. They can sit and watch the waves. They can buy food at the snack bars. The snack bars are open from 8 A.M. to 10 P.M. *Opinions:* Sandy Point Beach is perfect! People have more fun there than anywhere else. It is much more fun than going to a lake or to the mountains. It is even more fun than going to an amusement park.

Skill Points

✓ A **fact** is a statement that can be proved true or false.

✓ An **opinion** is a statement that tells a person's thoughts, feelings, or ideas. Statements of opinion cannot be proved true or false. Valid opinions are supported by facts or stated by experts. Faulty statements of opinion are not supported by facts.

Look at the picture. **Read** the paragraph.

• Identify the facts and the opinions in the paragraph.

• **Write** four facts and four opinions in the chart below.

Sandy Point Beach

Sandy Point Beach is perfect! During the summer, the water at Sandy Point Beach is about 68 degrees. People have more fun there than anywhere else in the world. They can swim in the ocean. They can sit on the beach and watch the waves. They can buy food at the snack bars, which are open from eight o'clock in the morning until ten o'clock at night. It is much more fun than going to a lake or to the mountains. It is even more fun than going to an amusement park.

Facts	Opinions

Vocabulary Activities and Word Cards

Copy the Word Cards on pages 24–25 as needed for the following activities.
Use the blank card for an additional word that you want to teach.
Also see suggestions for teaching vocabulary in the ELL and Transition Handbook.

Parts-of-Speech Word Sort	Clue Game	Fill in the Blanks
• Give each student a complete set of Word Cards. • Have each student prepare a three-column chart with *Nouns, Adjectives,* and *Verbs* as the headings. • Remind students what kinds of words belong in each column. • Have students write each vocabulary word in the appropriate column. • When all students have completed the exercise, ask volunteers to explain what each word means.	• Reproduce one set of Word Cards. Write the definition of each vocabulary word on the back of its card. • Have one student read the definition and ask the others to try to guess the word. • Once the students correctly identify the word, ask several students to create sentences using the word.	• Give each student a complete set of Word Cards. Have the students place the cards face up on their desks or tables. • Choose one vocabulary word and think of a context in which it can be used. Describe the context, omitting the word. For example: *Many people give money to _____ that help people, rescue animals, or protect the environment.* • Have students examine their Word Cards and choose the word that best fits the context. • Repeat the context clue several times as students search for the correct word.

basin

charities

equator

erosion

evaporates

exported

industrial

recycled

tropics

Multilingual Summaries

Saving the Rain Forests

There are three types of rain forest. They are tropical, cloud, and temperate rain forests. More than half of the world's plants and animals live in rain forests. Trees help maintain the water cycle. They release oxygen into the air. Trees absorb some of the rainfall. Tree roots help keep soil in place.

Many rain forests are being cut down. People want to use the land for farms. The wood from rain forest trees is valuable. Sometimes rain forests are cut down so miners can reach minerals in the ground.

It is important to save the rain forests. Scientists have not yet found all the plants and animals there. Rain forest plants may cure diseases. They might also be new sources of food. People must find a way to live and work in rain forests without destroying them.

Salvar las selvas

Hay tres tipos de selvas. Hay selvas tropicales, nubladas y templadas. Más de la mitad de las plantas y los animales del mundo viven en las selvas. Los árboles ayudan a mantener el ciclo de las aguas. Ellos liberan oxígeno en el aire. Los árboles absorben parte de las lluvias. Las raíces de los árboles ayudan a mantener el suelo en su lugar.

Muchas selvas han sido cortadas. La gente quiere usar esas tierras para granjas. La madera de los árboles de la selva es valiosa. Algunas veces se talan las selvas para que los mineros encuentren minerales en el suelo.

Es importante salvar las selvas. Los científicos no han encontrado todavía todas las plantas y los animales que viven en ellas. Las plantas de las selvas pueden curar enfermedades. También pueden ser nuevas fuentes de alimentos. La gente tiene que encontrar una forma de vivir y trabajar en las selvas sin destruirlas.

Multilingual Summaries

拯救雨林

　　地球上的雨林分為三種類型，分別是熱帶雨林、雲霧雨林和溫帶雨林。世界上一半以上的動植物都生活在雨林裡。樹木可以幫助水份保持循環，並且把氧氣釋放到空氣裡。樹木也可以吸收部分雨水，樹根可以緊緊抓牢土壤，不讓土壤流失。

　　人們大量砍伐雨林，因為他們想清出土地種田，而且雨林裡的木材非常值錢。還有些是因為要開礦，必須把雨林砍掉才挖得到礦物。

　　拯救雨林是一件相當重要的任務，因為到現在為止，雨林裡還有動植物是科學家還沒發現的。雨林裡的植物可以消弭天然災害，也可能是人類食物的新來源。人們必須找出新方法，讓大家利用雨林來居住和工作的同時，也能夠保持雨林原貌，不破壞環境。

Giữ Gìn Những Khu Rừng Mưa

　　Có ba loại rừng mưa. Rừng mưa nhiệt đới, rừng mưa mây, và rừng mưa ôn đới. Hơn phân nửa số cây và thú vật trên thế giới sống ở rừng mưa. Cây giúp duy trì chu kỳ nước. Cây nhả khí ô-xy vào không khí. Cây hấp thụ nước mưa. Rễ cây giúp giữ đất.

　　Nhiều rừng mưa đang bị đốn đi. Người ta muốn lấy đất rừng để làm trang trại. Gỗ từ rừng mưa rất quý giá. Thỉnh thoảng rừng mưa bị đốn đi để những người thợ mỏ có thể lấy các chất khoáng từ trong đất.

　　Giữ gìn rừng mưa là điều quan trọng. Các nhà khoa học vẫn chưa tìm hết các loại thực vật và thú sống ở đó. Các cây từ rừng mưa có thể chữa được bệnh. Chúng cũng có thể là nguồn thực phẩm mới. Con người phải tìm ra cách để sinh sống và làm việc trong rừng mưa mà không hủy hoại chúng.

Multilingual Summaries

Korean

열대 우림 보호

열대 우림에는 열대림, 운무림, 온대림 세 종류가 있으며 세계 동식물의 절반 이상이 열대 우림에 서식한다. 나무들은 물의 순환을 유지하도록 돕고 공기 중에 산소를 배출하며 빗물을 흡수한다. 나무 뿌리는 토양이 제자리에 계속 있도록 돕는다.

많은 열대 우림이 벌목되고 있다. 사람들은 땅을 농작지로 사용하고 싶어하는데 열대 우림에서 자란 목재가 값이 나가기 때문이다. 때때로 광부들은 땅속에서 광물을 찾으려고 나무를 베기도 한다.

열대 우림을 보호하는 일은 중요하다. 과학자들은 아직 열대 우림의 모든 동식물들을 발견해내지 못했다. 열대 우림에 서식하는 식물은 질병을 치료할지도 모르고 새로운 식품의 자원이 될지도 모른다. 사람들은 숲을 훼손하지 않고 더불어 살며 일하는 방법을 찾아야 한다.

Hmong

Kev Cawm Cov Hav Zoov Los Nag

Muaj peb hom hav zoov los nag. Ib lub hu ua tropical, ib lub hu ua huab cua, thiab ib lub hu ua nruab nrab. Tshaj li ib nrab cov nroj tsuag thiab cov tsiaj txhu nyob rau hauv hav zoov los nag. Cov tsob ntoo pab kom yeej muaj dej. Cov tsob ntoo tso pa oxygen rau hauv cua. Lawv ntxaum dej ib feem ntawm cov nag uas los. Tsob ntoo kuj pab kom av txhob raug kuav lawm.

Cov hav zoov los nag feem coob raug kev txiav ntoo. Cov tib neeg kuj xav siv thaj av kom muaj chaw ua qoob ua loo. Cov ntoo uas nyob rau hauv hav zoov los nag muaj nuj nqis heev. Qee zaum hav zoov los nag raug txiav kom cov neeg khaws pobzeb muaj nqis muaj peev xwm txhob rau hauv av.

Yog ib qhov tseem ceeb pab cawm cov hav zoov los nag. Cov kws kawm txuj ci tseem tsis tau paub txog tag nrho cov nroj tsuag thiab cov tsiaj txhu uas nyob rau ntawd. Cov nroj tsuag tej zaum yuav muaj peev xwm kom kab mob zoo lawm. Nyaj yuav muaj cov nroj tsuag tshiab uas cov neeg yuav nyiam noj. Tib neeg yuav tsum nrhiav tau ib txog kev ke ua hauj lwm thiab nyob rau hauv hav zoov los nag ke txhob muab lawv puas tsuaj tas.

When Crowbar Came Student Edition pages 116–131

Week at a Glance	Customize instruction every day for your English Language Learners.				
	Day 1	**Day 2**	**Day 3**	**Day 4**	**Day 5**
Teacher's Edition	Use the ELL Notes that appear throughout each day of the lesson to support instruction and reading.				
ELL Poster 5	• Assess Prior Knowledge • Develop Concepts and Vocabulary	• Preteach Tested Vocabulary	• Review Fact and Opinion	• Who's that Animal?	• Monitor Progress
ELL Teaching Guide	• Picture It! Lesson, pp. 29–30 • Multilingual Summaries, pp. 33–35	• ELL Reader Lesson, pp. 220–221	• Vocabulary Activities and Word Cards, pp. 31–32 • Multilingual Summaries, pp. 33–35		
ELL Readers	• Reread *A Visit to El Yunque*	• Teach *Horses and Their Trainers*	• Reread *Horses and Their Trainers* and other texts to build fluency		
ELL and Transition Handbook	Use the following as needed to support this week's instruction and to conduct alternative assessments: • Phonics Transition Lessons • Grammar Transition Lessons • Assessment				

Picture It! Comprehension Lesson
Fact and Opinion

Use this lesson to supplement or replace the skill lesson on pages 112–113 of the Teacher's Edition.

Teach

Distribute copies of the Picture It! blackline master on page 30.
• Have students describe the picture. Then read the paragraph aloud.
• Ask: *What is one fact from the paragraph? One opinion?*
• Share the Skill Points (at right) with students.
• Ask students how they would prove the statements of fact.

Practice

Read aloud the directions on page 30. Have students complete the graphic organizer. Have them keep their organizers for later reteaching.

Answers for page 30: *Facts:* Crows are large black birds. American crows live all over the United States. They eat fruits, seeds, vegetables, and small animals. *How to Prove?* Answers will vary. *Opinion:* Crows are not nice birds. They are very ugly. Everyone wishes they would go somewhere else. *How to Support?* Answers will vary.

Skill Points

✓ Statements of **fact** can be proved true or false. They can be proven by reading, observing, or asking an expert.

✓ Statements of **opinion** are judgments or beliefs. They cannot be proven true or false, but they can be supported by facts and logic.

Look at the picture. **Read** the paragraph.

- Which sentences state facts? **Write** the sentences in the *Fact* box. In the box labeled *How to Prove?* tell how you would prove the facts.

- Which sentences state opinions? **Write** the sentences in the *Opinion* box. In the box labeled *How to Support?* tell how you would support the opinions.

Crows

Crows are large black birds. American crows live all over the United States. They eat fruits, seeds, vegetables, and small animals such as snakes and frogs. Crows are not nice birds. They are very ugly. Everyone wishes they would go somewhere else.

Fact	How to Prove?
1.	
2.	
3.	

Opinion	How to Support?
1.	
2.	
3.	

Vocabulary Activities and Word Cards

Copy the Word Cards on pages 31–32 as needed for the following activities.
Use the blank card for an additional word that you want to teach.
Also see suggestions for teaching vocabulary in the ELL and Transition Handbook.

Spot the Suffix	Synonym Concentration	Home Language Clues
• Have each student create a three-column chart with the headings *-ive*, *-ion*, and *-ed*. • Review the meanings of these endings with students. • Place one set of Word Cards face up so that all students can see them. Have one student select a Word Card. Ask the student if the vocabulary word belongs in any of the three categories. If it does, have the student place the word in the appropriate category. • For words ending in *-ion* and *-ed*, ask students to identify the root verb and explain what it means.	• Write the following words on blank cards: *forceful, notice, doubtfully, discouragement, stamped, appear, movement, sneaky, permitted.* Give a set of these cards and a set of Word Cards to each pair. • Explain that *synonyms* are words that mean the same or almost the same thing. Ask pairs to match each word with its synonym. • Next, students mix the cards together, and then lay them face down in a grid. They take turns choosing two cards. If the cards show synonyms, the student keeps them.	• Pair students who have writing proficiency in the same home language, and give each student a set of Word Cards. • Have students work together to write translations of the words in their home language on the back of each card. (See the Multilingual Lesson Vocabulary beginning on page 272 for suggested translations.) • Have partners lay out the cards with the home language sides facing up. • Have each student choose a card, read the home language translation, and then say the vocabulary word in English.

aggressive

detect

dubiously

frustration

imprinted

materialize

migration

secretive

tolerated

Multilingual Summaries

When Crowbar Came

The George family took in wild animals. One crow fell from a nest. They fed him and named him Crowbar. The children, Craig, Twig, and Luke, played with Crowbar. The bird walked to the school bus with them. He slept in their apple tree. He came into the house when he wanted to.

Crowbar was smart. He would go to the school at lunch. He stole the students' milk money. They did not know where he hid it. They found out that Crowbar hid the money in a rainspout.

One day, the family saw many crows in their yard. The crows were making a lot of noise. They were going to fly to a warmer place. They wanted Crowbar to migrate with them. At first, he stayed with the family. The crows came back each day. On the fifth day, Crowbar flew away with them.

Cuando llegó Crowbar

La familia George protegía los animales salvajes. Un día, un cuervo se cayó del nido. Ellos lo alimentaron y lo llamaron Crowbar. Los niños, Craig, Twig y Luke, jugaban con Crowbar. El pájaro iba al autobús con ellos. Él dormía en el manzano de la casa. También, entraba en la casa cuando quería.

Crowbar era inteligente. Él iba a la escuela a la hora del almuerzo. Robaba el dinero de la leche de los estudiantes. Ellos no sabían dónde él lo escondía. Ellos descubrieron que Crowbar escondía el dinero en un canalón de desagüe de lluvia.

Un día, la familia vio a muchos cuervos en el patio. Los cuervos estaban haciendo mucho ruido. Se iban volando a un lugar más cálido. Ellos querían que Crowbar emigrara con ellos. Al principio él se quedó con la familia. Los cuervos regresaban todos los días. Al quinto día, Crowbar se fue volando con ellos.

Multilingual Summaries

鴉霸來了

喬治家喜歡收養野生動物。有一次，他們看到一隻烏鴉掉出鳥巢，所以就收養了牠，還幫牠取了一個名字叫「鴉霸」。喬治家的小孩克雷格、瑞格和路加，都喜歡跟鴉霸玩。鴉霸會送他們上學校巴士，牠睡覺的地方是在院子裡的蘋果樹，興致一來，牠還會飛到屋子裡玩耍。

鴉霸很聰明，會挑午餐時間去學校偷學生的牛奶錢，藏在隱密的地方，沒有人知道牠到底把錢藏到哪裡去了。後來才發現原來是藏在排水管裡面。

有一天，喬治一家人發現院子裡突然出現了很多烏鴉，呱呱地亂叫，很吵耳。原來牠們要飛去溫暖的地方過冬，希望鴉霸跟牠們一塊去。第一次，鴉霸沒跟著去，因為牠想待在喬治家。之後烏鴉們每天都來找鴉霸，終於在第五天的時候，鴉霸告別喬治一家人，跟同伴一起飛走了。

Khi Chú Quạ Crowbar Đến

Gia đình nhà họ George nuôi những con thú hoang. Một con quạ rơi từ tổ xuống. Họ cho nó ăn và đặt tên cho nó là Crowbar. Các đứa con, Craig, Twig, và Luke, chơi với Crowbar. Chú chim đi đón xe buýt đưa đi học với chúng. Chú chim ngủ trên cây táo của gia đình. Nó được tự do vào nhà.

Chú quạ Crowbar thông minh. Chú đến trường vào giờ ăn trưa. Chú ăn cắp tiền sữa của các học sinh. Các em này không biết quạ giấu tiền ở đâu. Họ khám phá ra là Crowbar giấu tiền trên máng xối.

Ngày kia, gia đình thấy có nhiều quạ trong sân nhà. Các con quạ đang làm ồn ào. Chúng sẽ bay đến một nơi ấm áp hơn. Chúng muốn Crowbar bay theo chúng đến nơi khác ấm hơn. Thoạt tiên, chú quạ ở lại với gia đình. Mỗi ngày những con quạ trở lại. Đến ngày thứ năm, Crowbar bay đi với chúng.

Multilingual Summaries

크로우바가 왔을 때

조지 가족은 야생 동물들을 데리고 와 기른다. 가족은 둥지에서 떨어진 까마귀 한 마리에게 먹이를 주고 크로우바라고 이름 붙인다. 크레이그, 트위그, 루크 세 아이는 크로우바와 함께 놀며 지낸다. 새는 아이들과 함께 스쿨버스 타는 곳까지 간다. 크로우바는 사과나무에서 잠을 자고 집으로 돌아오고 싶을 때 돌아온다.

크로우바는 영리해서 점심시간에 학교로 날아가 학생의 우유값을 훔치곤 하는데 아이들은 크로우바가 돈을 어디에 숨겼는지 모른다. 사람들은 크로우바가 돈을 홈통에 숨겨놓은 것을 알아낸다.

어느 날 가족은 정원에 있는 많은 까마귀들을 본다. 까마귀들은 상당히 시끄러운 소리를 내고 있었는데 더 따뜻한 곳으로 날아가려는 것이었다. 새들은 크로우바와 함께 떠나고 싶어한다. 크로우바는 처음에 가족과 함께 남지만 까마귀들이 매일 같이 되돌아오자 다섯째 날 새들과 함께 날아가 버린다.

Thaum Crowbar Tuaj

Tsev Neeg George nqa tsiaj txhu qus los tsevlb tug uab lag poob qho nws lub zes. Lawv pub nws noj thiab tis npe rau nws hu ua Crowbar. Cov me nyuam, Craig, Twig, thiab Luke, nrog Crowbar ua si. Tus noog nrog lawv mus kev mus rau tom qhov chaw tos tsheb npav. Nws pw rau hauv lawv tsob ntoo av paum. Nws los tsev thaum nws siab xav ua li ntawd.

Crowbar txawj ntse heev. Nws mus tom tsev kawm ntawv thaum cov me nyuam noj su. Nws nyiag cov tub ntxhais nyiaj yuav kua miv nyuj. Lawv tsis tau paub xyov nws muab lawv nyiaj npis tso rau qhov twg. Ntev ntev tom qab lawv pom tias Crowbar tso lawv cov nyiaj rau hauv ib lub qhov txais dej.

Muaj ib hnub, tsev neeg pom ntau ntau cov uab lag nyob rau hauv lawv qab tsib taug. Cov uab lag nrov heev quaj ub quaj no. Lawv npaj tawm ya mus rau ib qhov chaws sov zog. Lawv xav kom Crowbar nrog lawg ya mus nram qab teb thiab. Thaum xub thawj, nws nrog tsev neeg ntawd nyob. Tab sis cov uab lag rov qab los txhua txhua hnub. Hnub tsib ces Crowbar ya plaws mus nrog lawv.

The Universe   Student Edition pages 150–161

Week at a Glance	Customize instruction every day for your English Language Learners.				
	Day 1	**Day 2**	**Day 3**	**Day 4**	**Day 5**
Teacher's Edition	Use the ELL Notes that appear throughout each day of the lesson to support instruction and reading.				
ELL Poster 6	• Assess Prior Knowledge • Develop Concepts and Vocabulary	• Preteach Tested Vocabulary	• Come to the Planetarium	• A Universe of Words	• Monitor Progress
ELL Teaching Guide	• Picture It! Lesson, pp. 36–37 • Multilingual Summaries, pp. 40–42	• ELL Reader Lesson, pp. 222–223	• Vocabulary Activities and Word Cards, pp. 38–39 • Multilingual Summaries, pp. 40–42		
ELL Readers	• Reread *Horses and Their Trainers*	• Teach *Eyes in the Skies*	• Reread *Eyes in the Skies* and other texts to build fluency		
ELL and Transition Handbook	Use the following as needed to support this week's instruction and to conduct alternative assessments: • Phonics Transition Lessons • Grammar Transition Lessons • Assessment				

Picture It! Comprehension Lesson
Main Idea and Details
Use this lesson to supplement or replace the skill lesson on pages 146–147 of the Teacher's Edition.

Teach
Distribute copies of the Picture It! blackline master on page 37.
• Have students describe the picture. Then read the paragraph aloud.
• Ask: *What is this paragraph all about?* (astronomy clubs)
• Share the Skill Points (at right) with students.
• Have students find the main idea of the paragraph and the supporting details.

Practice
Read aloud the directions on page 37. Have students answer the questions about the paragraph. Have them keep their work for later reteaching.

Answers for page 37: 1. astronomy clubs **2.** Possible answer: Joining an astronomy club is a good idea for amateur astronomers. **3.** Joining a club is a great way to learn about astronomy and to meet other people who share the same interest. Members of astronomy clubs share information about what is happening in the night sky. They also meet to look at the sky together.

Skill Points
✓ To find the topic of a paragraph, ask yourself, *What is this all about?*

✓ To find the **main idea,** ask yourself, *What is the most important idea about this topic?*

✓ To help find the main idea, look for **supporting details.**

✓ Supporting details explain or tell about the main idea.

Look at the picture. **Read** the paragraph.

- What is the topic of this paragraph? **Write** the words below.
- What is the main idea? **Write** it in a sentence below.
- Which sentences provide supporting details? **Write** them below.

Watching the Stars

Cities all over the world have astronomy clubs. Joining an astronomy club can be a good way to learn about astronomy and to meet other people who share the same interest. Members of astronomy clubs share information about what is happening in the night sky. They also meet to look at the sky together.

1. What is the topic of this paragraph?

_____

2. What is the main idea?

_____

_____

3. What are the supporting details?

_____

_____

_____

_____

_____

Vocabulary Activities and Word Cards

Copy the Word Cards on page 39 as needed for the following activities.
Use the blank cards for additional words that you want to teach.
Also see suggestions for teaching vocabulary in the ELL and Transition Handbook.

Charades	Parts-of-Speech Word Sort	True or False?
• Place one set of Word Cards face up so that all students can see them. • Divide students into pairs or small groups. Give each group one Word Card. • Have each group discuss how to act out their vocabulary word. • Have the groups take turns acting out scenes while the others try to guess the words, using the displayed set of Word Cards as clues.	• Give each student a complete set of Word Cards. • Have each student prepare a three-column chart with *Nouns*, *Verbs*, and *Adjectives* as the column headings. • Remind students what kinds of words belong in each column. • Have students write each vocabulary word in the appropriate column. • When all students have completed the exercise, ask volunteers to explain what each word means.	• Create one set of Word Cards. • Ask a student to choose a card. • Make up a sentence using the vocabulary word, and ask the student if the sentence is true or false. For example: *The Sun is a star in the Milky Way galaxy.* (true) • Ask the rest of the group whether they agree with the student's answer. • Repeat the exercise until all students have had a chance to choose a card.

astronomer

collapse

collide

compact

galaxy

particle

Multilingual Summaries

The Universe

The moon is the closest object to us in space. The sun is the closest star. Distances in space are measured in light years. One light year is the distance light can travel in one year.

Scientists have seen what look like new planets forming. Stars are born from clouds of gas and dust. Red giant stars are older stars that give off hot gas. No one knows what happens to stars when they die.

The galaxy we live in is called the Milky Way. We have many stars in our galaxy. Galaxies have four basic shapes. Scientists think there are at least one hundred billion galaxies in the universe.

Black holes are mysterious. Matter is sucked into them and never returns. Quasars are the bursts of energy a star gives off before it is pulled into a black hole. They are a mystery too.

Spanish

El universo

La Luna es el objeto del espacio más cercano a nosotros. El Sol es la estrella más cercana. La distancia en el espacio se mide en años luz. Un año luz es la distancia en que la luz viaja en un año.

Los científicos han visto algo que parece de nuevas planetas formándose. Las estrellas nacen de nubes de gas y polvo. Las estrellas rojas gigantes son estrellas viejas emiten gas caliente. Nadie sabe qué les sucede a las estrellas cuando mueren.

La galaxia donde vivimos se llama Vía Láctea. Nosotros tenemos muchas estrellas en nuestra galaxia. Las galaxias tienen cuatro formas diferentes. Los científicos creen que debe haber, por lo menos, cien billones de galaxias en el universo.

Los huecos negros son misteriosos. La materia es absorbida por ellos y nunca regresa. Los cuasares son ráfagas de energía que una estrella emite cuando es atraída dentro de un hueco negro. Los cuasares son misteriosos también.

Multilingual Summaries

宇宙

在太空中，月亮是最接近我們的星體，太陽則是最接近的恆星。太空中量度距離的單位是光年，一光年是光在一年內所能行進的距離。

科學家已經了解行星形成的過程。星體從瓦斯雲和灰塵中誕生，紅巨星是年紀較大的星體，會散發熱氣。沒有人知道星體滅亡時的實際狀況到底是什麼。

我們所居住的星系叫做銀河系，銀河系裡有很多星體。宇宙中的星系有四種基本形狀，科學家認為在宇宙裡至少有一千億個星系。

黑洞很神祕，物體一被吸進去就再也不能出來。類星體是星體被吸入黑洞前所發射出來的能量，同樣也是個謎。

Vũ Trụ

Mặt trăng là vật gần chúng ta nhất trong không gian. Mặt trời là ngôi sao gần nhất. Khoảng cách trong không gian được đo lường bằng các năm ánh sáng. Một năm ánh sáng là khoảng cách mà ánh sáng có thể du hành trong một năm.

Các nhà khoa học đã thấy một sự kiện giống như các hành tinh đang được hình thành. Các vì sao được tạo thành từ chất khí và bụi. Những tinh cầu khổng lồ màu đỏ là những vì sao xa xưa phát ra chất khí nóng. Không ai biết được những tinh cầu sẽ ra sao khi chúng lịm tắt.

Thiên hà mà chúng ta đang sống được gọi là Dãy Ngân Hà. Chúng ta có nhiều tinh cầu trong dãy ngân hà của chúng ta. Các thiên hà có ba hình dạng chính. Các nhà khoa học cho là có ít nhất một tỉ thiên hà trong vũ trụ.

Các lỗ đen bí ẩn. Vật chất bị hút vào những lỗ đen này và không bao giờ trở lại. Các chuẩn tinh là những luồng năng lượng mà một ngôi sao phát ra trước khi bị hút vào một lỗ đen. Chuẩn tinh cũng là một điều bí ẩn.

Multilingual Summaries

우주

달은 우주에서 우리와 가장 가까이에 있는 행성이고 태양은 가장 가까이에 있는 항성이다. 우주에서의 거리는 광년으로 측정되며 1광년은 빛이 1년 동안 갈 수 있는 거리이다.

과학자들은 새로운 행성이 형성되는 모습을 관찰해왔다. 별들은 가스와 먼지 구름으로부터 탄생하는데 붉은 빛을 띠는 거대한 별들은 뜨거운 가스를 발산하는 오래된 별들이다. 아무도 아직까지 별들이 소멸될 때 어떤 일이 일어나는지를 밝혀내지 못했다.

우리가 살고 있는 은하는 은하계라고 불리며 매우 많은 별들이 있다. 은하에는 네 개의 기본 형태가 있는데 과학자들은 우주에 적어도 1,000억 개의 은하가 있을 것이라고 추측한다.

블랙홀은 신비에 싸여있다. 물체가 블랙홀 안으로 빨려 들어가면 결코 되돌아오지 못한다. 준항성체는 별이 블랙홀에 끌려들어가기 전에 방출하는 에너지의 폭발로 블랙홀과 마찬가지로 신비롭기만 하다.

Lub Qab Ntuj Khwb

Lub hli yog qhov khoom uas nyob ze peb tshaj nyob rau sab qaum ntuj nrauv. Lub hnub yog lub hnub qub ua nyob ze tshaj. Qhov deb nyob rau sab qaum ntuj nrauv tau coj los muab ntsuas ua xyoo teeb. Ib xyoo teeb ntsuas hais tias ib xyoo no, teeb must au deb npaum li cas.

Cov kws kawm txog ntiaj teb tau pom tias ntxim li muaj ib co ntiaj teb tshiab ua tau tsim los. Hnub qub nraug puab los ntawm pa roj zeb ntsuam thiab hmoov av. Cov hnub qub loj loj thiab liab liab yog cov qub tshaj plaws thiab tso ib co pab roj zeb ntsuam kub kub tawm. Tsis muaj leej twg paub tias ua cas rau tej hnub qub thaum lawv tuag lawm.

Peb nyob rau hauv lub qab ntuj uas hua ua Kab Lig Ntuj. Peb muaj hnub qub ntau ntau nyob rau peb lub qab ntuj no. Tej qab ntuj muaj nraug puas uas plaub yam. Cov kws kawm txog ntiaj teb xav tias qhov tshawg kawg mas yeej muaj li ib phav txhiab lab ntuj nyob rau qab ntuj khwb no.

Muaj tej lub qhov dub uas peb tsis paub txog. Khoom dabtsi los yog raug nqus mus hauv lawm ces yeej tsis rov qab los. Quasars yog qhov uas ib lub hnub qub tso tawg ua dej nws raug nqus mus rau hauv ib lub qhov dub lawm. Qhov ntawv los kuj tsis muaj leej twg paub tias yog ua cas thiab.

Dinosaur Ghosts   Student Edition pages 172–187

Week at a Glance	Customize instruction every day for your English Language Learners.				
	Day 1	Day 2	Day 3	Day 4	Day 5
Teacher's Edition	Use the ELL Notes that appear throughout each day of the lesson to support instruction and reading.				
ELL Poster 7	• Assess Prior Knowledge • Develop Concepts and Vocabulary	• Preteach Tested Vocabulary	• A Day in Prehistory	• Prehistoric Adjectives	• Monitor Progress
ELL Teaching Guide	• Picture It! Lesson, pp. 43–44 • Multilingual Summaries, pp. 47–49	• ELL Reader Lesson, pp. 224–225	• Vocabulary Activities and Word Cards, pp. 45–46 • Multilingual Summaries, pp. 47–49		
ELL Readers	• Reread *Eyes in the Skies*	• Teach *The Story of Sue*	• Reread *The Story of Sue* and other texts to build fluency		
ELL and Transition Handbook	Use the following as needed to support this week's instruction and to conduct alternative assessments: • Phonics Transition Lessons • Grammar Transition Lessons • Assessment				

Picture It! Comprehension Lesson
Main Idea and Details

Use this lesson to supplement or replace the skill lesson on pages 168–169 of the Teacher's Edition.

Teach

Distribute copies of the Picture It! blackline master on page 44.
• Have students describe the picture. Then read the paragraph aloud.
• Ask: *What is the woman in the picture looking at?* (a fossil)
• Share the Skill Points (at right) with students.
• Ask students what the topic of this paragraph is. Then ask them to identify the main idea and supporting details.

Practice

Read aloud the directions on page 44. Have students complete the graphic organizer. Have them keep their organizers for later reteaching.

Answers for page 44: Possible answers: *Main Idea:* Fossils help scientists learn about dinosaurs. *Supporting Details:* Fossils tell us what dinosaurs looked like. They show what dinosaurs ate. They show when and how long dinosaurs lived.

Skill Points

✓ The **main idea** is the most important idea about the topic. Sometimes the main idea is given in a sentence. If it is not, you must find it on your own.

✓ **Supporting details** are smaller pieces of information that tell more about the main idea.

Look at the picture. **Read** the paragraph.

- What is the main idea of this story? **Write** a sentence in the graphic organizer.

- What details support this main idea? **Write** them in the graphic organizer.

Learning from Fossils

Dinosaurs once lived on Earth. We know this because some clues have survived. When an animal or plant dies, it sometimes leaves hardened bones or an outline of itself in the ground. Scientists study those bones and outlines, called fossils, to learn what dinosaurs looked like. They also study fossils to try to figure out what dinosaurs ate. Fossils can even help scientists learn when and how long dinosaurs lived.

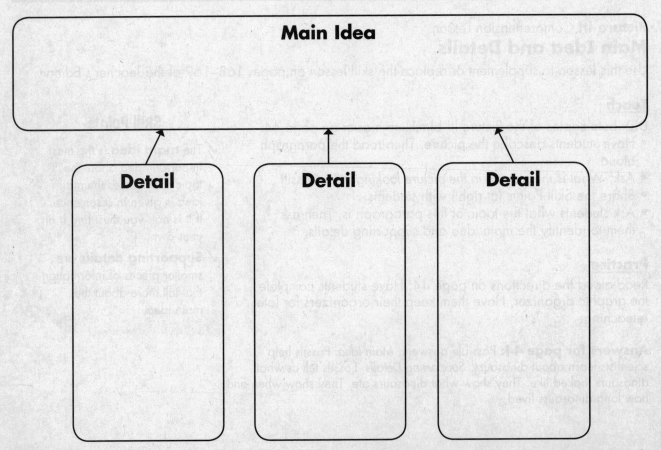

Main Idea

Detail

Detail

Detail

© Scott Foresman 6

Vocabulary Activities and Word Cards

Copy the Word Cards on page 46 as needed for the following activities.
Use the blank card for an additional word that you want to teach.
Also see suggestions for teaching vocabulary in the ELL and Transition Handbook.

Adjective Hunt	Poster Game	Home Language Clues
• Give each student a complete set of Word Cards.	• Reproduce one set of Word Cards for students to use in a poster game.	• Pair students who have writing proficiency in the same home language, and give each student a set of Word Cards.
• Remind students that adjectives are words that describe.	• Have students take turns choosing a Word Card without letting others see it.	• Have students work together to write translations of the vocabulary words in their home language on the back of each card. (See the Multilingual Lesson Vocabulary beginning on page 272 for suggested translations.)
• Have each student put all of the vocabulary words that are adjectives into one pile.	• Ask a student to point to a scene or detail on the ELL Poster, and then give clues about the word without saying it until other students guess the word.	
• When they have finished, point out some typical suffixes for adjectives (*-ish, -ous, -ic*).	• Repeat the process until all students have participated in the activity.	• Have partners lay out the cards with the home language sides facing up.
• Ask each student to try to explain what one of the adjective vocabulary words means.		• Have each student choose a card, read the home language translation, and then say the vocabulary word in English.

fragile

poisonous

prey

sluggish

specimens

treacherous

volcanic

Multilingual Summaries

English

Dinosaur Ghosts

Many *Coelophysis* dinosaurs died at Ghost Ranch. In 1947, Ned Colbert and his team found many *Coelophysis* skeletons there. They wondered why so many dinosaurs were buried in one place. Why did they all die at the same time?

Scientists studied *Coelophysis* for fifty years. They learned many things about the animal. The scientists formed several possible explanations for the mysterious deaths.

The scientists used facts to help them decide that some of the explanations were probably wrong. The best explanation was that there was a drought and then a flood. But no one really knows what happened to the dinosaurs. Scientists are still working on the problem. They may find new explanations.

Spanish

Fantasmas de dinosaurios

Muchos dinosaurios *Coelophysis* murieron en *Ghost Ranch* (Rancho Fantasma). En 1947, Ned Colbert y su equipo encontraron muchos esqueletos de *Coelophysis* allí. Ellos estaban asombrados de tantos dinosaurios enterrados en un solo lugar. ¿Por qué todos murieron al mismo tiempo?

Los científicos han estudiado los *Coelophysis* por cincuenta años. Ellos han aprendido muchas cosas de este animal. Los científicos pensaron en diferentes explicaciones para sus muertes misteriosas.

Los científicos usaron la información como ayuda para decidir que algunas explicaciones probablemente estaban equivocadas. La mejor explicación es que hubo una sequía y después una inundación. Pero nadie sabe realmente qué les pasó a los dinosaurios. Los científicos están todavía trabajando en este problema. Es posible que encuentren nuevas explicaciones.

Multilingual Summaries

恐龍幽靈

很多空骨龍都死在幽靈墓場。1947 年，奈德·柯伯特和他的工作團隊在那裡找到了許多空骨龍的遺骸。他們不明白為什麼會有那麼多恐龍死在同一個地方，而且是同一個時間死掉。

科學家研究空骨龍已經有 50 年了，他們知道許多關於空骨龍的事情，所以對幽靈墓牧場大批恐龍死亡的神秘事件，也想出了幾種可能的解釋。

科學家根據事實，判斷出哪些解釋可能是錯誤的，然後得出最好的解釋：先發生了旱災，然後又來了一個水災。但還是沒有人確實知道這群恐龍到底發生了什麼事。科學家仍然在研究這個問題，相信不久之後，他們就可以找到新答案了。

Những Con Ma Khủng Long

Nhiều khủng long loại Coelophysis chết ở Trang Trại Ma (Ghost Ranch). Vào năm 1947, Ned Colbert và toán của ông tìm thấy nhiều bộ xương loại Coelophysis ở đó. Họ tự hỏi tại sao có nhiều khủng long bị chôn vùi trong một nơi như vậy. Tại sao tất cả những con này lại chết cùng một lúc?

Các nhà khoa học đã nghiên cứu Coelophysis trong năm mươi năm. Họ học được nhiều điều về loại thú này. Các nhà khoa học đã lập vài giải thích khả dĩ về cái chết bí ẩn của loại này.

Các khoa học gia đã dùng những dữ kiện để giúp họ quyết định là một vài giải thích có thể bị sai. Giải thích tốt nhất là đã từng có một cơn hạn hán rồi đến một cơn lụt. Nhưng không ai thật sự biết điều gì đã xảy ra với những con khủng long. Các nhà khoa học vẫn còn đang cố giải quyết vấn đề này. Họ có thể tìm ra những giải thích mới.

Multilingual Summaries

유령이 된 공룡들

수많은 코엘로피시스 공룡이 유령농장(Ghost Ranch)에서 죽었다. 1947년 네드 콜버트와 그의 팀은 그곳에서 많은 코엘로피시스의 뼈를 찾아냈고 그들은 왜 그렇게도 많은 공룡들이 한 곳에 묻혔는지 궁금해했다. 왜 그들은 모두 동시에 죽었던 것일까?

과학자들은 50년간 코엘로피시스를 연구하는 동안 이 동물에 대해 많은 것을 알게 됐고 불가사의한 죽음에 대한 몇 가지 가능한 설명을 만들어냈다.

과학자들은 사실에 근거하여 그 설명들 중 몇 개는 틀린 것이라고 결정지었다. 가장 믿을만한 설명은 그 당시에 가뭄이 있었고 그 이후에 홍수가 발생했다는 것이다. 하지만 실제로 공룡한테 어떤 일이 일어났는지 아는 사람은 아무도 없다. 과학자들은 여전히 연구를 계속하고 있으며 아마 곧 새로운 설명을 찾게 될지도 모른다.

Dab Daisnausxauj (Dinosaur)

Muaj coob leej daisnausxauj hu ua Coelophysis uas tau tuag nyob rau Dab Vaj Dab Tsev (Ghost Ranch). Thaum ib txhiab cuaj pua plaub caug xya, Ned Colbert thiab nws pab neeg ua hauj lwm tau nrhiav pom ntau tus Coelophysis pob txa nyob rau qhov ntawd. Lawv xav tsis thoob tias ua cas ntau tus daisnausxauj tau raug faus nyob rau ib qhov chaws xwb. Ua cas lawv sawvdaws ho tuag tag tib lub caij?

Cov neeg kawm txuj kawm ci (scientists) tau kawm txog cov Coelophysis ntawd tau tsib caug xyoo. Lawv kawm tau ntau tsav ntau yam txog tus tsiaj ntawd. Cov scientists xav tau ob peb lub tswvyim los piav qhia txog cov tsiaj tuag ntawd.

Cov scientists tau sim tej yam uas muaj tseeb los pab lawv txiav txim siab tias muaj tej lub tswvyim tsis muaj tseeb. Lub tswvyim zoo tshaj plaws piav tias tau muaj ib caij uas ntuj qhuav teb nkig ces tom qab ntawd tau muaj ib lub caij uas dej nyab. Tiam si yeej tsis muaj leej twg uas paub tias saib ua cas thiam thiam rau cov daisnausxauj. Cov scientists tseem nyiaj hnub nyiam no tsuas qhov tabmeem ntawd. Tej zaum lawv yuav nrhiav tau ib co tswvyim tshiab.

A Week in the 1800s

Week at a Glance	Customize instruction every day for your English Language Learners.				
	Day 1	**Day 2**	**Day 3**	**Day 4**	**Day 5**
Teacher's Edition	Use the ELL Notes that appear throughout each day of the lesson to support instruction and reading.				
ELL Poster 8	• Assess Prior Knowledge • Develop Concepts and Vocabulary	• Preteach Tested Vocabulary	• Review Compare and Contrast	• Words from History	• Monitor Progress
ELL Teaching Guide	• Picture It! Lesson, pp. 50–51 • Multilingual Summaries, pp. 54–56	• ELL Reader Lesson, pp. 226–227	• Vocabulary Activities and Word Cards, pp. 52–53 • Multilingual Summaries, pp. 54–56		
ELL Readers	• Reread *The Story of Sue*	• Teach *The Corbin Farm*	• Reread *The Corbin Farm* and other texts to build fluency		
ELL and Transition Handbook	Use the following as needed to support this week's instruction and to conduct alternative assessments: • Phonics Transition Lessons • Grammar Transition Lessons • Assessment				

Picture It! Comprehension Lesson
Graphic Sources

Use this lesson to supplement or replace the skill lesson on pages 194–195 of the Teacher's Edition.

Teach

Distribute copies of the Picture It! blackline master on page 51.
• Have students read the dates and descriptions in the time line. Then read the paragraph aloud.
• Ask: *When did Illinois become a state?* (1818)
• Share the Skill Points (at right) with students.
• Ask students how the time line helped them understand the paragraph.

Practice

Read aloud the directions on page 51. Have students use the time line and the paragraph to answer the questions. Have them keep their work for later reteaching.

Answers for page 51: 1. Native Americans **2.** the French **3.** Great Britain **4.** twenty years

Skill Points

✓ **Graphic sources** such as charts, diagrams, and time lines organize information in a way that shows something about the topic.

✓ While reading, compare the information in a graphic source with information you read in the text.

✓ Sometimes making your own graphic source can help you understand and remember information better.

Look at the time line. **Read** the paragraph.

• Use the paragraph and the time line to **answer** the questions below.

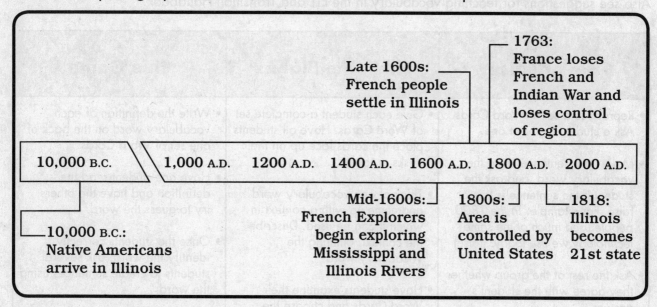

The History of Illinois

For thousands of years, people have lived in the area that is now Illinois. Native Americans lived in the area more than 12,000 years ago. For thousands of years, they were the only people there. Then, in the 1600s, French explorers arrived. France controlled Illinois and other areas around the Mississippi River until the 1700s. In 1763, France lost control of the region to Great Britain. Great Britain controlled Illinois for the next 20 years. After the American Revolution, Americans began settling the state. In 1818, Illinois became the 21st state.

1. Who were the first people to live in Illinois?

_____

2. Who were the first Europeans to live in Illinois?

_____

3. Who controlled Illinois after France lost the French and Indian War?

_____

4. How long did Great Britain control Illinois?

_____

Vocabulary Activities and Word Cards

Copy the Word Cards on page 53 as needed for the following activities.
Use the blank cards for additional words that you want to teach.
Also see suggestions for teaching vocabulary in the ELL and Transition Handbook.

True or False?	Fill in the Blanks	Clue Game
• Reproduce a set of Word Cards. Ask a student to select one. • Make up a sentence using the vocabulary word, and ask the student if the sentence is true or false. For example: *In the 1800s, people used much of the same technology we use today.* (false) • Ask the rest of the group whether they agree with the student's answer. • Repeat the activity until all students have had a chance to choose a card.	• Give each student a complete set of Word Cards. Have all students place the cards face up on their desks or tables. • Think of one vocabulary word and come up with a context in which it can be used. Describe the context, omitting the vocabulary word. • Have students examine their Word Cards and choose the word that best fits the context. • Repeat the context clue several times as students search for the correct word.	• Write the definition of each vocabulary word on the back of one set of Word Cards. • Have one student read the definition and have the others try to guess the word. • Once the students correctly identify the word, ask several students to create sentences using the word.

counselor

identity

physical

surplus

technology

Multilingual Summaries

English

A Week in the 1800s

Kings Landing in New Brunswick, Canada is a living museum. A group of young students spend a week there. They learn to live like people lived in the 1800s.

They get into costume. The students settle in. They help out with the chores and eat meals with the families in Kings Landing.

The girls work indoors. They sew, clean, and bake. The girls are not allowed to run or do the work that the boys do. The boys work in the fields. They help the blacksmith. The boys swim in the river.

The children like some things about living in the 1800s. The experience helps them to appreciate the things that they have today, such as electricity and more freedoms for women.

Spanish

Una semana en el siglo XIX

Kings Landing es un museo viviente que está en New Bruswick, Canadá. Un grupo de jóvenes estudiantes pasan una semana allí. Aprenden a vivir como vivía la gente en el siglo XIX.

Se visten como ellos. Los estudiantes se establecen allí. Ellos ayudan en las tareas y comen con las familias de Kings Landing.

Las muchachas trabajan dentro de la casa. Ellas cosen, lavan y hornean. A las muchachas no les permiten correr o hacer el trabajo que los muchachos hacen. Los muchachos trabajan en el campo. Ellos ayudan al herrero. Los muchachos nadan en el río.

A los estudiantes les gustan algunos aspectos de la vida del siglo XIX. La experiencia los ayuda a apreciar las cosas que tienen hoy, como la electricidad y más libertad para las mujeres.

Multilingual Summaries

Chinese

不一樣校外教學
體驗十九世紀的一星期

加拿大新伯倫瑞克省的金斯蘭登是活生生的博物館。有一群年輕的學生在那裡住了一星期，學習十九世紀人類的生活方式。

學生們穿上古代的服裝，開始適應十九世紀的生活。他們幫忙做些雜務，連吃飯也跟當地的居民一起。

女孩子待在家裡工作，負責縫紉、打掃和烘焙麵包，不可以做男孩子的工作。男孩子要到田裡工作，也要幫鐵匠打鐵，還可以到河裡游泳。

孩子們覺得十九世紀的生活方式有些地方很有趣。體驗過這些事情之後，讓他們更懂得珍惜現在所擁有的一切，例如有電可以用，以及女性擁有較多的自由。

Vietnamese

Một Tuần Lễ trong Các Thập Niên 1800

Kings Landing ở New Brunswick, Canada là một viện bảo tàng sống. Một nhóm học sinh trẻ đến ở đó một tuần. Họ học cách sống như người ta đã sống trong những thập niên 1800.

Họ mặc quần áo hóa trang. Các học sinh ổn định đâu vào đấy. Họ giúp làm các công việc và ăn uống với các gia đình ở Kings Landing.

Các cô gái làm việc ở trong nhà. Họ may, dọn rửa, và nấu nướng. Các cô gái không được phép chạy hoặc làm công việc của các cậu con trai làm. Các cậu con trai làm việc ngoài đồng. Họ giúp người thợ rèn. Các cậu bơi lội dưới sông.

Các trẻ em thích một vài điều về cuộc sống trong những thập niên 1800. Kinh nghiệm này giúp họ biết quý những điều mà ngày nay họ có được, như điện và tự do hơn cho phụ nữ.

Multilingual Summaries

최고의 현장학습
1800년대 일주일 체험하기

캐나다의 뉴 브런스위크에 위치한 킹스 랜딩은 살아있는 박물관이다. 어린 학생들의 한 무리가 그 곳에서 일주일을 보내기로 하고 그들은 1800년대에 살았던 사람들과 같은 방식으로 생활하는 법을 배운다.

학생들은 그 시대의 의상을 입고 거처를 정한 다음 잡일을 하고 킹스 랜딩에 있는 가족들과 식사를 한다.

소녀들은 집안에서 바느질을 하고 청소를 하며 빵을 굽는다. 소녀들은 뛰어 다니거나 소년들이 하는 일을 하지 못하게 되어 있다. 소년들은 들에서 일하고 대장장이를 도우며 강에서 수영을 하기도 한다.

아이들은 1800년대의 생활에서 어떤 점들은 좋아하게 되는데 이번 경험으로 아이들은 전기나 여성들에게 허용된 보다 많은 자유와 같이 오늘날 자신들이 누릴 수 있는 것에 대해 감사히 여길 수 있게 되었다.

Kev Mus Ua Si Zoo Tshaj Plaws
Ib Ab Thim Nyob Rau Lub Caij 1800

Kings Landing nyob rau New Brunswick, Canada, yog ib lub tsev liv xwm (museum) uas tseem tuav siav niaj hnub niam no. Ib pab tub kawm ntawv tau mus nyob rau pev tau ib as thim. Lawv tau kawm nyob zoo li tib neeg ua nyob rau lub caij ib txhiab yim pua ntawd nyob.

Lawv tau hnav tsoos tshob li txeej thauv. Cov tub kawm ntawv tau los nyob. Lawv pab ua hauj lwm thiab noj mov nrog cov yim neeg nyob rau Kings Landing.

Cov ntxhais ua hauj lwm hauv vaj hauv tsev. Lawv xaws tsoos tshob, tu vaj tu tsev, thiab ua zaub ua mov no. Lawv txwv tsis pub cov ntxhais khiav lossis ua tej tub tej hauj lwm. Cov tub ua hauj lwm pem liaj pem teb. Lawv pab cov kws ntaus hlaus. Cov tub ua luam dej nram tus dej.

Cov menyuam kuj nyiam teb yam txog kev ua neej nyob rau lub caij ib txhiab yim pua ntawd. Lawv kev kawm ntawd tau pab lawv saib tej khoom uas lawv muaj nyiaj hnub niam no rau nqi, xwb li fe fab thiab kev ywj phem rau poj niam.

Good-bye to the Moon
Student Edition pages 224–237

Week at a Glance	Customize instruction every day for your English Language Learners.				
	Day 1	Day 2	Day 3	Day 4	Day 5
Teacher's Edition	Use the ELL Notes that appear throughout each day of the lesson to support instruction and reading.				
ELL Poster 9	• Assess Prior Knowledge • Develop Concepts and Vocabulary	• Preteach Tested Vocabulary	• Review Compare and Contrast	• Commercial of the Future	• Monitor Progress
ELL Teaching Guide	• Picture It! Lesson, pp. 57–58 • Multilingual Summaries, pp. 61–63	• ELL Reader Lesson, pp. 228–229	• Vocabulary Activities and Word Cards, pp. 59–60 • Multilingual Summaries, pp. 61–63		
ELL Readers	• Reread *The Corbin Farm*	• Teach *The Day the Earthmen Came*	• Reread *The Day the Earthmen Came* and other texts to build fluency		
ELL and Transition Handbook	Use the following as needed to support this week's instruction and to conduct alternative assessments: • Phonics Transition Lessons • Grammar Transition Lessons • Assessment				

Picture It! Comprehension Lesson
Compare and Contrast
Use this lesson to supplement or replace the skill lesson on pages 220–221 of the Teacher's Edition.

Teach
Distribute copies of the Picture It! blackline master on page 58.
• Have students describe the people in the drawing.
• Ask: *In what ways do the two people look different?* (one is tall, one is short; one is a man, one is a woman)
• Share the Skill Points (at right) with students.
• Read the paragraph aloud. Ask students if they have had a teacher who reminds them of Mr. Rodriguez or Mrs. Johnson.

Practice
Read aloud the directions on page 58. Have students fill in the graphic organizer. Have them keep their organizers for later reteaching.

Answers for page 58: *Mrs. Johnson:* 60 years old, short, green eyes, math teacher, woman; *Mr. Rodriguez:* 30 years old, brown eyes, tall, reading teacher, man; *Both:* dark hair, second-grade teachers, liked by students

Skill Points
✓ When you **compare,** you tell how two or more things are alike.

✓ When you **contrast,** you tell how two or more things are different.

✓ While you are reading, compare and contrast the characters by asking yourself, *How are these two characters alike and different?*

Name _____

Look at the picture. **Read** the paragraph. **Complete** the diagram.

- What traits does Mrs. Johnson have that Mr. Rodriguez does not? **Write** them in the section labeled *Mrs. Johnson.*

- What traits does Mr. Rodriguez have that Mrs. Johnson does not? **Write** them in the section labeled *Mr. Rodriguez.*

- How are Mrs. Johnson and Mr. Rodriguez similar? **Write** the answers in the *Both* section.

Two Teachers

In second grade, I had two teachers. My math teacher was Mrs. Johnson. She was about 60 years old. She was short. She had dark hair and green eyes. Everyone in our class liked Mrs. Johnson. Our reading teacher was Mr. Rodriguez. He had dark hair too. His eyes were brown. He was about 30 years old. He was very tall. Mr. Rodriguez made reading fun. We liked him too.

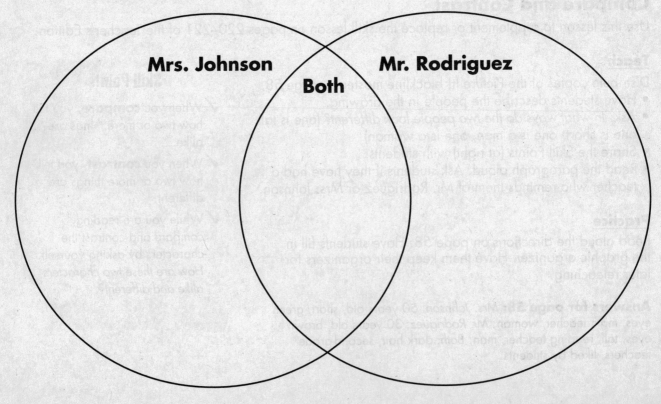

Mrs. Johnson   **Both**   **Mr. Rodriguez**

© Scott Foresman 6

Vocabulary Activities and Word Cards

Copy the Word Cards on page 60 as needed for the following activities.
Use the blank card for an additional word that you want to teach.
Also see suggestions for teaching vocabulary in the ELL and Transition Handbook.

Suffix Hunt	Poster Game	Home Language Clues
• Give one set of Word Cards to each student. • Remind students what a suffix is. Then ask them to find all of the Word Cards with suffixes. • When they have finished, ask each student to name one of the words he or she found that contains a suffix. • Ask students what the *-ing*, *-ed*, and *-tion* suffixes may tell them about the word's meaning.	• Reproduce one set of Word Cards for students to use in a poster game. • Have students take turns choosing a Word Card without letting others see it. • Ask a student to point to a scene or detail on the ELL Poster, and then give clues about the word without saying it until other students guess the word. • Repeat the process until all students have participated in the activity.	• Pair students who have writing proficiency in the same home language, and give each student a set of Word Cards. • Have students work together to write translations of the vocabulary words in their home language on the back of each card. (See the Multilingual Lesson Vocabulary beginning on page 272 for suggested translations.) • Have partners lay out the cards with the home language sides facing up. • Have each student choose a card, read the home language translation, and then say the vocabulary word in English.

combustion

dingy

lunar

negotiate

traversed

waft

waning

Multilingual Summaries

Good-bye to the Moon

Kepler was the first person to be born on the Moon. His father is the Governor of Moon. They must travel to Earth. Kepler has never been to Earth before.

Kepler does not know what to expect. He says goodbye to his girlfriend. He will miss her. He will be on Earth for six months. Kepler thinks about how Moon and Earth are different from each other. There is very little water on the Moon. On the shuttle, Kepler is amazed to see Earth's oceans.

The descent through Earth's atmosphere is rough. Kepler has never felt Earth gravity. Earth's gravity makes him feel much heavier. He gets a bloody nose. The next day he will have two black eyes. It is hard for him to walk on Earth. When he gets off the shuttle, Kepler is amazed at clouds, birds, and real air. He cannot wait to see all the sights on Earth.

Spanish

Adiós a la Luna

Kepler fue la primera persona que nació en la Luna. Su padre es el Gobernador de la Luna. Ellos tienen que viajar a la Tierra. Kepler no ha visto nunca antes la Tierra.

Kepler no sabe qué esperar. Le dice adiós a su amiga. La extrañará. Estará en la Tierra seis meses. Kepler piensa en cómo la Luna y la Tierra son diferentes una de la otra. En la Luna hay muy poca agua. En la nave, Kepler está asombrado de ver los océanos de la Tierra.

El descenso a la atmósfera de la Tierra es brusco. Kepler nunca sintió la gravedad. La gravedad de la Tierra lo hace sentir más pesado. A Kepler le sangra la nariz. El próximo día tendrá los dos ojos negros. Es difícil para él caminar en la Tierra. Cuando se baja de la nave, Kepler está asombrado de las nubes, los pájaros y el aire real. Está impaciente por ver todo lo que hay en la Tierra.

Multilingual Summaries

月球再見

克普勒是第一個在月球上出生的孩子，他爸爸是月球總督。克普勒和爸爸必須去地球一趟，他以前從來沒去過地球。

克普勒不知道這趟去地球會發生什麼事。他跟女朋友說再見，他將會很想念她。克普勒會在地球上待 6 個月，他很好奇月球和地球到底有些什麼分別。月球上的水很少，所以從太空梭上看到地球的海洋時，他覺得非常驚訝。

從太空降落到地球表面必須穿過大氣層，這中間的過程非常辛苦。克普勒以前從來沒有體會過地球的地心引力，地心引力讓他覺得自己變得很重，他的鼻子還流了鼻血！第二天肯定會有兩個黑眼圈。在地球上走路對克普勒來說也很辛苦，可是當他從太空梭走出來看到雲朵、小鳥，呼吸到真正的空氣時，他覺得很驚訝，急不及待地要把地球上的風景全部看個夠。

Tạm Biệt Trăng

Kepler là người đầu tiên sanh ở Mặt Trăng. Ba của cậu là Thống Đốc Mặt Trăng. Họ phải du hành đến Trái Đất. Kepler chưa từng đến Trái Đất bao giờ.

Kepler không biết sẽ thấy gì. Cậu từ giã cô bạn gái. Cậu sẽ nhớ cô. Cậu sẽ ở Trái Đất sáu tháng. Kepler nghĩ về sự khác nhau giữa Mặt Trăng và Trái Đất. Có rất ít nước trên Mặt Trăng. Trên phi thuyền con thoi, Kepler ngạc nhiên khi thấy những đại dương trên Trái Đất.

Việc bay vào tầng khí quyển của Trái Đất là điều khó khăn. Kepler chưa bao giờ cảm nhận sức hút của Trái Đất. Sức hút của Trái Đất làm cho cậu thấy mình nặng hơn. Cậu bị chảy máu mũi. Ngày hôm sau cậu bị bầm hai mắt. Đi trên Trái Đất là việc khó khăn. Khi cậu bước ra khỏi phi thuyền con thoi, Kepler ngạc nhiên thấy mây, chim, và không khí thật sự. Cậu nôn nóng muốn được thưởng ngoạn mọi cảnh vật trên Trái Đất.

Multilingual Summaries

달이여! 잘 있거라

케플러는 달에서 태어난 최초의 인간으로 그의 아버지는 달의 통치자다. 케플러는 지구에 가 본 적이 없지만 그들 부자는 지구로 여행을 하기로 했다.

케플러는 지구 여행에서 무엇을 기대해야 하는지도 모른 채 여자친구에게 작별의 인사를 한다. 그는 그녀를 그리워할 것이다. 케플러는 지구에서 6개월을 머물 예정이다. 그는 달과 지구의 차이점에 대해 생각하며 달에는 물이 거의 없다는 것을 생각한다. 그러다 우주 왕복선 안에서 지구의 바다를 보고 놀라게 된다.

지구의 대기를 통과하기란 쉽지 않다. 케플러는 지구의 중력을 느껴본 적이 한 번도 없었기 때문에 지구에서의 자신이 훨씬 무겁게 느껴진다. 그는 코피가 난다. 다음 날에는 두 눈이 멍이 들 것이다. 케플러에게 지구 위를 걷기란 힘든 일이다. 왕복선에서 내렸을 때 케플러는 구름, 새, 그리고 진짜 공기에 놀란다. 그는 지구 위의 모든 볼거리들에 대해 무척 기대하고 있다.

Sib Ntsib Dua Lub Hli

Kepler yog thawj tug neeg uas yug los nyob saum lub hli. Nws txiv yog lub hli tus tswv xeev. Lawv yuav tsum nqis los rau ntiaj teb no. Kepler tsis tau tuaj txog ntiaj teb no duab li.

Kepler tsis paub yuav xav li cas. Nws hais rau nws tus hluas nkauj tias nkawv mam sib tsib duab. Nws yuav nco nws. Nws yuav los nyob rau lub hlis rau ntiaj teb no. Kepler xav tias lub hli thiab ntiaj teb no txawv npaum li cas ib leeg ntawm ib lub. Tsis muaj dej ntau nyob saum lub hli. Nyob saum nyooj hoom, Kepler xav tsis thoob thaum nws pom ntiaj teb no tej dej hiavtxwv.

Thaum nqis los dhau ntiaj teb tej huab cua ua rau nyooj hoom ua yog koog. Kepler tsis tau hnov ntiaj teb kev nqus (gravity) dua li. Kev nqus nyob ntiaj teb no ua rau nws txim hnyav tshaj. Nws qhov tswg los ntshav. Hnub tom qab, nws muaj ob lub qhov muag xyiav tuaj. Mus kev nyob ntiaj teb no nyuab heev rau nws. Thaum nws nqis nyooj hoom, Kepler xav tsis thoob txog tej huab cua, tej noog, thiab txoj pa. Nws tos tsis tau mus xyuas teb xyuas chaws nyob rau ntiaj teb no.

Week at a Glance	Customize instruction every day for your English Language Learners.				
	Day 1	**Day 2**	**Day 3**	**Day 4**	**Day 5**
Teacher's Edition	Use the ELL Notes that appear throughout each day of the lesson to support instruction and reading.				
ELL Poster 10	• Assess Prior Knowledge • Develop Concepts and Vocabulary	• Preteach Tested Vocabulary	• Travelogue	• Review Graphic Sources	• Monitor Progress
ELL Teaching Guide	• Picture It! Lesson, pp. 64–65 • Multilingual Summaries, pp. 68–70	• ELL Reader Lesson, pp. 230–231	• Vocabulary Activities and Word Cards, pp. 66–67 • Multilingual Summaries, pp. 68–70		
ELL Readers	• Reread *The Day the Earthmen Came*	• Teach *The Art of Making Mummies*	• Reread *The Art of Making Mummies* and other texts to build fluency		
ELL and Transition Handbook	Use the following as needed to support this week's instruction and to conduct alternative assessments: • Phonics Transition Lessons • Grammar Transition Lessons • Assessment				

Picture It! Comprehension Lesson
Graphic Sources

Use this lesson to supplement or replace the skill lesson on pages 244–245 of the Teacher's Edition.

Teach

Distribute copies of the Picture It! blackline master on page 65.
• Have students study the map. Ask them what it shows. Then read the paragraph aloud.
• Ask: *Where do most people in Egypt live?*
• Share the Skill Points (at right) with students.
• Ask students how the map helped them understand the paragraph.

Practice

Read aloud the directions on page 65. Have students use the map and the paragraph to answer the questions. Have them keep their work for later reteaching.

Answers for page 65:
1. Cairo **2.** along the Nile River **3.** Alexandria, Port Said
4. Possible response: because it is a desert

Skill Points

✓ **Graphic sources** such as charts, diagrams, and time lines organize information in a way that shows something about the topic.

✓ While reading, compare the information in a graphic source with information you read in the text.

✓ Sometimes graphic sources are used to make complicated information easier to understand.

Look at the map. **Read** the paragraph.

• Use the paragraph and the map to **answer** the questions below.

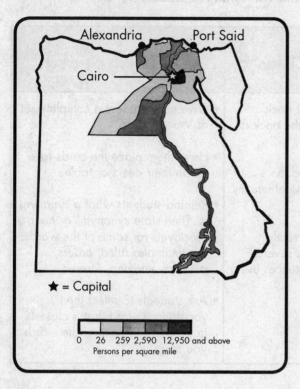

Life in Egypt

For thousands of years, the Nile River has allowed people to farm and live in Egypt. Most of the country is a desert, where it is difficult to raise crops. But the land around the Nile is rich. Many crops, including cotton, grow in this area. That is why most of Egypt's population lives near the Nile River. Some people also live in cities located along Egypt's coast.

1. What is the capital of Egypt?

_____

2. Where does most of the population live?

_____

3. What are two cities along the coast?

_____

4. Why do you think that few people live in the western part of Egypt?

_____

Vocabulary Activities and Word Cards

Copy the Word Cards on page 67 as needed for the following activities.
Use the blank card for an additional word that you want to teach.
Also see suggestions for teaching vocabulary in the ELL and Transition Handbook.

Riddle Game	Definition Clues	Synonym Search
• Divide students into pairs or small groups, and give each group a set of Word Cards. • Have students place the cards face down in a pile and take turns choosing a card and making up a riddle about the word for others to guess. • Provide a model for the riddle, such as: *This word starts with the letter _____. It ends with the letter _____. It means _____.*	• Write the definition of each vocabulary word on the back of a set of Word Cards. • Have one student read the definition and have the others try to guess the word. • Once the students correctly identify the word, ask several students to create sentences using the word.	• Give each student a complete set of Word Cards. • Have them place the cards face up on their desks or tables. • Remind students what a synonym is. Then state synonyms or near synonyms for some of the words. For example: *ruled, orders, plentiful, undying, forever.* • Ask students to select the vocabulary word that is closest in meaning to each of the words you say.

abundant

artifacts

decrees

eternity

immortal

receded

reigned

Multilingual Summaries

Egypt

Menes became the first pharaoh of ancient Egypt around 3100 B.C. Menes brought together all the people of Egypt. Ancient Egypt had upper, middle, and lower classes of people. Most Egyptian people lived in houses made from mud bricks. They slept on mats on the floor.

The Egyptians had a rainy season, a planting season, and a harvesting season. The people shared the land with many different kinds of animals.

Ancient Egyptian writing is called hieroglyphics. Pictures and symbols stood for letters and words. The ancient Egyptians had another tradition. When people died, many were made into mummies. Some pharaohs had pyramids built as tombs for their afterlife. Other pharaohs had tombs in the earth. Some of these tombs have not been found.

Egipto

Menes fue el primer faraón de Egipto alrededor del 3100 a.C. Menes unió a todas las personas de Egipto. El Egipto antiguo dividía a las personas en clases altas, medias y bajas. La mayoría de los egipcios vivían en casas hechas de ladrillos de barro. Dormían en alfombrillas en el piso.

Los egipcios tenían una estación de lluvias, una estación de sembrado y una estación de cosecha. Las personas compartían la tierra con diferentes tipos de animales.

Los egipcios escribían en jeroglíficos. Las figuras y los símbolos representaban letras y palabras. Los egipcios antiguos tenían otra tradición. Cuando las personas morían, muchas de ellas eran convertidas en momias. Algunos faraones se hacían construir tumbas en forma de pirámides para su vida después de la muerte. Otros faraones tenían tumbas en la tierra. Algunas de estas tumbas no se han encontrado.

Multilingual Summaries

埃及

約在西元前 3100 年，曼尼斯王登基成為古埃及的第一個法老王，統一了整個埃及。當時埃及社會分成上、中、下三大階級。大部分的埃及人都住在泥磚蓋成的房子裡，在地板上鋪上蓆子睡覺。

埃及有雨季、播種季節和收成季節，古埃及人和許多不同種類的動物分享大地資源。

古埃及的文字叫作象形文字，圖像符號代表字母和單字。古埃及還有另一個傳統，就是將去世的人做成木乃伊。有些法老王會建金字塔當墳墓，好為來生做準備，有些法老王把墳墓蓋在地下，所以到現在還沒有被發現。

Ai Cập

Menes trở thành vị vua đầu tiên của Ai Cập cổ xưa vào khoảng 3100 B.C (trước Công Nguyên). Menes thống nhất mọi người dân trong xứ Ai Cập. Ai Cập cổ xưa có lớp thượng lưu, trung lưu, và hạ lưu. Hầu hết những người Ai Cập sống trong những ngôi nhà làm từ gạch bùn. Họ ngủ trên những tấm thảm trải trên sàn nhà.

Người Ai Cập có mùa mưa, mùa trồng trọt, và mùa thu hoạch. Con người cùng sinh sống với nhiều loại thú khác nhau.

Chữ viết Ai Cập cổ xưa được gọi là chữ tượng hình. Hình ảnh và các ký hiệu tượng trưng cho chữ cái và từ ngữ. Người Ai Cập cổ xưa còn có một tục lệ khác nữa. Khi người ta chết, nhiều người được làm thành xác ướp. Nhiều vị vua cho xây những kim tự tháp làm mồ để họ dùng sau khi chết. Những vị vua khác có mộ chôn trong lòng đất. Một vài ngôi mộ này vẫn chưa được tìm ra.

Multilingual Summaries

이집트

　메네스는 기원전 3100년경 고대 이집트 최초의 파라오가 되었다. 메네스는 이집트의 모든 사람들을 한데 모았다. 고대 이집트 사람들은 상류, 중류, 하류 계급으로 나뉘어져 있었고 대부분의 사람들은 진흙 벽돌로 만든 집에서 살았으며 땅바닥 위에 매트를 깔고 잠을 잤다.

　이집트인들은 우기, 농번기, 그리고 수확기가 있었고 사람들은 여러 동물들과 함께 같은 땅에서 살았다.

　고대 이집트의 문자는 상형문자인데 여기서 그림은 글자를, 기호는 단어를 의미한다. 고대 이집트인들은 다른 풍습을 갖고 있었고 이것은 사람이 죽었을 때 미라로 만드는 것이다. 어떤 파라오들은 내세를 위한 무덤으로 피라미드를 지었고 다른 파라오들은 지상에 피라미드를 지었다. 아직까지 이 무덤들 중 일부는 발견되지 않고 있다.

Ivyis (Egypt) Teb Chaws

Menes tau raug tsa los ua huab tais Ivyis teb txheej tau hu ze ntawm li peb txhiaj ib puas xyoo ua dej Yesus los. Menes tau sau tas nrho cov neeg nyob Ivyis los ua ib phawm. Txheej thaum ub nyob Ivyis muaj peb thiam neeg. Ib thiam neeg siab, ib thiam neeg nrab, thiab ib thiam neeg qis. Cov neeg Ivyis feem coob nyob tsev thwvcib uas siv av nkos los ua. Lawv pu saum lev hauv av.

Neeg Ivyis muaj ib lub caij los nag, ib lub caij cog noob cog zaub, thiab ib lub caij sau noob sau zaub. Tib neeg faib teb faib chaws nrog coob yam tsiaj.

Ivyis txheej thaum ub kev sau ntawv hu ua hislauskivfiv (hieroglyphics). Lawv teeb duab thiab cim cov los txhais ua ntawv thiab lus. Neeg Ivyis nyob txheej thaum thaum ub kuj muaj lwm yam kev cai thiab. Thaum neeg tuag, lawv muab coob leej coob tub los tu tseg cia ua masmis (mummies). Ib cov huab tais tau ua ib cov tsev hu ua pislasmiv (pyramids) los ua tsev faus lawv rau lub neej dhau kev tuag. Lwm cov huab tais ua tsev faus lawv rau hauv av sab hauv. Niaj hnub niam no,luag tseem ntshiab tsis tau tau ib txhia tsev faus ntawd.

Hatchet Student Edition pages 278–291

Week at a Glance	**Customize instruction every day for your English Language Learners.**				
	Day 1	**Day 2**	**Day 3**	**Day 4**	**Day 5**
Teacher's Edition	Use the ELL Notes that appear throughout each day of the lesson to support instruction and reading.				
ELL Poster 11	• Assess Prior Knowledge • Develop Concepts and Vocabulary	• Preteach Tested Vocabulary	• Talk Show Challenge	• Wildlife Twenty Questions	• Monitor Progress
ELL Teaching Guide	• Picture It! Lesson, pp. 71–72 • Multilingual Summaries, pp. 75–77	• ELL Reader Lesson, pp. 232–233	• Vocabulary Activities and Word Cards, pp. 73–74 • Multilingual Summaries, pp. 75–77		
ELL Readers	• Reread *The Art of Making Mummies*	• Teach *How to Survive in the Desert*	• Reread *How to Survive in the Desert* and other texts to build fluency.		
ELL and Transition Handbook	Use the following as needed to support this week's instruction and to conduct alternative assessments: • Phonics Transition Lessons • Grammar Transition Lessons • Assessment				

Picture It! Comprehension Lesson

Sequence

Use this lesson to supplement or replace the skill lesson on pages 274–275 of the Teacher's Edition.

Teach

Distribute copies of the Picture It! blackline master on page 72.
• Have students describe each picture. Then read the paragraph aloud.
• Ask: *How did Cam lose her sister?* (She stopped to look in the store window, and her sister kept walking.)
• Share the Skill Points (at right) with students.
• Have students identify the sequence of events by retelling the seven events described in the paragraph.

Practice

Read aloud the directions on page 72. Have students identify the sequence of events described in the paragraph.

Answers for page 72: 1. Cam and her sister went shopping.
2. Cam saw a pretty blouse in a store window. **3.** Cam stopped to look at the blouse. **4.** Cam didn't see her sister. **5.** Cam became worried. **6.** Cam saw her sister. **7.** Cam hugged her sister.

Skill Points

✓ **Sequence** is the order of events in a story.

✓ Sometimes clue words such as *next* and *then* indicate the sequence of events.

✓ Some events in a story happen at the same time. Clue words such as *when* and *during* help you recognize that events occur at the same time.

Name _____

Look at the pictures. **Read** the paragraph.

• What do you see in the pictures? **Describe** what you see.

Lost and Found

One day Cam and her older sister, Han, went shopping together. Cam saw a pretty blouse in a store window. She stopped to look at it.

When Cam turned around, she did not see Han. Cam became worried.

At last she saw Han. Cam was so relieved that she hugged her sister with joy.

Write the events of the story in order.

1. _____

2. _____

3. _____

4. _____

5. _____

6. _____

7. _____

Vocabulary Activities and Word Cards

Copy the Word Cards on page 74 as needed for the following activities.
Use the blank card for an additional word that you want to teach.
Also see suggestions for teaching vocabulary in the ELL and Transition Handbook.

Verb Hunt	True or False?	Fill in the Blanks
• Give each student a complete set of Word Cards for a verb hunt.	• Reproduce one set of Word Cards for a true-or-false activity.	• Give each student a complete set of Word Cards. Have students place the cards face up on their desks or tables.
• Remind students that a verb is a word that tells what someone or something does.	• Ask a student to choose a card.	• Choose one vocabulary word and think of a context in which it can be used. Describe the context, omitting the vocabulary word. For example: *I want to make a fire. First I have to _____ this match.*
• Have each student sort all of the vocabulary words that are verbs into one pile.	• Make up a sentence using the vocabulary word and ask the student if the sentence is true or false. For example: *Porcupines have sharp quills.* (true)	
• When they have finished, ask each student to name one of the verbs he or she found and tell what it means.	• Ask the rest of the group if they agree with the student's answer.	• Have students choose the word that best fits the context.
	• Repeat the exercise until all students have had a chance to choose a card.	• Repeat the context clue several times as students search for the correct word.

hatchet

ignite

painstaking

quills

registered

smoldered

stiffened

Multilingual Summaries

Hatchet

Brian survives a plane crash in the woods. He is alone, and his only tool is a hatchet. A porcupine sticks him with its quills. He falls asleep. He dreams about his father and his friend. He cannot understand what they say. He wakes up in pain.

Brian tries to start a fire. He hits the cave wall with his hatchet and makes sparks. The sparks do not start a fire. He tries over and over. He uses grass, twigs, and bark. The fire will not catch.

Brian does not stop trying. He remembers that fire needs oxygen. He tries blowing on the sparks. He blows them out. He tries again. Then he blows just enough and he starts a fire. He feels safer because he has a fire.

Spanish

El hacha

Brian sobrevive a un accidente de avión en el bosque. Está solo, y su única herramienta es un hacha. Un puercoespín lo hiere con sus púas. Él se duerme. Sueña con su padre y su amigo. Él no puede entender qué dicen ellos. Se despierta con mucho dolor.

Brian trata de encender un fuego. Le pega a la pared de la cueva con su hacha y hace chispas. Las chispas no prenden el fuego. Él lo intenta una y otra vez. Usa hierba, ramitas y cortezas. El fuego no se enciende.

Brian no se detiene y sigue intentándolo. Recuerda que el fuego necesita oxígeno. Intenta soplar sobre las chispas. Las apaga. Vuelve a intentarlo. Sopla con cuidado y enciende el fuego. Brian se siente a salvo porque tiene un fuego.

Multilingual Summaries

布萊恩的斧頭

布萊恩乘坐的飛機發生空難，他掉到樹林裡，不過卻幸運地活下來。他只有一個人，身邊唯一能用的工具是一把斧頭。有隻豪豬想用身上的刺攻擊他，幸好有斧頭趕走討厭的豪豬。布萊恩睡著了，他夢見他的爸爸和朋友跟他說話，可是布萊恩不了解他們到底在說什麼。最後布萊恩在一陣痛苦中醒來。

布萊恩試著生火，他用斧頭敲擊洞穴裡的岩壁，想製造些火花出來，可是試了半天那些火花卻都生不起火來。布萊恩不放棄，試了一遍又一遍，他還用草、小樹枝和樹皮，可是火就是點不起來。

布萊恩不氣餒，他想起火燃燒時需要氧氣，所以他試著把火花吹成火，可是不小心卻把火花吹熄了，布萊恩還是繼續試著生火，終於有一次他吹的氣恰到好處，把火點燃了。有了火之後，布萊恩就覺得自己安全多了。

Cây Rìu

Brian được sống sót sau một tai nạn rớt máy bay trong rừng. Cậu chỉ có một mình, và dụng cụ duy nhất của cậu là cây rìu. Một con nhím đâm cậu với những chiếc lông nhọn của nó. Cậu ngủ thiếp đi. Cậu mơ thấy ba và bạn của mình. Cậu không hiểu được họ nói gì. Cậu thức dậy vì đau đớn.

Brian cố làm ra lửa. Cậu đập cây rìu vào vách hang và những tia lửa bắn ra. Những tia lửa không làm ra lửa. Cậu cố làm đi làm lại. Cậu dùng cỏ, cành cây, và vỏ cây. Lửa cũng không bén được.

Brian không ngừng cố gắng. Cậu nhớ là lửa cần có khí ô-xy. Cậu cố thổi vào những tia lửa. Cậu thổi tắt những tia lửa này. Cậu thử lần nữa. Rồi cậu thổi vừa đúng để bắt đầu có lửa. Cậu thấy an toàn hơn vì cậu có được lửa.

Multilingual Summaries

손도끼

　　브라이언은 숲으로 추락한 비행기에서 살아남는다. 그는 혼자이며 그가 가진 유일한 도구는 손도끼이다. 브라이언은 고슴도치 가시에 찔린다. 그는 곧 잠에 빠져들고 아빠와 친구들 꿈을 꾸지만 그들이 무엇을 얘기하는지 알 수가 없다. 그는 고통 속에서 잠을 깬다.

　　브라이언은 불을 피우려고 한다. 그는 손도끼로 동굴 벽을 쳐서 불똥을 만들지만 불이 지펴지지 않는다. 그는 풀과 작은 가지 그리고 나무 껍질을 가지고 계속 시도해보지만 불은 붙지 않는다.

　　브라이언은 불 피우려는 시도를 멈추지 않는다. 그는 불을 만들려면 산소가 필요하다는 것을 기억해내고 불똥에 대고 바람을 분다. 바람 때문에 불똥을 꺼뜨리지만 그는 다시 해본다. 결국 그는 적당한 만큼만 바람을 불어 불을 피운다. 브라이언은 불이 있어 더욱 안전하다고 느낀다.

Rab Taus

　　Ib lub nyooj hoom poob rau pem hav zoov tiam is Brian tsis tuag. Nws ib leeg, thiab nws tsuas muaj ib rab taus xwb. Ib tug tsaug tua nws nrog nws cov koob. Nws cia li tsaug zog. Nws ua npau suav txog nws txiv thiab nws cov phooj ywg. Nws tsis tau taub lawv hais li cas. Nws mob ib ce tag thaum nws sawv los.

　　Brian sim piv zes hluav taws. Nws siv nws rab taus ntaus lub qhov tsua thiab tawm txim liab vog. Cov txim tsis zes hluas taws. Nws rov sim duab ob peb lwm. Nws siv nroj, pas ntoo, thiab tawv ntoo. Tsis zes hluav taws li.

　　Brian tsis tsum li. Nws nco qab tias hluav taws yuav tsum rau pa. Nws sim tshuab cov txim. Nws muab lawv tshuab tuag lawm. Nws sim ua duab. Ces nws tshuab kom tab tom txaus thiab zest au hluav taws lawm. Nws tsis ntshai lawm vim tias nws muaj hluav taws lawm.

When Marian Sang

Student Edition pages 302–315

Week at a Glance	Customize instruction every day for your English Language Learners.				
	Day 1	**Day 2**	**Day 3**	**Day 4**	**Day 5**
Teacher's Edition	Use the ELL Notes that appear throughout each day of the lesson to support instruction and reading.				
ELL Poster 12	• Assess Prior Knowledge • Develop Concepts and Vocabulary	• Preteach Tested Vocabulary	• Art Is All Around Us	• Exploring Culture	• Monitor Progress
ELL Teaching Guide	• Picture It! Lesson, pp. 78–79 • Multilingual Summaries, pp. 82–84	• ELL Reader Lesson, pp. 234–235	• Vocabulary Activities and Word Cards, pp. 80–81 • Multilingual Summaries, pp. 82–84		
ELL Readers	• Reread *How to Survive in the Desert*	• Teach *Louis Armstrong, Jazz Artist*	• Reread *Louis Armstrong, Jazz Artist* and other texts to build fluency.		
ELL and Transition Handbook	Use the following as needed to support this week's instruction and to conduct alternative assessments: • Phonics Transition Lessons • Grammar Transition Lessons • Assessment				

Picture It! Comprehension Lesson
Generalize

Use this lesson to supplement or replace the skill lesson on pages 298–299 of the Teacher's Edition.

Teach

Distribute copies of the Picture It! blackline master on page 79.
• Have students describe the picture and then tell you what the paragraph is about.
• Ask: *What generalization is made in this paragraph?* (Marian Anderson sang in countries all over Europe.)
• Share the Skill Points (at right) with students.
• Have students find the sentence in the paragraph that gives a generalization. Then have them find the sentences that support the generalization with facts.

Practice

Read aloud the directions on page 79. Have students fill in the generalization and support in the graphic organizer.

Answers for page 79: *Generalization*: Marian Anderson sang in countries all over Europe. *Support*: She performed in France and England. She sang in Russia and Austria. Audiences applauded for her in Norway and Sweden.

Skill Points

✓ **Generalizations** are broad statements that apply to many examples. Clue words such as *most, all, always,* and *never* can help identify generalizations.

✓ Generalizations supported by facts and logic are called *valid generalizations. Faulty generalizations* are not supported by facts.

Name _____

Look at the picture. **Read** the paragraph.

- Which sentence makes a generalization about where Marian Anderson performed? **Write** that sentence in the *Generalization* box.

- Which sentences support the generalization with facts? **Write** those sentences in the *Support* boxes.

Singing All Over the World

Marian Anderson sang in countries all over Europe. She performed in France and England. She sang in Russia and Austria. Audiences applauded for her in Norway and Sweden.

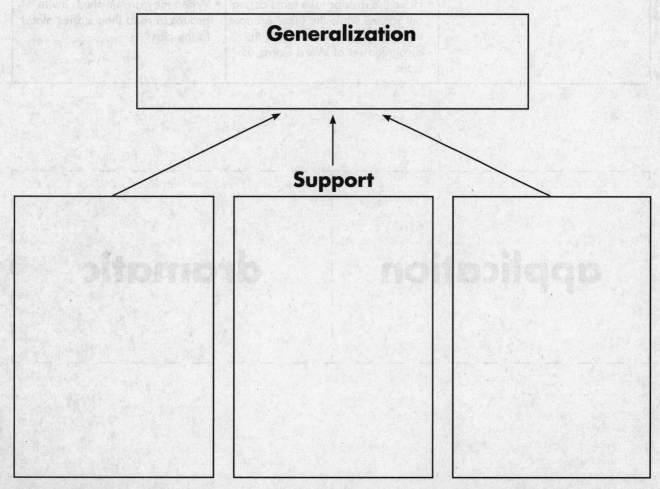

Generalization

Support

Vocabulary Activities and Word Cards

Copy the Word Cards on pages 80–81 as needed for the following activities.
Use the blank card for an additional word that you want to teach.
Also see suggestions for teaching vocabulary in the ELL and Transition Handbook.

Clue Game	Charades	Success Story
• Write the definition of each vocabulary word on the back of a set of Word Cards for students to use in a clue game. • Have one student read the definition and have the others guess the word. • Once the students correctly identify the word, invite volunteers to create sentences using the word.	• Reproduce two sets of Word Cards, and have students play charades. • Place one set of Word Cards face up so that all students can see them. • Divide students into pairs or small groups. Give each group one Word Card. • Have each group discuss how to act out the meaning of its word. • Have the groups take turns acting out scenes while the other groups try to guess the word, using the displayed set of Word Cards as clues.	• Form small groups of students to write a success story. Give each group a set of Word Cards. • Tell groups to use at least six of the Word Cards in a short story about a character who finds a way to achieve a dream. • Give each group a sheet of chart paper. Ask the students to write the story on the paper, taping the Word Cards at the appropriate places. • When they are finished, invite groups to read their stories aloud to the class.

application　　dramatic

enraged

formal

momentous

opera

prejudice

privileged

recital

Multilingual Summaries

English

When Marian Sang

Marian was seven. Everyone wanted to hear her sing. She sang in a church choir. She sang in the People's Chorus.

When Marian was eighteen, she tried to go to music school. In 1915, the school would not teach black people. So Marian studied in her neighborhood. She sang with choirs, and performed sometimes.

Later, Marian went to many states to sing. Sometimes traveling was difficult because she was black. Marian studied with a famous voice teacher. But she wanted to study in Europe. She went and studied there. She sang all over Europe.

When Marian came home, she could not find a place to sing in Washington, D. C. No one would allow Marian to use their hall to sing in. Finally, Marian sang at the Lincoln Memorial. After that, she sang for many people. She received many awards. She sang with the Metropolitan Opera in New York City.

Spanish

Cuando Marian cantó

Marian tenía siete años. Todos querían escucharla cantar. Ella cantaba en el coro de la iglesia. También cantaba en el Coro del Pueblo.

Cuando Marian tenía dieciocho años, trató de ir a la escuela de música. En 1915, la escuela no le enseñaba a las personas de raza negra. Entonces Marian estudió en el barrio. Ella cantaba en coros y algunas veces actuaba.

Más tarde, Marian fue a muchos estados a cantar. Algunas veces tenía dificultades en los viajes porque ella era negra. Marian estudió con un famoso profesor de canto. Pero ella quería estudiar en Europa. Ella fue y estudió allí. Ella cantó por toda Europa.

Cuando Marian regresó a casa, no pudo encontrar un lugar donde cantar en Washington D.C. Nadie le permitía a Marian usar su sala para que cantara. Finalmente, Marian cantó en el Monumento a Lincoln. Después de eso, ella cantó para muchas personas. Recibió muchos premios. Cantó en la Ópera Metropolitana de la Ciudad de Nueva York.

Multilingual Summaries

瑪莉安的悠揚歌聲

瑪莉安七歲時就很會唱歌，每個人都想聽她唱。她參加教堂的唱詩班，也曾經在人民合唱團裡唱歌。

瑪莉安十八歲時想進音樂學校唸書，可是這所學校在 1915 年的時候不收黑人學生，所以瑪莉安就在家附近的學校唸書。當時，她還在唱詩班裡唱歌，有時候還會登台表演。

之後，瑪莉安又去了許多地方表演唱歌，可是因為她是黑人，所以旅行的時候有時會遇到麻煩。她跟一位很有名的聲樂老師學唱歌，不過她真正嚮往的地方是歐洲，她想去那裡唸音樂。後來她真的去了歐洲，而且還在歐洲各地表演唱歌。

儘管如此，瑪莉安回到美國時，還是沒有辦法在首都華盛頓找到地方表演，因為沒有人願意把表演廳借給她。最後，她終於找到林肯紀念堂答應讓她表演。之後，瑪莉安繼續為大家唱歌，也得了很多獎項，而且還在紐約市的大都會歌劇院裡表演。

Khi Marian Hát

Marian bảy tuổi. Mọi người muốn nghe cô hát. Cô hát trong ban hát của nhà thờ. Cô hát trong Ca Đoàn Nhân Dân.

Khi Marian mười tám tuổi, cô cố đi học ở trường âm nhạc. Vào năm 1915, trường này không dạy người Mỹ đen. Vì vậy Marian đi học ở khu phố của mình. Cô hát với các ban hát, và thỉnh thoảng đi trình diễn.

Về sau, Marian đi hát ở nhiều tiểu bang. Đôi khi việc du hành bị khó khăn vì cô là người da đen. Marian học với một thầy dạy hát nổi tiếng. Nhưng cô muốn đi học ở Âu Châu. Cô đi sang đó học. Cô hát khắp nơi ở Âu Châu.

Khi Marian quay về, cô không tìm được một chỗ để hát ở thủ đô Washington, D.C. Không ai cho Marian dùng hội trường của họ để hát. Cuối cùng, Marian hát ở Dinh Kỷ Niệm Tổng Thống Lincoln. Sau đó, cô đi hát cho nhiều người. Cô được nhiều giải thưởng. Cô hát với Đoàn Hát Metropolitan Opera ở Thành phố New York.

Multilingual Summaries

마리안이 노래부를 때

마리안이 7 살이었을 때 모든 사람들은 그녀의 노래를 듣고 싶어했다. 그녀는 교회 성가대와 시민 합창단에서 노래를 불렀다.

마리안이 18살이었을 때 그녀는 음악 학교에 가려고 했지만 1915년이었던 당시 학교에서는 흑인을 가르치려 하지 않았다. 그래서 마리안은 집 근처에서 공부하고 성가대에서 노래 부르며 가끔씩 공연을 했다.

나중에 마리안은 노래를 부르러 여러 주를 다녔는데 때때로 그녀가 흑인이라는 이유로 여행이 어려워지기도 했다. 마리안은 유명한 성악 교사와 공부를 했지만 유럽에서 공부하고 싶어서 유럽으로 가서 공부했고 결국 그녀는 유럽 전역에서 노래를 불렀다.

마리안이 집으로 돌아왔을 때 그녀는 워싱턴 DC에서 노래부를 곳을 찾을 수가 없었다. 아무도 마리안이 노래를 하도록 홀을 내주지 않았지만 결국 그녀는 링컨 기념관에서 노래를 불렀다. 그 일 이후 그녀는 많은 사람들을 위해 노래를 불렀고 여러차례 상을 받았으며 뉴욕시의 메트로폴리탄 오페라와 함께 노래를 불렀다.

Thaum Marian Hu Nkauj

Marian muaj xya xyoo. Txhua leek txhua tus xav mloog nws hu nkauj. Nws hu nkauj nrog pab hu nkauj pem ib lub tshawj. Nws tau hu nkauj nrog pab hu ua hais tias Tib Neeg Pab Hu Nkauj (People's Chorus).

Thaum Marian muaj kaum yim xyoo, nws tau sim mus kawm ntawv nyob rau ib lub tsev kawm qhia txog kev hu nkauj ntaus phe. Nyob rau xyoo ib txhiab ncuaj pua kaum tsib, lub tsev qhia ntawv ntawd tsis kam qhia neeg khej dub. Yog li ntawv, Marian thiaj li kawm nyob hauv nws zej zog. Nws tau hu nkauj nrog ob peb pab hu nkauj, thiab muaj tej zaum uas nws tau ua yeeb yam thiab.

Tom qab ntawd, Marian tau mus rau ntau lub xyeev mush u nkauj. Muaj tej zaum uas kuj nyuab rau nws pem duab kev rau qhov nws yog neeg khej dub. Marian tau kawm nrog ib tug nais khus qhia neeg hu nkauj uas nto npe heev. Tiam si nws xav mus kawm nyob rau sab Aws Laus. Nws tau mus kawm ntawd. Nws tau hu nkauj nyob tau plaws Aws Laus.

Thaum Marian los tsev, nws nrhiav tsis tau ib qhov chaws hu nkauj nyob rau Washington D.C. Tsis muaj leej twg ua yuav pub Marian siv lawv tej tsev los hu nkauj li. Thaum kawg, Marian hu nkauj nyob rau pem qhov chaws uas tau tsim nco txog (Memorial) Lincoln. Tom qab ntawd, nws tau hu nkauj rau coob leej coob tus neeg. Nws tau txais ntau lub nqi zog. Nws tau hu nkauj nrog pab Metropolitan Opera nyob rau New York City.

Learning to Swim Student Edition pages 326–339

Week at a Glance	Customize instruction every day for your English Language Learners.				
	Day 1	**Day 2**	**Day 3**	**Day 4**	**Day 5**
Teacher's Edition	Use the ELL Notes that appear throughout each day of the lesson to support instruction and reading.				
ELL Poster 13	• Assess Prior Knowledge • Develop Concepts and Vocabulary	• Preteach Tested Vocabulary	• Review Sequence	• The Calm Before the Storm	• Monitor Progress
ELL Teaching Guide	• Picture It! Lesson, pp. 85–86 • Multilingual Summaries, pp. 89–91	• ELL Reader Lesson, pp. 236–237	• Vocabulary Activities and Word Cards, pp. 87–88 • Multilingual Summaries, pp. 89–91		
ELL Readers	• Reread *Louis Armstrong, Jazz Artist*	• Teach *Alta Peak*	• Reread *Alta Peak* and other texts to build fluency		
ELL and Transition Handbook	Use the following as needed to support this week's instruction and to conduct alternative assessments: • Phonics Transition Lessons • Grammar Transition Lessons • Assessment				

Picture It! Comprehension Lesson
Sequence

Use this lesson to supplement or replace the skill lesson on pages 322–323 of the Teacher's Edition.

Teach

Distribute copies of the Picture It! blackline master on page 86.
• Have students describe each picture. Then read the paragraph aloud.
• Ask: *What is the girl doing in the first picture?* (She is watching her mother swim.)
• Share the Skill Points (at right) with students.
• Have students identify sequence words in the paragraph.
• Ask them to identify the sequence of events.

> ## Skill Points
> ✓ **Sequence** is the order of events in a story.
> ✓ Clue words such as *before* and *after* help you know the order in which things happen.

Practice

Read aloud the directions on page 86. Have students identify the sequence of events described in the paragraph and answer the questions.

Answers for page 86: 1. Jenny watches her mother swim. **2.** Jenny puts on her goggles. **3.** Jenny gets into the pool.

Look at the pictures. **Read** the paragraph.

Going for a Swim

Jenny and her mother are at the pool. Before she gets into the pool herself, Jenny watches her mother swim back and forth.

After watching her for a while, Jenny puts on her goggles.

She gets into the pool to swim too.

Answer the questions below.

1. What is the first thing that happens in this paragraph?

_____

2. What is the next thing that happens?

_____

3. What is the last thing that happens?

_____

Vocabulary Activities and Word Cards

Copy the Word Cards on page 88 as needed for the following activities.
Use the blank cards for additional words that you want to teach.
Also see suggestions for teaching vocabulary in the ELL and Transition Handbook.

Can You Guess?	Riddle Game	True or False?
• Reproduce one set of Word Cards for a guessing game. • Place all of the Word Cards face down in a pile. • Have one student choose a card and give verbal or visual clues that will help the rest of the group guess the word. • Repeat the process until all students have had a chance to provide clues.	• Divide students into pairs or small groups to play a riddle game. Give each group a set of Word Cards. • Have students place the cards face down in a pile and take turns choosing a card and making up a riddle about the word for others to solve. • Provide a model for the riddle, such as: *This word starts with the letter _____. It ends with the letter _____. It means _____.*	• Reproduce one set of Word Cards for a true-or-false activity. • Ask a student to choose a card. • Make up a sentence using the vocabulary word and ask the student if the sentence is true or false. For example: *It is customary to greet your teacher with a small gift each day.* (false) • Ask the rest of the group whether they agree with the student's answer. • Repeat the activity until all students have had a chance to choose a card.

customary

emphasized

frantic

stunned

treaded

Multilingual Summaries

English

Learning to Swim

A girl wants to be a better swimmer. Her mother teaches her to swim. The girl wants to swim farther in the school swimming test. She is a faster runner than other children. However, the other children are faster swimmers.

The girl knows it will take hard work to be a better swimmer. Her mother teaches her strokes and helps her practice in the river all summer.

One day, the family goes to the sea. The girl and her mother play in the waves. Then the current carries them far from shore. The girl is afraid. They might drown. They swim to some rocks and are safe. Later, the girl wins the race at school.

Spanish

Aprender a nadar

Una niña quiere ser mejor nadadora. La madre le enseña a nadar. La niña quiere llegar más lejos en el examen de la escuela de natación. Ella corre más rápido que los otros niños. Sin embargo, los otros niños nadan más rápido que ella.

La niña sabe que le costará mucho trabajo ser mejor nadadora. Su madre le enseña diferentes estilos de nadar y la ayuda en su práctica en el río todo el verano.

Un día, la familia va al mar. La niña y la madre juegan en las olas. Luego la corriente las arrastra lejos de la orilla. La niña tiene miedo. Ellas pueden ahogarse. Ellas nadan hacia unas rocas y están a salvo. Después, la niña gana en la competencia de la escuela.

Multilingual Summaries

Chinese

學游泳

有個女孩想把游泳練好，她媽媽答應教她。女孩想在學校游泳考試中游得更遠一些。跟別的小朋友比起來，她跑得比較快，可是游泳卻輸給其他人。

女孩知道要游泳進步便要辛勤地練習。整個夏天，媽媽都教她划水，並且陪她在河裡練習游泳。

有一天，女孩一家人去海邊玩，女孩和媽媽在海浪中玩耍，突然有個大浪把她們捲離了岸邊。女孩覺得很害怕，她和媽媽可能都會淹死。幸好她們會游泳，兩個人一起努力游到岩石上，終於安全了。後來，女孩在學校的游泳比賽裡得了冠軍。

Vietnamese

Học Bơi

Một cô gái muốn trở thành một người bơi giỏi hơn. Mẹ của cô dạy cho cô bơi. Cô muốn bơi xa hơn trong kỳ thi bơi lội ở trường. Cô là người chạy nhanh hơn những trẻ khác. Tuy nhiên, các đứa trẻ khác là người bơi nhanh hơn cô.

Cô gái biết là phải gắng nhiều công sức để trở thành một người bơi giỏi hơn. Mẹ của cô dạy cho cô những động tác bơi và giúp cô tập dợt bơi dưới sông cả mùa hè.

Một ngày kia, gia đình đi ra biển. Cô gái và mẹ của cô chơi đùa trong sóng nước. Rồi dòng nước đưa họ ra xa bờ. Cô gái lo sợ. Họ có thể bị chết đuối. Họ bơi đến những hòn đá và được an toàn. Về sau, cô gái thắng kỳ bơi đua ở trường.

Multilingual Summaries

수영 배우기

한 소녀가 남들보다 수영을 잘 하고 싶어한다. 그녀의 엄마는 그녀에게 수영하는 법을 가르쳐 준다. 소녀는 교내 수영대회에서 앞서고 싶어한다. 그녀는 다른 아이들보다 더 빨리 달리지만 다른 아이들은 그녀보다 더 빨리 헤엄친다.

그 소녀는 훌륭한 수영선수가 되려면 고된 노력이 필요하다는 것을 알고 있다. 소녀의 엄마는 소녀에게 여름 내내 강가에서 수영을 가르치고 연습하는 걸 돕는다.

어느 날 소녀의 가족이 바다에 가게 되고 소녀와 엄마는 파도 속에서 물놀이를 한다. 그 때 파도가 그들을 해안에서 먼 곳으로 실어가고 소녀는 겁이 난다. 그들이 빠져 죽을 지도 모른다고 생각했기 때문이다. 소녀와 엄마는 바위로 헤엄쳐가고 이제는 안전하다. 그 후 소녀는 학교 수영대회에서 우승한다.

Kawm Ua Luam Dej

Ib tug ntxhais xav kawm ua luam dej kom keej tshaj. Nws niam qhia nws ua luam dej. Tub ntxhais xav ua luam dej kom deb tshaj kev sib xeem pem tsev kawm ntawv. Nws qhia ceev tshaj lwm cov menyuam. Tiam si, lwm cov menyuam luam tau dej ceev dua.

Tub ntxhais paub tias nws yuav tsum rau siab rho kawm nws thiaj li ua tau luam kom keej tshaj. Nws niam qhia nws tias yuav tsum luam li cas thiab pab nws xaum hauv tub dej tas cim ntuj sov.

Muaj ib hnub uas lawv tsev neeg mus rau nram hiavtxwv. Tub ntxhais thiab nws niam nkawv ua si hauv dej. Ces dej nqa nkawv mus deb ntawm nrug dej lawm. Tub ntxhais ntshai. Tej zaum nkawv yuav poob dej. Nkawv ua luam dej mus rau pem ib cov pobzeb thiab nkawv siab kaj lawm. Tom qab, tub ntxhais yeej kev sib tw tom tsev kawm ntawv.

Juan Verdades Student Edition pages 350–363

Week at a Glance	Customize instruction every day for your English Language Learners.				
	Day 1	**Day 2**	**Day 3**	**Day 4**	**Day 5**
Teacher's Edition	Use the ELL Notes that appear throughout each day of the lesson to support instruction and reading.				
ELL Poster 14	• Assess Prior Knowledge • Develop Concepts and Vocabulary	• Preteach Tested Vocabulary	• I Trust You	• Review Generalize	• Monitor Progress
ELL Teaching Guide	• Picture It! Lesson, pp. 92–93 • Multilingual Summaries, pp. 96–98	• ELL Reader Lesson, pp. 238–239	• Vocabulary Activities and Word Cards, pp. 94–95 • Multilingual Summaries, pp. 96–98		
ELL Readers	• Reread *Alta Peak*	• Teach *Golden Sea Farm*	• Reread *Golden Sea Farm* and other texts to build fluency		
ELL and Transition Handbook	Use the following as needed to support this week's instruction and to conduct alternative assessments: • Phonics Transition Lessons • Grammar Transition Lessons • Assessment				

Picture It! Comprehension Lesson
Generalize

Use this lesson to supplement or replace the skill lesson on pages 346–347 of the Teacher's Edition.

Teach

Distribute copies of the Picture It! blackline master on page 93.
• Have students describe what the paragraph is about.
• Ask: *What generalization is made in this paragraph?* (People who work on ranches are always busy.)
• Share the Skill Points (at right) with students.
• Have students find the sentence in the paragraph that gives a generalization. Then have them find the sentences that support the generalization with examples.

Practice

Read aloud the directions on page 93. Have students write the generalization and examples in the graphic organizer. Have students keep their organizers for later reteaching.

Answers for page 93: *Generalization*: People who work on ranches are always busy. *Examples*: They must take care of cattle. They must plant trees. When the fruit on the trees is ripe, they must pick the fruit.

Skill Points

✓**Generalizations** are broad statements that apply to many examples.

✓Sometimes authors generalize about a group of people or things.

✓Valid generalizations are supported by examples or facts. Invalid generalizations are not supported.

Look at the picture. **Read** the paragraph.

- Which sentence makes a generalization about what life is like for people who work on ranches? **Write** that sentence in the *Generalization* box.

- Which sentences support the generalization with examples? **Write** those sentences in the *Example* boxes.

Working on a Ranch

People who work on ranches are always busy. They must take care of cattle. They must plant trees. When the fruit on the trees is ripe, they must pick the fruit.

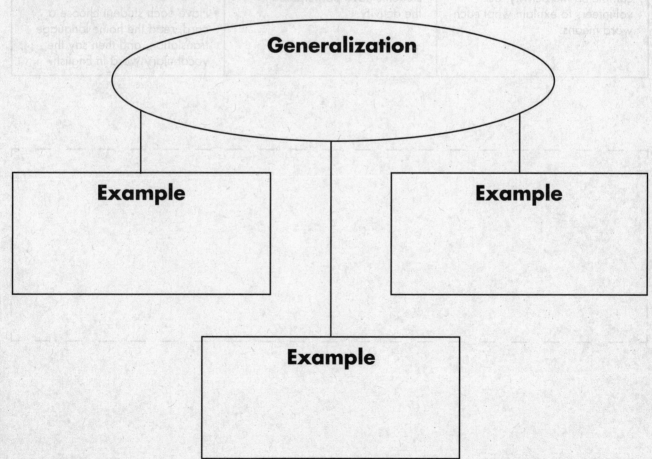

Generalization

Example

Example

Example

© Scott Foresman 6

Vocabulary Activities and Word Cards

Copy the Word Cards on page 95 as needed for the following activities.
Use the blank cards for additional words that you want to teach.
Also see suggestions for teaching vocabulary in the ELL and Transition Handbook.

Parts-of-Speech Word Sort	Poster Game	Home Language Clues
• Give each student a set of Word Cards for a word sort activity. • Have each student prepare a four-column chart with *Nouns, Verbs, Adjectives,* and *Adverbs* as the headings. • Remind students what kinds of words belong in each column. • Have students write each vocabulary word in the appropriate column. • When all students have completed the activity, ask volunteers to explain what each word means.	• Reproduce one set of Word Cards for students to use in a poster game. • Have students take turns choosing a Word Card without letting others see it. • On their turn, ask students to point to a scene or detail on the ELL Poster, and then give clues about their word without saying it until other students guess the word. • Repeat the process until all students have participated in the activity.	• Pair students who have writing proficiency in the same home language, and give each student a set of Word Cards. • Have students work together to write translations of the vocabulary words in their home language on the back of each card. (See the Multilingual Lesson Vocabulary beginning on page 272 for suggested translations.) • Have partners lay out the cards with the home language sides facing up. • Have each student choose a card, read the home language translation, and then say the vocabulary word in English.

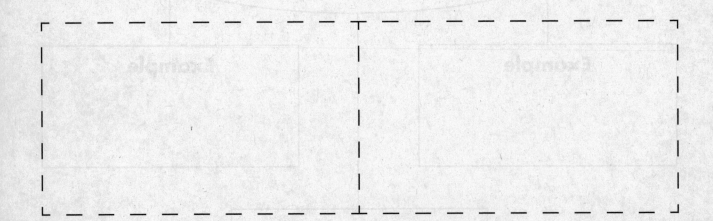

confidently

dismounted

distressed

flourish

fulfill

permission

repay

vigorously

Multilingual Summaries

Juan Verdades:
The Man Who Couldn't Tell a Lie

Don Ignacio has the best apple tree in the land. He is very proud of the apples. He also has a foreman called Juan Verdades. Juan cannot tell a lie. Don Arturo makes a bet with Don Ignacio. He bets that he can make Juan tell a lie. He bets his ranch.

Don Arturo goes home to tell his wife and daughter. They make a plan. The daughter makes Juan fall in love with her. Then, she asks him to pick all the apples. She and her family think that Juan will lie to Don Ignacio about the apples.

Juan picks all the apples. But he cannot lie to Don Ignacio. Juan tells a riddle that tells the truth. Don Ignacio is happy that Juan tells the truth. He wins the bet. Don Ignacio gives Don Arturo's ranch to Juan. Juan and Don Arturo's daughter will marry.

Juan Verdades:
El hombre que no podía mentir

Don Ignacio tiene el mejor manzano del lugar. Él está muy orgulloso de sus manzanas. También tiene un capataz llamado Juan Verdades. Juan no puede decir una mentira. Don Arturo hace una apuesta con Don Ignacio. Apuesta que él puede hacer que Juan diga una mentira. Cada uno apuesta su rancho.

Don Arturo regresa a casa y les cuenta a su esposa y a su hija. Ellos hacen un plan. La hija hace que Juan se enamore de ella. Luego, le pide que recoja todas las manzanas para ella. Ella y su familia piensan que Juan le dirá a Don Ignacio una mentira sobre las manzanas.

Juan recoge todas las manzanas. Pero no puede mentirle a Don Ignacio. Juan dice un acertijo que cuenta la verdad. Don Ignacio está feliz de que Juan haya dicho la verdad. Él gana la apuesta. Don Ignacio le da el rancho de Don Arturo a Juan. Juan y la hija se casarán.

Multilingual Summaries

Chinese

朱安・凡達帝斯
不會說謊的人

唐・伊格納西歐有全世界最好的蘋果樹，他對這棵樹長出來的蘋果感到非常自豪，他還有一個不會說謊的領班，名字叫朱安・凡達帝斯。唐・阿楚若跟伊格納西歐打賭，他有辦法讓朱安說謊，要是輸了就把農場送給伊格納西歐。

阿楚若回家之後跟妻子和女兒說了這件事，他們想了一個計畫，讓朱安愛上他們的女兒，然後女兒再叫朱安去偷摘所有蘋果。這家人以為，朱安一定會為了蘋果跟伊格納西歐說謊。

朱安果真摘了所有的蘋果，但是他沒有辦法對伊格納西歐說謊，於是編了一個謎語，讓他的主人從這個謎語裡知道了一切真相。伊格納西歐覺得非常高興，因為朱安說了實話，他打賭贏了！伊格納西歐把阿楚若的農場送給朱安，朱安還娶到了阿楚若的女兒。

Vietnamese

Juan Verdades
Người Không Thể Nói Dối

Don Ignacio có cây táo ngon nhất trong vùng. Ông rất hãnh diện về những trái táo của mình. Ông cũng có một người quản đốc tên Juan Verdades. Juan không thể nói dối. Don Arturo cá cược với Don Ignacio. Ông ta cá là ông có thể làm cho Juan nói dối. Ông cá trang trại của mình.

Don Arturo về nhà nói cho vợ và con gái nghe. Họ đặt ra một kế hoạch. Người con gái làm cho Juan phải lòng yêu thương cô. Kế đến, cô kêu anh ta hái hết những trái táo. Cô và gia đình nghĩ là Juan sẽ nói dối với Don Ignacio về những trái táo.

Juan hái hết mấy trái táo. Nhưng anh ta không thể nói dối với Don Ignacio. Juan đặt ra câu đố để nói sự thật. Don Ignacio vui mừng là Juan nói sự thật. Ông ấy thắng kỳ cá cược. Don Ignacio trao trang trại của Don Arturo cho Juan. Juan và con gái Don Arturo sẽ kết hôn.

Multilingual Summaries

후안 베르다데스
거짓말을 하지 못한 사나이

돈 이그나시오는 그 지역에서 가장 좋은 사과 나무를 갖고 있고 그는 그 사과들을 매우 자랑스럽게 여긴다. 그는 또한 후안 베르다데스라고 불리는 감독관도 데리고 있는데 후안은 거짓말을 하지 못한다. 돈 알투로는 자기가 후안을 거짓말하도록 만들 수 있다고 돈 이그나시오와 내기를 하고 자신의 목장을 내기에 건다.

돈 알투로는 부인과 딸에게 가서 이 사실을 얘기하고 그들은 계획을 세운다. 딸이 후안을 자신과 사랑에 빠지도록 만들고 나서 그에게 그 사과들을 모두 따라고 간청하는 것이다. 그녀 가족은 후안이 그 사과들에 대해서 돈 이그나시오에게 거짓말을 할 것이라고 생각한다.

후안은 사과를 모두 딴다. 하지만 그는 돈 이그나시오에게 거짓말을 할 수 없다. 후안은 진실을 담은 수수께끼를 내고 돈 이그나시오는 후안이 사실대로 얘기해준 데 대해 기뻐하며 내기에서 이긴 다. 돈 이그나시오는 후안에게 돈 알투로의 목장을 주고 나중에 후안과 그 딸은 결혼한다.

Tus Txiv Neej Uas Tsis Txawj Dag

Don Ignacio muaj tub ntoo av pooj (apple) uas zoo tshaj plaws nyob rau daim av ntawd. Nws rau siab rau nws cov av paum kawg. Nws kuj muaj ib tug pab nais hu ua Juan Verdades thiab. Juan tsis txawj dag li. Don Arturo tau npav nrog don Ignacio. Nws npav tias nws yuav ua tau kom Juan dag kom tau. Nws npav nws lub vaj lub tsev.

Don Arturo mus tsev mus hais qhia rau nws tus poj niam thiab nws tus ntxhais. Lawv npaj in lub tswv yim. Tus ntxhais uas kom Juan nyiam nws. Ces, nws hnug kom nws de tas nrho cov av paum. Nws thiab nws tsev neeg xav tias Juan yuav dag rau Don Ignacio hais txog cov txiv av paum.

Juan de tas nrho cov av paum. Tiam si he tsis txawj dag rau Don Ignacio. Juan piav ib zaj dab neeg uas txhaib qhov tseeb. Don Ignacio zoo siab tias Juan qhia qhov tseeb. Nws yeej qhov npav. Don Ignacio muab Don Arturo lub vaj lub tsev rau Juan. Juan thiab tus ntxhais sib yuav.

Elizabeth Blackwell   Student Edition pages 376–395

Week at a Glance	\multicolumn{5}{c}{**Customize instruction every day for your English Language Learners.**}				
	Day 1	**Day 2**	**Day 3**	**Day 4**	**Day 5**
Teacher's Edition	Use the ELL Notes that appear throughout each day of the lesson to support instruction and reading.				
ELL Poster 15	• Assess Prior Knowledge • Develop Concepts and Vocabulary	• Preteach Tested Vocabulary	• Opportunity Knocks	• I Have a Dream	• Monitor Progress
ELL Teaching Guide	• Picture It! Lesson, pp. 99–100 • Multilingual Summaries, pp. 103–105	• ELL Reader Lesson, pp. 240–241	• Vocabulary Activities and Word Cards, pp. 101–102 • Multilingual Summaries, pp. 103–105		
ELL Readers	• Reread *Golden Sea Farm*	• Teach *Alice Hamilton*	• Reread *Alice Hamilton* and other texts to build fluency.		
ELL and Transition Handbook	Use the following as needed to support this week's instruction and to conduct alternative assessments: • Phonics Transition Lessons • Grammar Transition Lessons • Assessment				

Picture It! Comprehension Lesson

Draw Conclusions

Use this lesson to supplement or replace the skill lesson on pages 372–373 of the Teacher's Edition.

Teach

Distribute copies of the Picture It! blackline master on page 100.
- Have students describe what they see in the picture. Then read the paragraph aloud.
- Ask: *What do you notice about the people in the picture?* (Half are men, and half are women.)
- Share the Skill Points (at right) with students.
- Ask students what conclusion they draw about who studies to become a doctor today. Then have them find facts that support this conclusion.

Practice

Read aloud the directions on page 100. Have students write the conclusion in the graphic organizer. Have them write supporting facts.

Answers for page 100: *Conclusion*: Both men and women can become doctors. *Fact*: Half the students in Maria's class are women and half are men. *Fact*: Half the doctors at her brother's hospital are women. *Real Life*: I saw both men and women doctors when I visited a hospital.

Skill Points

✓ When you draw a conclusion, you decide what to think about something. You form an opinion that makes sense.

✓ Conclusions should be **based on facts**. What you read should support your conclusion.

✓ You can also use **what you know about real life** to help you draw conclusions.

Look at the picture. **Read** the paragraph.

- What conclusion can you draw from this paragraph? **Write** the conclusion in the *Conclusion* box.

- Which sentences helped you draw the conclusion? **Write** them in the *Fact* boxes.

- Are there any facts from real life that helped you draw the conclusion? **Write** them in the *Real Life box.*

Medical Student

Maria is in medical school. She is studying to become a doctor. Half of the students in her class are men, and half are women. Maria's brother is a doctor. Half of the doctors at his hospital are women.

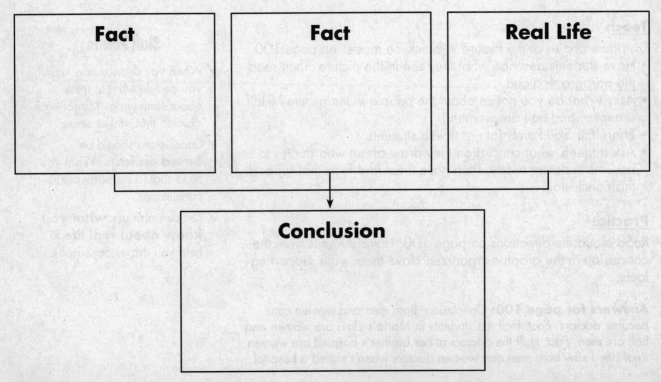

Fact	**Fact**	**Real Life**

Conclusion

Vocabulary Activities and Word Cards

Copy the Word Cards on pages 101–102 as needed for the following activities.
Use the blank card for an additional word that you want to teach.
Also see suggestions for teaching vocabulary in the ELL and Transition Handbook.

Clue Game	Fill in the Blanks	Secret Word
• Write the definition of each vocabulary word on the back of one set of Word Cards for students to use in a clue game.	• Give each student a complete set of Word Cards. Have students place the cards face up on their desks or tables.	• Divide students into pairs for a Secret Word activity. Give each pair of students a complete set of Word Cards.
• Have one student choose a card and read the definition. Have the others guess the word.	• Choose one vocabulary word and think of a context in which it can be used. Describe the context, omitting the vocabulary word. For example: *Miguel smiled as he received his _____ at graduation.*	• Have students place the Word Cards face up on a desk or table so that both students can see them.
• Once students correctly identify the word, invite volunteers to create sentences using the word.	• Have students choose the word that best fits the context.	• Have one student secretly choose a word and give verbal and visual clues that will help the other student guess the word. Have the student pause after each clue so that his or her partner can guess the word.
	• Repeat the context clue several times as students search for the correct word.	• Have students take turns giving clues and guessing words.

absurd

behalf

candidate

dean

delirious

diploma

hovers

obedient

reject

Multilingual Summaries

Elizabeth Blackwell: Medical Pioneer

Elizabeth Blackwell studied with a fine doctor. She wanted to go to medical school. No school would accept her. In that time, medical schools would not teach women. Finally, Geneva Medical College took her. She graduated with honors. Elizabeth wanted to be a surgeon.

Elizabeth went to Paris to work as a student nurse. She got an infection in her eye that almost blinded her. She had to go home. She regained some of her sight later. She studied practical medicine instead of surgery.

Elizabeth opened a clinic in New York City. The clinic was for immigrants. She worked very hard. Once, when a patient died, a crowd of people grew angry. One immigrant said Elizabeth was a fine doctor. Then the people were thankful for Elizabeth's hard work.

Spanish

Elizabeth Blackwell: Pionera de la medicina

Elizabeth Blackwell estudió con un distinguido médico. Ella quería ir a la escuela de medicina. Ninguna escuela de medicina la aceptaba. En aquel tiempo, las escuelas de medicina no aceptaban a las mujeres. Finalmente, el Colegio Geneva de Medicina la aceptó. Ella se graduó con honores. Elizabeth quería ser cirujana.

Elizabeth fue a París a trabajar como enfermera estudiante. Contrajo una infección en un ojo que casi la deja ciega. Tuvo que regresar a casa. Recuperó parte de la visión después. Ella estudió medicina práctica en vez de cirugía.

Elizabeth abrió una clínica en la Ciudad de Nueva York. La clínica era para inmigrantes. Trabajó muy duro. Una vez, cuando un paciente murió, un grupo de personas se pusieron furiosas. Uno de los inmigrantes dijo que Elizabeth era una buena doctora. Luego la gente agradeció el trabajo duro que hizo Elizabeth.

Multilingual Summaries

伊莉莎白・布蕾克威爾
歷史上第一位女醫生

　　伊莉莎白跟著一位優秀的醫生學習，她想進醫學院唸書，可是沒有學校肯收她，因為在那個年代，醫學院不收女學生。最後，日內瓦醫學院答應讓她入學。伊莉莎白以優異的成績畢業，她想當外科醫生。

　　伊莉莎白到巴黎當護士學生，可是卻因為眼睛感染了傳染病，嚴重到幾乎看不見東西，所以她只好回家。幸好回家休養後，視力恢復了一些。後來她決定放棄當外科醫生，改唸實用醫學。

　　之後，伊莉莎白在紐約市開了一家診所，專門為移民看病，她非常努力工作。有一回，病人不幸去世，有些人覺得很生氣，怪伊莉莎白醫術不好，可是有個移民卻挺身為伊莉莎白說話，他說伊莉莎白是個好醫生。後來大家了解伊莉莎白的付出之後，都非常感激她。

Elizabeth Blackwell
Nhà Tiên Phong Y Học

Elizabeth Blackwell theo học với một bác sĩ giỏi. Cô muốn đi học trường y. Không có trường nào nhận cô. Vào thời đó, các trường y khoa không dạy phụ nữ. Cuối cùng, Trường Đại Học Y Khoa Geneva nhận cô. Cô tốt nghiệp với bằng danh dự. Elizabeth muốn trở thành một bác sĩ phẫu thuật.

Elizabeth đi đến Paris để làm một y tá thực tập. Cô bị nhiễm trùng mắt nặng suýt làm cô bị mù. Cô phải trở về nhà. Sau đó cô thấy lại được chút ít. Cô học y khoa thực dụng thay vì phẫu thuật.

Elizabeth mở một y viện ở Thành phố New York. Y viện này dành cho di dân. Cô rất cần cù làm việc. Có lần, một bệnh nhân bị chết, đám đông giận dữ. Một di dân nói Elizabeth là một bác sĩ giỏi. Rồi người ta cám ơn Elizabeth vì sự cần cù của cô.

Multilingual Summaries

엘리자베스 블랙웰
의학 선구자

엘리자베스 블랙웰은 한 저명한 의사 밑에서 공부하며 의과 대학에 가길 원했다. 하지만 그녀를 받아주는 학교가 없었다. 왜냐하면 당시에는 여성을 가르치려는 의과 대학이 없었기 때문이다. 마침내 제네바 의과 대학이 그녀를 받아주었고 그녀는 우수한 성적으로 졸업했다. 엘리자베스는 외과의사가 되고 싶었다.

엘리자베스는 학생 간호사로 일하기 위해 파리로 갔는데 거기서 그녀는 안질환을 얻어 거의 실명 위기에 처해 집으로 돌아와야만 했다. 후에 그녀는 약간의 시력을 되찾았고 수술 대신 실용 의학을 공부했다.

엘리자베스는 뉴욕시에 이민자들을 위한 병원을 열고 매우 열심히 일했다. 한 번은 어떤 환자가 죽어 사람들이 화를 낸 적이 있었는데 한 이민자가 엘리자베스를 훌륭한 의사라고 말하자 사람들은 엘리자베스의 노고에 감사를 표시했다.

Elizabeth Blackwell

Elizabeth Blackwell tau kawm ua hauj lwm nrog ib tug kw tshuaj nto npe heev. Nws xav mus kawm ua kws tshuaj. Tsis muaj leej twg ua kam txiaj nws. Thaum lub sib hawm ntawd, tsev kho mob qhia neeg ua kw tshuaj tsis kam qhia poj niam. Thaum kawg, lub tsev kawm ntawd Geneva Medical College txais nws. Nws tau kawm tas nrog qib siab kawg. Elizabeth xav los ua ib tug kws khob mob pais neeg.

Elizabeth mus rau Paris mus ua hauj lwm ua ib tug ntxhais kawm ua hauj lwm ua nawj (nurse). Nws tau ib tug mob kis nws lub qhov muag ua rau nws yuav luag dig muag. Nws tau mus tsev. Lwm hnub nws rov pom kev duab. Nws tau los kawm ua kw khob mob xwb es tsis pais neeg lawm.

Elizabeth qib ib lub tsev khob mob nyob rau New York City. Lub tsev khob mob yog rau neeg ua nyuam qhuav tuaj teb chaws no. Nws khwv heev. Muab ib zaug, thaum ib tug neeg mob tuag, ib pab neeg tau chim heev. Ib tug neeg nyuaj qhuav tuaj hais tias Elizabeth yogi b tug kw khob mob zoo heev. Ces cov neeg txawm li ua Elizabeth tsaug rau nws txoj kev rau siab tso ua hauj lwm khob neeg.

Into the Ice

Student Edition pages 412–425

<div style="text-align:center">**Week at a Glance**</div>	Customize instruction every day for your English Language Learners.				
	Day 1	**Day 2**	**Day 3**	**Day 4**	**Day 5**
Teacher's Edition	Use the ELL Notes that appear throughout each day of the lesson to support instruction and reading.				
ELL Poster 16	• Assess Prior Knowledge • Develop Concepts and Vocabulary	• Preteach Tested Vocabulary	• My Own Expedition	• Super Synonyms	• Monitor Progress
ELL Teaching Guide	• Picture It! Lesson, pp. 106–107 • Multilingual Summaries, pp. 110–112	• ELL Reader Lesson, pp. 242–243	• Vocabulary Activities and Word Cards, pp. 108–109 • Multilingual Summaries, pp. 110–112		
ELL Readers	• Reread *Alice Hamilton*	• Teach *Matthew Henson's Story*	• Reread *Matthew Henson's Story* and other texts to build fluency		
ELL and Transition Handbook	Use the following as needed to support this week's instruction and to conduct alternative assessments: • Phonics Transition Lessons • Grammar Transition Lessons • Assessment				

Picture It! Comprehension Lesson

Cause and Effect

Use this lesson to supplement or replace the skill lesson on pages 408–409 of the Teacher's Edition.

Teach

Distribute copies of the Picture It! blackline master on page 107.
- Have students describe the picture. Then read the paragraph aloud.
- Ask: *Why did Richard Peary spend years of his life exploring?* (because he wanted to reach the North Pole)
- Share the Skill Points (at right) with students.
- Have students identify the cause in the paragraph. Then have them identify the effect.

Practice

Read aloud the directions on page 107. Have students fill in causes and effects in the graphic organizer. Have them keep their organizers for later reteaching.

Answers for page 107: *Cause 1:* Robert Peary wanted to be the first person to visit the North Pole *Effect 1:* So he spent more than 20 years exploring very cold places. *Cause 2:* He learned as much as he could about places very far north. *Effect 2:* In 1909 he finally achieved his goal of reaching the North Pole.

Skill Points

✔ An **effect** is something that happens. A **cause** is the reason something happens. To find a cause, ask yourself, *Why did this happen?* To find an effect, ask yourself, *What happened because of this?*

✔ Clue words, such as *because, so,* and *due to* can help you spot cause-and-effect relationships.

Look at the picture. **Read** the paragraph.

• Which sentences identify causes? **Write** them in the *Cause* boxes.

• Which sentences identify the effects of those causes? **Write** them in the *Effect* boxes.

Reaching the North Pole

Robert Peary wanted to be the first person to visit the North Pole. So he spent more than 20 years exploring very cold places. He learned as much as he could about places very far north. Thanks to all his hard work, in 1909 he finally achieved his goal of reaching the North Pole.

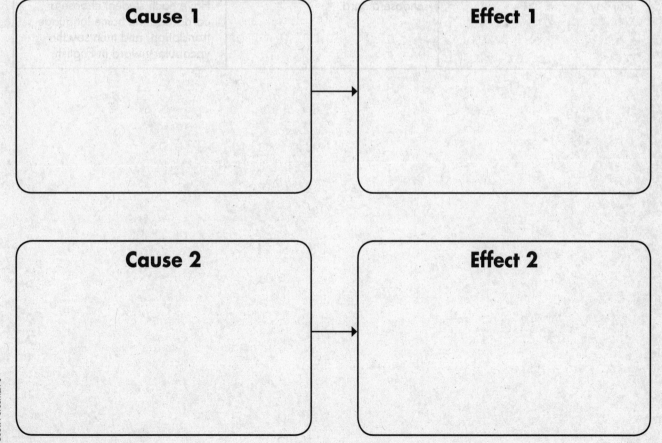

Cause 1

Effect 1

Cause 2

Effect 2

© Scott Foresman 6

Vocabulary Activities and Word Cards

Copy the Word Cards on page 109 as needed for the following activities.
Use the blank card for an additional word that you want to teach.
Also see suggestions for teaching vocabulary in the ELL and Transition Handbook.

Synonym Search	True or False?	Home Language Clues
• Give each student a set of Word Cards for a synonym search.	• Reproduce one set of Word Cards for a true-or-false activity.	• Pair students who have writing proficiency in the same home language, and give each student a set of Word Cards.
• Have students place the cards face up on their desks or tables.	• Ask a student to choose a card.	
• Remind students that synonyms are words that mean the same thing. Then state the following synonyms or near synonyms for the vocabulary words: *journey, pilot, covered, aloneness, fate, defeat, confirm.*	• Make up a sentence using the vocabulary word and ask the student if the sentence is true or false. For example: *Most people enjoy being in isolation.* (false)	• Have students work together to write translations of the vocabulary words in their home language on the back of each card. (See the Multilingual Lesson Vocabulary beginning on page 272 for suggested translations.)
• Ask students to select the vocabulary word that is closest in meaning to each of the words you say.	• Ask the rest of the group whether they agree with the student's answer.	• Have partners lay out the cards with the home language sides facing up.
	• Repeat the activity until all students have had a chance to choose a card.	• Have each student choose a card, read the home language translation, and then say the vocabulary word in English.

conquer

destiny

expedition

insulated

isolation

navigator

verify

Multilingual Summaries

Into the Ice:
The Story of Arctic Exploration

Fridtjof Nansen explored the Arctic in 1893. He and another man left their ship and took some dog sleds across the ice. They set the first record for traveling farthest into the Arctic.

Another explorer, Salomon Andrée, tried to reach the North Pole by hot air balloon. The balloon ran out of gas. The men in the balloon died on the ice.

An American named Robert E. Peary went on his first Arctic expedition in 1886. On that trip, he ran out of supplies. He and his men had to turn back. In 1909, Peary claimed to have finally reached the North Pole. Another man, Dr. Cook, claimed he had reached the North Pole a year earlier. Neither claim has been proven. The first person to reach the Pole by plane was Joseph Fletcher, in 1952.

Dentro el hielo:
La historia de la exploración del Ártico

Fridtjof Nansen exploró el Ártico en 1893. Él y otro hombre dejaron su embarcación y viajaron a través del hielo en unos trineos de perros. Ellos establecieron el primer récord del viaje más largo dentro del Ártico.

Otro explorador, Salomon Andrée, trató de llegar al polo norte en un globo de aire caliente. El globo se quedó sin gas. Los hombres murieron en el hielo.

Un norteamericano llamado Robert E. Peary fue en su primera expedición al Ártico en 1886. En ese viaje, se quedó sin provisiones. Él y sus compañeros tuvieron que regresar. En 1909, Peary afirmó que finalmente había llegado al polo norte. Otro hombre, Dr. Cook, afirmó que él había llegado al polo norte un año antes. Ninguna de las dos afirmaciones ha sido probada. La primera persona en llegar al polo norte en avión fue Joseph Fletcher en 1952.

Multilingual Summaries

深入冰原
北極探險的故事

1893 年，弗里特約夫·南森前往北極探險，他和同伴下了船之後，就乘著狗拉的雪橇穿越冰原。他們創下在北極旅行距離最遠的紀錄。

另一個探險家－所羅門·安德烈－嘗試乘坐熱氣球到達北極點，可是熱氣球的瓦斯卻半途用光了，安德烈不幸死在冰原中。

1886 年，有個名叫羅伯特·皮列的美國人展開他第一次的北極探險之旅，但糧食在半路上就吃完了，他和探險隊隊員只好折返。1909 年，皮列宣稱他終於抵達了北極點，不過，另一個探險家－庫克博士－也說他早在一年前就到達北極點了。皮列和庫克的說法都沒有辦法證明是真的。而在 1952年第一個乘坐飛機抵達北極點的是喬瑟夫·弗勒契。

Đi Vào Băng Đá
Câu Chuyện Thám Hiểm Bắc Cực

Fridtjof Nansen đi thám hiểm Bắc Cực vào năm 1893. Ông và một người nữa rời tàu của họ và dẫn theo những con chó trượt tuyết đi qua băng đá. Họ lập kỷ lục đầu tiên vì đã du hành xa nhất vào Bắc Cực.

Một người thám hiểm khác, Salomon Andrée, cố đi đến Bắc Cực bằng khinh khí cầu. Quả cầu hết khí. Những người trong quả cầu chết trên băng.

Một người Mỹ tên Robert E. Peary bắt đầu cuộc hành trình Bắc Cực đầu tiên của ông vào năm 1886. Trong chuyến đi đó, ông bị hết đồ dự trữ. Ông và những người theo ông phải quay trở lại. Vào năm 1909, Peary tuyên bố là cuối cùng ông đã đến được Bắc Cực. Một người khác, Bác Sĩ Cook, tuyên bố là ông đã đến Bắc Cực một năm trước đó. Cả hai lời tuyên bố đều không chứng thực được. Người đầu tiên đi đến Bắc Cực bằng máy bay là Joseph Fletcher, vào năm 1952.

Multilingual Summaries

빙하 속으로
북극 탐험 이야기

프리됴프 난센은 1893년에 북극을 탐험했다. 그와 다른 한 명은 타고 온 배를 떠나 개 썰매를 타고 빙하를 가로질렀다. 이것으로 그들은 최초로 북극으로 가장 멀리 탐험한 기록을 세웠다.

또 다른 탐험가인 살로몬 앙드레는 열기구로 북극에 도달하려고 했지만 열기구의 연료가 바닥이 나서 사람들이 얼음 위에서 죽었다.

로버트 E. 피어리라는 미국인이 1886년 처음으로 북극 탐험 길에 올랐다. 그 원정에서 피어리는 물자가 바닥이 났고 그와 그의 동료들은 되돌아와야만 했다. 1909년 피어리는 마침내 북극에 도달했다고 주장했고 쿡 박사라는 사람은 그가 피어리보다 1년 전에 북극에 도달했다고 주장했다. 하지만 두 사람의 주장 모두 증명되지 않고 있다. 최초로 비행기로 북극에 도착한 사람은 조셉 플레처로 1952년의 일이었다.

Nyob Rau Hauv Nab Kuab
Zaj Dab Neeg Piav Txog Kev
Nrhiav Sab Artic Teb

Fridtjof Nansen nrhiav pom sab Artic teb nyob rau xyoo ib txhiab yim pua cuaj caum peb. Nws thiab lwm tus txiv neej tau tso lawv lub nkoj tseg thiab tau caij ib cov laub uas aub cab hla nab kuab. Nkawv tau sau thawj zag xeev xwm txheej uas tau mus txog sab teb Artic deb tshaj plaws.

Lwm tus neeg nrhiav teb chaws, Salomon Andrée, tau sim caij ib lub zais rau roj pa kub (hot air balloon) mus kom txog rau North Pole teb. Lub zais roj tag lawm. Cov txiv neej caij lub zais tau tuag saum nab kuab lawm.

Ib tug miskas hu ua Robert E. Peary tau mus nrhiav txog sab Artic teb thawj thawj zaug thaum xyoo ib txhiab yim pua yim caum rau. Zaum ntawd, nws cov zaub cov mov tag lawm. Nws thiab nws cov neeg tau tig rov qab. Thaum ib txhiab cuaj pua cuaj, nws tau tshaj tawm tias he tau mus txog North Pole lawm. Lwm tus txiv neej, Dr. Cook, tau tshaj tawm tias nws tau mus txog North Pole ib xyoo ua dej ntawd lawm. Tsis muaj leej twg ho los paiv qhia kom tau kiag. Thawj thawj tug neeg uas tau caik nyooj hoom mus txog lub Pole yog Joseph Fletcher, nyob rau xyoo ib txhiab cuaj pua tsib caug ob.

The Chimpanzees I Love
Student Edition pages 434–447

Week at a Glance	Customize instruction every day for your English Language Learners.				
	Day 1	**Day 2**	**Day 3**	**Day 4**	**Day 5**
Teacher's Edition	Use the ELL Notes that appear throughout each day of the lesson to support instruction and reading.				
ELL Poster 17	• Assess Prior Knowledge • Develop Concepts and Vocabulary	• Preteach Tested Vocabulary	• More Room for the Bears	• Animal Guessing Game	• Monitor Progress
ELL Teaching Guide	• Picture It! Lesson, pp. 113–114 • Multilingual Summaries, pp. 117–119	• ELL Reader Lesson, pp. 244–245	• Vocabulary Activities and Word Cards, pp. 115–116 • Multilingual Summaries, pp. 117–119		
ELL Readers	• Reread *Matthew Henson's Story*	• Teach *Jane Goodall*	• Reread *Jane Goodall* and other texts to build fluency		
ELL and Transition Handbook	Use the following as needed to support this week's instruction and to conduct alternative assessments: • Phonics Transition Lessons • Grammar Transition Lessons • Assessment				

Picture It! Comprehension Lesson
Author's Purpose

Use this lesson to supplement or replace the skill lesson on pages 430–431 of the Teacher's Edition.

Teach

Distribute copies of the Picture It! blackline master on page 114.
• Have students describe the picture. Ask: *What do you think the author's purpose was for writing this paragraph?* Then read the paragraph aloud.
• Share the Skill Points (at right) with students.
• Then have them look for clues to the author's purpose as they read. After they have finished reading, ask them if the author met his purpose. Then have them tell you how he or she did so.

Practice

Read aloud the directions on page 114. Have students fill in the graphic organizer. Have them keep their organizers for later reteaching.

Answers for page 114: *Before Reading:* Purpose is to persuade readers that chimpanzees are smart. *During Reading:* Chimps use tools to crack open nuts; they throw rocks at enemies; they can remember people years after they last saw them; they can be taught to ride bicycles, to sew, and to paint. *After Reading:* Purpose was met by providing examples of chimps' intelligence.

> ## Skill Points
>
> ✓ Authors may write to persuade, to inform, to express ideas or feelings, or to entertain.
>
> ✓ Preview a selection to try to predict the **author's purpose.** After reading, ask yourself if the author met the purpose.

Name _____

Look at the picture. **Read** the paragraph.

- What is the author's purpose in writing this paragraph? **Write** the answer in the *Before Reading* box.

- Which sentences show how the author achieves his or her purpose? **Write** them in the *During Reading* box.

- Do you think the author achieved his or her purpose? Why or why not? **Write** your opinion in the *After Reading* box.

Our Intelligent Friends the Chimpanzees

Chimpanzees are very smart. They use tools to crack open nuts. They throw rocks at enemies. They can remember people years after they last saw them. They can be taught to ride bicycles, to sew, and to paint.

Before Reading	**During Reading**	**After Reading**

Vocabulary Activities and Word Cards

Copy the Word Cards on page 116 as needed for the following activities.
Use the blank card for an additional word that you want to teach.
Also see suggestions for teaching vocabulary in the ELL and Transition Handbook.

Fill in the Blanks	Rescue Story	Poster Game
• Give each student a complete set of Word Cards. Have students place the cards face up on their desks or tables.	• Form small groups of students to write a rescue story. Give each group a set of Word Cards.	• Reproduce one set of Word Cards for students to use in a poster game.
• Choose one vocabulary word and think of a context in which it can be used. Describe the context, omitting the vocabulary word. For example: *Endangered animals are safer in _____.*	• Tell groups to use at least five of the Word Cards in a short story about a rescue.	• Have students take turns choosing a Word Card without letting others see it.
• Have students choose the word that best fits the context.	• Give each group a sheet of chart paper. Ask them to write the story on the paper, taping the Word Cards at the appropriate places.	• On their turn, ask students to point to a scene or detail on the ELL Poster, and then give clues about their word without saying it until other students guess the word.
• Repeat the context clue several times as students search for the correct word.	• When they are finished, invite groups to read their stories aloud to the class.	• Repeat the process until all students have participated in the activity.

captive

companionship

existence

ordeal

primitive

sanctuaries

stimulating

Multilingual Summaries

The Chimpanzees I Love: Saving Their World and Ours

Jane Goodall has spent many years studying chimpanzees. She has found that their behavior is more complex than anyone imagined. Chimpanzees make tools from sticks. They make decisions. Some chimpanzees have learned sign language from humans.

Many chimpanzees have been taken from Africa. They are sometimes used to entertain people. Baby chimpanzees are sometimes taken to be pets. Chimpanzees may also be sold to scientists for research. Sometimes they are abused in laboratories. Chimpanzees in labs are often alone and unhappy.

Chimpanzees come from African forests. These forests are being destroyed for wood. Hunters kill the animals for food. Hunters kill some chimpanzees to steal their babies. There are not many wild chimpanzees left. Many people are trying to help and protect the chimpanzees.

Los chimpancés que amo: Salvar su mundo y el nuestro

Jane Goodall ha pasado muchos años estudiando a los chimpancés. Ella ha encontrado que su comportamiento es más complejo de lo que nadie puede imaginarse. Los chimpancés hacen herramientas de los palos. Saben tomar decisiones. Algunos chimpancés han aprendido el lenguaje de signos de los humanos.

Muchos chimpancés han sido sacados de África. A veces los usan para divertir a la gente. Los bebés chimpancés son algunas veces usados como mascotas. También se han vendido chimpancés a los científicos para investigaciones. En ocasiones han sido maltratados en los laboratorios. Los chimpancés en el laboratorio con frecuencia están solos y no son felices.

Los chimpancés son originarios de los bosques africanos. Esos bosques han sido destruidos para sacar madera. Los cazadores matan animales para comer. Los cazadores matan algunos chimpancés para robar a sus bebés. No quedan muchos chimpancés salvajes. Mucha gente está tratando de ayudar y de proteger a los chimpancés.

Multilingual Summaries

Chinese

我所喜愛的黑猩猩
救救他們，也救救我們自己

　　珍古德花了多年時間研究黑猩猩，她發現黑猩猩的行為比人們想像中的更為複雜。牠們會用樹枝製造工具，知道如何下決定，有些還學會了人類的手語。

　　許多黑猩猩都是從非洲抓來的，有些人會訓練黑猩猩，好讓牠們表演賺錢。有些黑猩猩寶寶會被當作寵物，有些甚至可能賣給科學家做實驗。黑猩猩有時會在實驗室裡遭到虐待，所以實驗室裡的黑猩猩通常都是孤獨和不快樂的。

　　黑猩猩的故鄉在非洲雨林，但是這些雨林現在卻因為人類砍伐木材而遭到破壞。獵人把動物殺來吃，他們還會殺死黑猩猩，搶走猩猩寶寶。目前，野生黑猩猩已經所剩不多，許多人都在想辦法幫助和保護黑猩猩。

Vietnamese

Những Con Tinh Tinh mà Tôi Yêu Mến:
Giữ Gìn Thế Giới Của Chúng và Của Chúng Ta

　　Jane Goodall đã trải qua nhiều năm quan sát các con tinh tinh. Bà tìm thấy rằng cách cư xử của chúng phức tạp hơn người ta tưởng tượng được. Tinh tinh lấy que gậy làm dụng cụ. Chúng biết quyết định. Vài tinh tinh còn học được ngôn ngữ cử chỉ từ con người.

　　Nhiều tinh tinh bị bắt đi từ Phi Châu. Thỉnh thoảng chúng được dùng để giải trí người ta. Tinh tinh con đôi khi bị bắt làm thú nuôi trong nhà. Tinh tinh cũng có thể bị đem bán cho những nhà khoa học nghiên cứu. Thỉnh thoảng chúng bị đối xử tệ trong các phòng thí nghiệm. Tinh tinh trong các phòng thí nghiệm thường cô độc và buồn bực.

　　Tinh tinh từ rừng Phi Châu. Những khu rừng này đang bị phá hủy để lấy gỗ. Những người đi săn giết thú vật làm thức ăn. Những người đi săn thỉnh thoảng giết tinh tinh để bắt tinh tinh con. Không có nhiều tinh tinh còn sống trong rừng hoang dại. Nhiều người đang cố giúp đỡ và bảo vệ tinh tinh.

Multilingual Summaries

내가 사랑하는 침팬지
그들과 우리의 세상을 지키며

제인 구달은 침팬지를 연구하며 수년을 보냈다. 그녀는 침팬지의 행동이 우리가 상상하는 것보다 훨씬 복잡하다는 걸 알게 되었다. 침팬지는 막대기로 도구를 만들고 결정을 내린다. 어떤 침팬지들은 인간한테 수화를 배우고 있다.

많은 침팬지들이 아프리카에서 왔다. 가끔 침팬지들은 인간의 흥미를 돋우기 위해 이용되고 때때로 아기 침팬지들은 애완용으로 길러지기도 한다. 또한 연구 목적으로 과학자들에게 팔릴 수도 있고 때때로 실험실에서 이용당하기도 한다. 실험실의 침팬지들은 종종 외로워하고 슬퍼한다.

침팬지들의 고향은 아프리카 밀림으로 여기 밀림이 목재로 사용되면서 파괴되고 있다. 사냥꾼들은 동물들을 식량감으로 죽이고 일부 침팬지를 죽여 침팬지 새끼들을 훔친다. 이제 야생 침팬지들은 얼마 남지 않았기 때문에 많은 사람들이 침팬지들을 돕고 보호하려고 노력하고 있다.

Cov Liab Chimpanzees Uas Kuv Hlub:
Pab Cawm Lawv Lub Teb
Lub Chaws thiab Peb Lub

Jane Goodall tau kawm txog cov liab chimpanzees tau ntau xyoo. Nws tau pom tias lawv coj lawv tus yeeb yam nyuab tshaj qhov ua peb xav tau. Cov liab chimpanzees ntawd siv ntoo cov los ua cuabyeej. Lawv txiav txim siab tau. Ib txhia liab chimpanzees tau kawm piav tes los ntawm neeg.

Cov tub liab chimpanzees tau raug coj tawm ntawm Africa tuaj. Muaj tej zaum uas lawv raug sim los ntxias neeg ua kev lom zem. Kuj muaj tej tus menyuam mob liab chimpanzees uas hluag coj mus tu ua lawv tus tsiaj nyob hauv tsev. Cov liab chimpanzees ntawd kuj raug muag tau rau kws tshuaj kawm mob kawm nkeeg (scientists) los rau lawv kawm. Muaj tej zaum uas lawv kuj raug tsim txom nyob rau hauv tej hoom kawm mob ntawd. Cov liab chimpanzees nyob hauv tej hoom kawm mob feem coob lawv nyob lawv ib leeg xwb thiab tsis muaj kev zoo siab li.

Cov liab chimpanzees ntawd tuaj pem tej hav zoov nyob Africa tuaj. Tej hav zoov ntawd raug puam tsuaj tag cov los ua ntoo. Neeg tua tej tsiaj los noj. Ib txhia neeg muab chimpanzees tua kom nyiag tau lawv cov menyuam liab. Tsis tshuav cov tus chimpanzees qus lawm. Muaj coob leej neeg uas pab tiv thaiv cov chimpanzees.

Black Frontiers   Student Edition pages 460–473

Week at a Glance	Customize instruction every day for your English Language Learners.				
	Day 1	Day 2	Day 3	Day 4	Day 5
Teacher's Edition	Use the ELL Notes that appear throughout each day of the lesson to support instruction and reading.				
ELL Poster 18	• Assess Prior Knowledge • Develop Concepts and Vocabulary	• Preteach Tested Vocabulary	• Review Cause and Effect	• Pioneer Words	• Monitor Progress
ELL Teaching Guide	• Picture It! Lesson, pp. 120–121 • Multilingual Summaries, pp. 124–126	• ELL Reader Lesson, pp. 246–247	• Vocabulary Activities and Word Cards, pp. 122–123 • Multilingual Summaries, pp. 124–126		
ELL Readers	• Reread Jane Goodall	• Teach Dunlap, Here We Come!	• Reread Dunlap, Here We Come! and other texts to build fluency		
ELL and Transition Handbook	Use the following as needed to support this week's instruction and to conduct alternative assessments: • Phonics Transition Lessons • Grammar Transition Lessons • Assessment				

Picture It! Comprehension Lesson
Cause and Effect

Use this lesson to supplement or replace the skill lesson on pages 456–457 of the Teacher's Edition.

Teach

Distribute copies of the Picture It! blackline master on page 121.
- Have students describe the picture. Ask: *What kind of job do you think the woman in the picture has?* Then read the paragraph aloud.
- Ask students if they see any words that identify a cause-effect relationship.
- Have students state the effect described in the paragraph.
- Then have them describe the causes.

Practice

Read aloud the directions on page 121. Have students fill in the graphic organizer. Have them keep their organizers for later reteaching.

Answers for page 121: *Effect:* As a result, more people of color have professional jobs today. *Causes:* Universities accepted more minority students. Companies hired more people of different backgrounds. The military promoted minorities to positions of power. The government hired companies owned by minorities.

Skill Points

✓ A **cause** tells why something happens. An **effect** is something that happens as a result of a cause. Sometimes several causes lead to one effect.

✓ Clue words and phrases, such as *consequently*, *as a result*, and *therefore*, can help you spot cause-effect relationships. Sometimes, though, there are no clue words.

Look at the picture. **Read** the paragraph.

- Which sentence identifies the effect? **Write** it in the *Effect* box.
- Which sentences identify the causes? **Write** them in the *Cause* boxes.

Important Changes

Seventy years ago, few doctors, lawyers, generals, and businesspeople were people of color. Since then, things have changed. Universities accepted more minority students. Companies hired more people of different backgrounds. The military promoted minorities to positions of responsibility. The government hired companies owned by minorities. As a result, more people of color have professional jobs today.

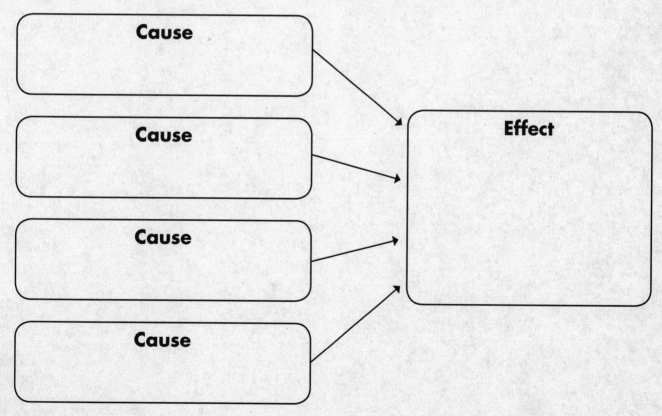

© Scott Foresman 6

Vocabulary Activities and Word Cards

Copy the Word Cards on page 123 as needed for the following activities.
Use the blank cards for additional words that you want to teach.
Also see suggestions for teaching vocabulary in the ELL and Transition Handbook.

Clue Game	True or False?	Riddle Game
• Write the definition of each vocabulary word on the back of one set of Word Cards for students to use in a clue game.	• Reproduce one set of Word Cards for a true-or-false activity.	• Divide students into pairs or small groups to play a riddle game. Give each group a set of Word Cards.
• Have one student choose a card and read the definition, and have the others guess the word.	• Ask a student to choose a card.	
	• Make up a sentence using the vocabulary word and ask the student if the sentence is true or false. For example: *Our school has an earthen roof.* (false)	• Have students place the cards face down in a pile and take turns choosing a card and making up a riddle about the word for others to solve.
• Once the students correctly identify the word, invite volunteers to create sentences using the word.	• Ask the rest of the group whether they agree with the student's answer.	• Provide a model for the riddle, such as: *This word starts with the letter _____. It ends with the letter _____. It means _____.*
	• Repeat the exercise until all students have had a chance to choose a card.	

bondage

commissioned

earthen

encounter

homesteaders

settlement

Multilingual Summaries

Black Frontiers

After the Civil War, some former slaves moved west to begin new lives. Many of them hoped to found African American homesteads and towns. One of the first black towns in the Midwest is now an historic landmark.

On the plains, homesteaders often built their homes out of sod. Some people dug homes into the ground. Some pioneer homes had no stove. People cooked over fires instead. They used buffalo chips for fuel.

Buffalo Soldiers were African Americans in the U.S. Army. Native Americans gave them that name. They said that the soldiers' hair was like a buffalo's coat. Buffalo Soldiers won awards for their service. They became proud of the name.

African Americans did many jobs out west. Some were miners and ranchers. Some were businessmen or cowboys. They helped build America's frontier.

Las fronteras negras

Después de la Guerra Civil, algunas personas anteriormente esclavizadas se mudaron al Oeste para comenzar una nueva vida. Muchos de ellos tenían la esperanza de encontrar haciendas y pueblos de afroamericanos. Uno de los primeros pueblos negros de la región central de Estados Unidos es ahora un punto de referencia histórico.

Era común que en las llanuras los colonos construyeran sus hogares de tepe. Algunas personas hacían sus casas debajo del suelo. Las primeras casas de los pioneros no tenían estufas. La gente cocinaba en fogatas. Ellos usaban grasa de búfalo como combustible.

Buffalo Soldiers eran soldados afroamericanos de la Armada de EE. UU. Los indígenas americanos le pusieron ese nombre. Ellos decían que el pelo de los soldados era como el pelaje del búfalo. Estos soldados ganaron condecoraciones por sus servicios. Ellos estaban orgullosos de su nombre.

Los afroamericanos hicieron diferentes trabajos en el Oeste. Algunos fueron mineros y rancheros. Algunos fueron comerciantes o vaqueros. Ellos ayudaron a construir la frontera americana.

Multilingual Summaries

Chinese

黑人開拓的邊疆

美國南北戰爭結束後，有些奴隸得到了自由，決定要搬到西部展開新生活，他們希望在那裡建立屬於自己的農莊和城鎮。而今天，在美國中西部出現的第一批黑人城鎮中，有一個已經被政府列為歷史性地標。

在廣大的草原上，開墾農莊的人通常利用草來蓋房子，有些人則把家建在地底下。有些人家裡沒有爐子，所以直接把東西放在火上面烤來吃，他們用水牛的大便當生火的燃料。

蠻牛戰士是指美國軍隊裡的黑人士兵，這是印地安人給他們取的名字，因為黑人士兵的頭髮很像水牛的毛。蠻牛戰士為國家做了很多貢獻，得到了許多獎項。他們為能夠擁有這個名稱而自豪。

美國黑人在開墾西部的時候做了許多事情，有些人當礦工或當牧場工人，有些人當商人或當牛仔。他們幫助國家建設邊疆，功勞實在不小。

Vietnamese

Vùng Định Cư của Người Da Đen

Sau cuộc Nội Chiến, vài người từng là nô lệ dọn đến miền tây để bắt đầu đời sống mới. Nhiều người trong số họ hy vọng thành lập những đô thị và các vùng đất do chính phủ cấp cho Người Mỹ Gốc Phi Châu. Một trong những đô thị đầu tiên của người da đen ở vùng Trung Tây hiện đã trở thành một di tích lịch sử.

Ở vùng đồng bằng, những người có đất do chính phủ cấp thường xây nhà của mình bằng cỏ. Vài người đào nhà sâu trong đất. Vài ngôi nhà của thời khai hoang không có lò bếp. Thay vào đó, người ta nấu ăn trên những đống lửa lộ thiên. Họ dùng phân trâu làm nhiên liệu.

Các Binh Sĩ Trâu (Buffalo Soldiers) là Người Mỹ gốc Phi Châu trong quân đội Hoa Kỳ. Người Mỹ gốc Da Đỏ đặt cho họ cái tên đó. Họ nói rằng tóc của những binh sĩ này giống như lông trâu. Binh Sĩ Trâu được giải thưởng vì sự phục vụ của họ. Họ trở nên hãnh diện với danh hiệu này.

Người Mỹ gốc Phi Châu làm nhiều công việc ở miền tây. Một số người làm nghề thợ mỏ và chủ trang trại. Một số khác là thương gia hoặc chăn bò. Họ giúp xây dựng vùng hoang dã của Hoa Kỳ.

Multilingual Summaries

흑인 개척자

　　미국 남북전쟁 이후 전에 노예였던 일부 흑인들이 새로운 삶을 시작하기 위해 서부로 옮겨갔고 그들 중 많은 이들은 흑인만의 정착지와 마을을 세우길 원했다. 미국 중서부 최초의 흑인 마을 중의 하나는 현재 역사적 명소로 되어 있다.

　　이주민들은 종종 평원에 뗏장으로 집을 지었고 어떤 이들은 땅을 파 집을 지었다. 일부 개척자들의 집에는 난로가 없어 대신 불 위에서 요리를 했고 버팔로 배설물을 연료로 이용했다.

　　버팔로 솔져는 인디언들이 미국 군대의 흑인 병사들에게 붙인 이름이다. 인디언들은 군인들의 머리가 버팔로 가죽과 같이 생겼다고 했다. 버팔로 솔져들은 공헌의 대가로 상을 받았고 그들은 그 이름을 자랑스럽게 여겼다.

　　흑인들은 서부에서 많은 일을 했는데 일부는 광산 또는 목장에서 일했고 또 일부는 사업가나 카우보이로 살았다. 흑인들은 미국을 개척하는 데 기여했다.

Cem Teb Dub

Tom qab kev ua tsov ua rog nyob rau Miskas teb no kom sawvdaws muaj tau kev ywj phej, ib txhia neeg uas yog qhev thaum ub tsiv mus nyob rau sab hnub poob mus pib ua neej tshiab. Lawv coob leej tau cia siab tias lawv yuav tau tsim zeb zog rau neeg khej dub nyob. Thawj thawj lub zos khej dub nyob rau thaj tsam duab nrab hauv Amiskas teb no thiab niaj hnub niam no yog tau raug cov los ua ib qhov chaws qhia keeb kwm lawm.

Nyob rau tej tiaj nras, tib neeg siv av thiab nroj los puas ua thwvcib coj los ua lawv tej tsev nyob. Ib txhia neeg ho khawb qhov ua tsev nyob. Neeg thaum ub nyob rau lub caij ntawd tsis muaj qhov cub. Neeg siv qhov cub taws los ua zaub ua mov noj xwb. Lawv ntais tawv twm qhuav qhuav lawm los ua roj taws xwb.

Luag muab Amiskas dub uas tua rog nrog thab ham Miskas hu ua Tub Rog Twm. Cov neeg Khab tau muab lawv tib npe li ntawd. Lawv hais tias cov tub rog ntawd cov plaub hau zoo li plaub twm li. Tub Rog Twm tau yeej kib rau lawv txoj kev pab ua rog. Lawv tau saib lub npe ntawd rau nqi kawg.

Amiskas dub tau ua ntau txoj hauj lwm nyob rau sab hnub poob. Ib txhia tau ua hauj lwm khawb qhov khawb tsua thiab ib txhia tau mus ua neeg zov nyuj zov twm zov nees. Ib txhia tau los ua lag ua luam lossis ua khos npuais (cowboys). Lawv pab tsim cem teb Miskas.

Space Cadets
Student Edition pages 482–493

Week at a Glance	Customize instruction every day for your English Language Learners.				
	Day 1	**Day 2**	**Day 3**	**Day 4**	**Day 5**
Teacher's Edition	Use the ELL Notes that appear throughout each day of the lesson to support instruction and reading.				
ELL Poster 19	• Assess Prior Knowledge • Develop Concepts and Vocabulary	• Preteach Tested Vocabulary	• Space Exploration Letter to the Editor	• Descriptive Planets	• Monitor Progress
ELL Teaching Guide	• Picture It! Lesson, pp. 127–128 • Multilingual Summaries, pp. 131–133	• ELL Reader Lesson, pp. 248–249	• Vocabulary Activities and Word Cards, pp. 129–130 • Multilingual Summaries, pp. 131–133		
ELL Readers	• Reread *Dunlap, Here We Come!*	• Teach *Space— and People's Ideas About Space*	• Reread *Space—and People's Ideas About Space* and other texts to build fluency		
ELL and Transition Handbook	Use the following as needed to support this week's instruction and to conduct alternative assessments: • Phonics Transition Lessons • Grammar Transition Lessons • Assessment				

Picture It! Comprehension Lesson

Draw Conclusions

Use this lesson to supplement or replace the skill lesson on pages 478–479 of the Teacher's Edition.

Teach

Distribute copies of the Picture It! blackline master on page 128.
- Have students describe the picture. Then read the paragraph aloud. Ask: *Did the creatures the astronauts met seem dangerous or peaceful?*
- Share the Skill Points (at right) with students.
- Have students draw a conclusion about the creatures the astronauts met. Then have them find facts or details from the paragraph to support their conclusion.

Practice

Read aloud the directions on page 128. Have students fill in the graphic organizer. Have them keep their organizers for later reteaching.

Answers for page 128: *Conclusion:* The creatures were friendly and gentle. *Details:* They moved slowly. They carried small boxes. They made soft sounds. The tallest one bowed slightly. All of the others sat down on the ground.

Skill Points

✓ When you **draw a conclusion,** you form an opinion about what you have read. Use what you know about real life to help you draw conclusions.

✓ Be sure that there are enough facts or information in the text to support your conclusions.

Look at the picture. **Read** the paragraph.

- What conclusion can you draw about the creatures the astronauts met?
  Write your answer in the *Conclusion* box.

- What facts or details led to this conclusion? **Write** them in the *Detail* boxes.

Which Kind of Creatures Are These?

We knew that two kinds of creatures lived on the planet. One kind of creature was dangerous and cruel. The other was friendly and gentle. We did not know which kind we would meet. Then we saw them. They came toward us slowly, carrying small boxes in their arms. When they reached us, they made soft sounds. The tallest one then bowed slightly. All of the others sat down on the ground.

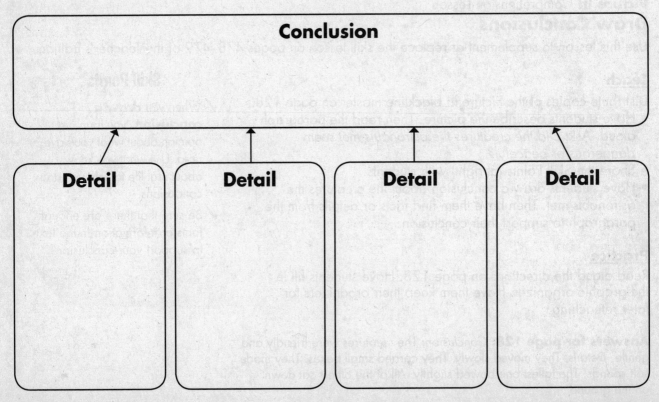

Conclusion

Detail

Detail

Detail

Detail

Vocabulary Activities and Word Cards

Copy the Word Cards on page 130 as needed for the following activities.
Use the blank cards for additional words that you want to teach.
Also see suggestions for teaching vocabulary in the ELL and Transition Handbook.

Parts-of-Speech Word Sort	Space Story	Home Language Clues
• Give each student a set of Word Cards for a word sort activity. • Have each student prepare a three-column chart with *Nouns*, *Verbs*, and *Adjectives* as the headings. • Remind students what kinds of words belong in each column. • Have students write each vocabulary word in the appropriate column. • When all students have completed the activity, ask volunteers to explain what each word means.	• Form small groups of students to write a space story. Give each group a set of Word Cards. • Tell groups to use at least five of the Word Cards in a short story about life in space. • Give each group a sheet of chart paper. Ask them to write the story on the paper, taping the Word Cards at the appropriate places. • When they are finished, invite groups to read their stories aloud to the class.	• Pair students who have writing proficiency in the same home language, and give each student a set of Word Cards. • Have students work together to write translations of the vocabulary words in their home language on the back of each card. (See the Multilingual Lesson Vocabulary beginning on page 272 for suggested translations.) • Have partners lay out the cards with the home language sides facing up. • Have each student choose a card, read the home language translation, and then say the vocabulary word in English.

aliens

barge

hospitable

molten

ore

refrain

universal

version

Multilingual Summaries

Space Cadets

A space ship has found a new planet. The First Officer has experience on a space ship. The Captain does not have experience. The Captain sends for two cadets to lead a mission.

Tom and Harold, the cadets, do not seem very intelligent. The Captain says that the cadets are going on a mission to greet the life on the new planet. He sends the First Officer with them.

On the planet, they see three aliens. The crew thinks that two of the aliens look like space dogs. They think the other alien looks like a cow. The crew is frightened when the cow touches Tom's head. The First Officer takes them back to the ship. The two space dog aliens agree that their meeting with the humans was strange.

Spanish

Cadetes del espacio

Una nave espacial ha encontrado un nuevo planeta. El Primer Oficial tiene experiencia en naves espaciales. El Capitán no tiene experiencia. El Capitán envía a dos cadetes al frente de la misión.

Tom y Harold, los cadetes, no parecen ser muy inteligentes. El Capitán dice que los cadetes van en una misión a saludar la vida del nuevo planeta. Él envía al Primer Oficial con ellos.

En el planeta, ellos ven tres extraterrestres. La tripulación piensa que dos de los extraterrestres parecen perros espaciales. Ellos piensan que el otro extraterrestre parece una vaca. La tripulación se aterroriza cuando la vaca toca la cabeza de Tom. El Primer Oficial los conduce a la nave. Los dos perros espaciales están de acuerdo en que su encuentro con los humanos fue extraño.

Multilingual Summaries

太空軍校學員

有艘太空船發現了新行星。副船長以前曾經乘坐太空船到太空旅行，但是船長沒有。船長決定派兩個太空軍校學員去完成任務。

那兩個太空軍校學員名字叫湯姆和哈洛德，看起來呆呆的，可是船長卻說他們兩個要負責這個任務，到新行星跟上面的外星人打招呼，他還派了副船長跟他們一起去。

在新行星上，他們看到了三個外星人，覺得其中兩個長得好像太空狗，另一個看起來好像乳牛。當那乳牛摸湯姆的頭時，三個人都覺得很害怕。副船長帶著兩個太空軍校學員回太空船，那兩隻太空狗也覺得人類長得很奇怪。

Thiếu Sinh Quân Vũ Trụ

Một chiếc phi thuyền vũ trụ đã tìm ra một hành tinh mới. Vị Phó Chỉ Huy Trưởng có kinh nghiệm trên chuyến tàu vũ trụ. Viên Chỉ Huy Trưởng không có kinh nghiệm. Viên Chỉ Huy Trưởng đưa hai thiếu sinh quân đi thi hành một nhiệm vụ.

Tom và Harold, hai thiếu sinh quân, không có vẻ thông minh lắm. Vị Chỉ Huy Trưởng nói rằng các thiếu sinh quân này sẽ đi với một nhiệm vụ là chào hỏi những người sống trên hành tinh mới. Ông ấy đưa vị Phó Chỉ Huy Trưởng đi với họ.

Trên hành tinh này, họ gặp ba người ở hành tinh xa lạ này. Phi hành đoàn nghĩ rằng hai trong số những người này trông giống như những con chó vũ trụ. Còn người hành tinh xa lạ kia thì họ nghĩ là trông giống như một con bò. Phi hành đoàn hoảng sợ khi con bò sờ đầu của Tom. Vị Phó Chỉ Huy Trưởng đưa họ trở lại phi thuyền. Hai chú chó vũ trụ đồng ý là cuộc gặp gỡ của chúng với con người là kỳ lạ.

Multilingual Summaries

우주 사관생

한 우주선이 새로운 행성을 발견한다. 1등 항해사는 우주선을 탄 경험이 있지만 선장은 그렇지 않다. 선장은 두 사관생을 보내 임무를 수행하도록 한다.

사관생인 톰과 해롤드는 그다지 똑똑해 보이지 않는다. 선장은 두 사관생이 새 행성의 생명체를 맞이할 임무를 수행할 것이라고 말하고 1등 항해사를 그들과 함께 보낸다.

행성에서 그들은 세 개의 외계생물을 본다. 대원들은 그것들 중 두 외계생물이 우주 개, 나머지는 소처럼 생겼다고 생각한다. 대원들은 그 소가 톰의 머리를 건드렸을 때 겁에 질린다. 1등 항해사는 그들을 우주선으로 돌려보낸다. 우주 개처럼 생긴 두 외계생물은 인간들과의 만남이 이상했다고 생각한다.

Tub Rog nyob Ntsuab Ntug

Ib lub nkoj ntsuab ntug tau nrhiav pom ib lub ntiaj teb. Thawj tug tus rog (First Officer) tau nyob ua hauj lwm sau ib lub nkoj ntsuab ntug dua los lawm. Tus kaspistej (captain) tseem tsis tau tau. Tus kaspistej (captain) xav ob tug tub rog mus ua ib txoj hauj lwm.

Tom thiab Harold, ob tug tub rog, tsis txim ntse li. Tus kaspistej (captain) hais tias ob tug tub rog nkawd txoj hauj lwm yog mus tos txais cov neeg uas nyob saum lub ntiaj teb tshiab no. Nws xav thawj tug tub rog (First Officer) qhov nkawd mus.

Nyob saum lub ntiaj teb ntawd, lawv pom peb tug alien. Lawv xav tias muaj ob tug alien uas zoo nkauv li aub ntsuab ntug. Lawv xav tias tus thib peb zoo li ib tug nyuj. Lawv sawvdaws ntshai tag thaum tus nyuaj kov Tom lub taub hau. Thawj tug tus rog (First Officer) coj lawv rov qab mus pem lub nkoj. Ob tug aub ntsuab ntug xav tias lawv kev tsib tib neeg tuaj ntiaj tej no tuaj txawv heev.

Inventing the Future
Student Edition pages 504–521

Week at a Glance	Customize instruction every day for your English Language Learners.				
	Day 1	**Day 2**	**Day 3**	**Day 4**	**Day 5**
Teacher's Edition	Use the ELL Notes that appear throughout each day of the lesson to support instruction and reading.				
ELL Poster 20	• Assess Prior Knowledge • Develop Concepts and Vocabulary	• Preteach Tested Vocabulary	• Create a Commercial	• Action Words	• Monitor Progress
ELL Teaching Guide	• Picture It! Lesson, pp. 134–135 • Multilingual Summaries, pp. 138–140	• ELL Reader Lesson, pp. 250–251	• Vocabulary Activities and Word Cards, pp. 136–137 • Multilingual Summaries, pp. 138–140		
ELL Readers	• Reread *Space—and People's Ideas About Space*	• Teach *Inventions Through Time in Rhyme*	• Reread *Inventions Through Time in Rhyme* and other texts to build fluency		
ELL and Transition Handbook	Use the following as needed to support this week's instruction and to conduct alternative assessments: • Phonics Transition Lessons • Grammar Transition Lessons • Assessment				

Picture It! Comprehension Lesson
Author's Purpose
Use this lesson to supplement or replace the skill lesson on pages 500–501 of the Teacher's Edition.

Teach
Distribute copies of the Picture It! blackline master on page 135.
• Have students describe the picture. Then read the paragraph aloud. Ask: *What are some of the things that Thomas Edison invented?* (phonograph, light bulb, movie camera)
• Share the Skill Points (at right) with students.
• Have students identify the author's purpose. Then have them show how the author achieved that purpose.

Practice
Read aloud the directions on page 135. Have students fill in the graphic organizer. Have them keep their organizers for later reteaching.

Answers for page 135: *Before Reading*: Purpose is to inform readers about Thomas Edison's inventions. *During Reading*: Edison invented the phonograph and the light bulb. He improved the telephone. He invented a movie camera. *After Reading:* The author achieved his purpose by providing facts and presenting them clearly.

> ### Skill Points
> ✓ Authors may write to persuade, inform, express, or entertain. Preview the title, headings, and pictures to help predict the **author's purpose.**
> ✓ When you finish reading, ask yourself, *How did the language or style meet the author's purpose?*

Look at the picture. **Read** the paragraph.

- What is the author's purpose in writing this paragraph? **Write** the answer in the *Before Reading* box.

- Which sentences show how he or she achieves that purpose? **Write** them in the *During Reading* box.

- Do you think the author achieves that purpose? Why or Why not? **Write** your opinion in the *After Reading* box.

Thomas Edison, Inventor

Thomas Edison developed hundreds of inventions. Some of them changed people's lives. He invented the phonograph and the light bulb. He improved the telephone. He also invented the first motion picture camera.

Before Reading	**During Reading**	**After Reading**

Vocabulary Activities and Word Cards

Copy the Word Cards on page 137 as needed for the following activities.
Use the blank cards for additional words that you want to teach.
Also see suggestions for teaching vocabulary in the ELL and Transition Handbook.

Past and Present Tenses	Clue Game	Poster Game
• Give each student a complete set of Word Cards. Have them place all the Word Cards facing up on their desks or tables. • Remind students that a verb tells what someone or something does. Then have them put all of the verbs in a pile. • Remind them how to identify a past tense verb. Then have them pull all of the past tense verbs out of the verb pile. • Read each word and invite a volunteer to say what it means. • Continue the activity until all students have had the opportunity to participate.	• Write the definition of each vocabulary word on the back of a set of Word Cards. • Have one student choose a card and read the definition, and have the others guess the word. • Once students correctly identify the word, invite volunteers to create sentences using the word.	• Reproduce one set of Word Cards for students to use in a poster game. • Have students take turns choosing a Word Card without letting others see it. • On their turn, ask students to point to a scene or detail on the ELL Poster, and then give clues about their word without saying it until other students guess the word. • Repeat the process until all students have participated in the activity.

converts

devise

efficiency

generated

percentage

proclaimed

reproduce

transmitted

Multilingual Summaries

Inventing the Future:
A Photobiography of Thomas Alva Edison

Thomas Alva Edison worked in a telegraph office in Boston, Massachusetts. Later, he quit that job to work on inventing a better telegraph machine. He invented many new things and patented many of them. He opened his own company in 1869. He worked very hard. He was often away from his family.

Edison invented more items. He also improved Alexander Graham Bell's telephone. One of Edison's favorite inventions was the phonograph. The model he made worked on the first try!

In 1879, Edison invented the first long-lasting light bulb. He invented other devices to help provide electricity to people's homes. Edison also created the first movie camera. His inventions helped to start the movie industry and the recording industry.

Spanish

Inventar el futuro:
Una fotobiografía de Thomas Alva Edison

Thomas Alva Edison trabajó en la oficina de telégrafos de Boston, Massachusetts. Luego, renunció a ese trabajo para dedicarse a la invención de una mejor máquina de telegráfica. Él inventó muchas cosas y patentó muchas de ellas. Abrió su propia compañía en 1869. Trabajó muy duro. Él estaba a menudo lejos de su familia.

Edison inventó más artículos. También mejoró el teléfono de Alexander Graham Bell. Uno de los primeros inventos favoritos de Edison fue el fonógrafo. ¡El modelo que inventó funcionó desde la primera prueba!

En 1879, Edison inventó la primera bombilla de larga duración. Él inventó otros dispositivos para proveer de electricidad a la gente en sus casas. Edison también creó la primera cámara de cine. Sus inventos ayudaron a crear a la industria del cine y la industria discográfica.

Multilingual Summaries

發明未來
愛迪生傳

托馬斯・阿爾瓦・愛迪生原本在美國麻州波士頓的一家電報公司工作，後來他辭掉工作，專心改良電報機。愛迪生發明了許多新東西，也得到很多專利，他在 1869 年開辦了自己的公司。愛迪生非常努力工作，所以和家人相聚的時間不多。

愛迪生不斷發明新東西，也改良了貝爾發明的電話。愛迪生自己最得意的發明是留聲機，因為他做出來的第一台留聲機竟然試一次就成功了！

1879 年，愛迪生發明了第一個可以長時間發光的燈泡。之後，他還發明了其他可以為家庭提供電力的機器。電影攝影機也是由愛迪生發明的，這項發明開創了電影業和唱片業。

Phát Minh Ra Tương Lai:
Ảnh Hồi Ký của Thomas Alva Edison

Thomas Alva Edison làm việc cho một văn phòng điện tín ở Boston, Massachusetts. Sau đó, ông nghỉ việc này để làm công việc phát minh một máy điện tín tốt hơn. Ông sáng chế ra nhiều vật mới và được có bằng sáng chế cho những vật này. Ông tự mở công ty vào năm 1869. Ông làm việc cần cù. Ông thường phải xa gia đình.

Edison phát minh thêm nhiều vật nữa. Ông ấy cũng cải tiến máy điện thoại của Alexander Graham Bell. Một trong những phát minh mà Edison ưa thích nhất là máy quay đĩa hát. Mẫu máy mà ông làm ra chạy được ngay vào lần thử nghiệm đầu tiên!

Vào năm 1879, Edison phát minh một bóng đèn đầu tiên cháy được lâu. Ông phát minh những dụng cụ khác để giúp cung cấp điện đến nhà người ta. Edison cũng chế tạo máy quay phim đầu tiên. Các sáng chế của ông giúp khởi sự nền kỹ nghệ phim ảnh và kỹ nghệ thu thanh.

Multilingual Summaries

미래를 만들어내다
사진으로 보는 토마스 알바 에디슨의 생애

토마스 알바 에디슨은 매사추세츠주의 보스턴에 있는 전신국에서 일했다. 후에 그는 보다 나은 전신 기를 발명하는 일을 하고자 그 일을 그만두었다. 그는 여러 새로운 것들을 발명해냈고 그들 중 많은 수를 특허 등록했다. 그는 1869년 자신의 회사를 열어 매우 열심히 일했으며 종종 가족을 떠나 있었다.

에디슨은 더 많은 것들을 발명했고 알렉산더 그레이엄 벨의 전화 또한 개선했다. 에디슨이 가장 좋아하는 발명품 중의 하나는 축음기로 그가 만든 시제품은 첫 번째 시도에 작동이 됐다.

1879년 에디슨은 최초로 오래가는 전구를 발명했고 집에 전기를 공급할 수 있는 여러 기계들을 발명했다. 에디슨은 또한 최초의 영화 카메라도 만들었고 그의 발명품들은 영화산업과 음반산업을 시작하는 데 일조했다.

Tsim Yav Tom Ntej
A Phau Duab Piav Txog
Thomas Alva Edison Lub Neej

Thomas Alva Edison tau ua hauj lwm hauv ib lub hoob kaas txais thiab xa xov telegraph nyob rau Boston, Massachusetts. Tom qab ntawd, nws tau tso nws txoj hauj lwm ntawd tseg mus tsim ib lub cav ntau telegraph kom zoo tshaj. Nws tau tsim ntau yam khoom tshiab thiab sau nws npe rau ntau yam khoom kom neeg thiaj li nyiag tsis tau lub tswvyim ua cov khoom ntawd. Nws tau qib nws lub hoob kaas thaum ib txhiab yim pua rau caum cuaj. Nws khwv kawg. Muaj ntau zaus uas nws tsis tau nyob nrog nws tsev neeg.

Edison tau tsim ntau yam khoom tsiv. Nws tau muab Alexander Graham Bell lub xov tooj ua kom zoo tshaj thiab. Ib qhov uas Edison tau tsim uas nws nyiam tshaj plaws yog lub cav xa suab hu ua phonograph. Lub cav uas nws tau tsim ntawd ua hauj lwm thawj thawj nws muab sim.

Thaum ib txhiab yim pua xya caum cuaj, Edison kuj tau tsim thawj lub teeb fe fab uas chim ntev tshaj plaws. Nws tau tsim lwm yam khoom uas pab kom neeg tej tsev muaj tau fe fab. Edison kuj tsim tau thawj lub koob thaij muv vim thiab. Tej khoom uas nws tau tsim ntawd tau pab neeg pib thaij mus vim thiab kaw phe.

The View from Saturday

Student Edition pages 540–557

Week at a Glance	Customize instruction every day for your English Language Learners.				
	Day 1	**Day 2**	**Day 3**	**Day 4**	**Day 5**
Teacher's Edition	Use the ELL Notes that appear throughout each day of the lesson to support instruction and reading.				
ELL Poster 21	• Assess Prior Knowledge • Develop Concepts and Vocabulary	• Preteach Tested Vocabulary	• A Day in the Life	• Family Tree	• Monitor Progress
ELL Teaching Guide	• Picture It! Lesson, pp. 141–142 • Multilingual Summaries, pp. 145–147	• ELL Reader Lesson, pp. 252–253	• Vocabulary Activities and Word Cards, pp. 143–144 • Multilingual Summaries, pp. 145–147		
ELL Readers	• Reread *Inventions Through Time in Rhyme*	• Teach *A Special Birthday in Mexico*	• Reread *A Special Birthday in Mexico* and other texts to build fluency		
ELL and Transition Handbook	Use the following as needed to support this week's instruction and to conduct alternative assessments: • Phonics Transition Lessons • Grammar Transition Lessons • Assessment				

Picture It! Comprehension Lesson

Plot

Use this lesson to supplement or replace the skill lesson on pages 536–537 of the Teacher's Edition.

Teach

Distribute copies of the Picture It! blackline master on page 142.
- Have students describe the picture. Then read the paragraph aloud. Ask: *What is the problem in this paragraph?* (The puppy almost jumps on the wedding cake.)
- Share the Skill Points (at right) with students.
- Have students find the sentence in the paragraph that describes the problem. Then have them find the sentence that describes the solution.

Practice

Read aloud the directions on page 142. Have students write in the problem, the solution, and the sentence that foreshadows the problem. Have students keep their answers for later reteaching.

Answers for page 142: *Foreshadowing:* Bringing a puppy to the wedding was a big mistake. *Problem:* The puppy almost jumps on the wedding cake. *Solution:* Jason stops the puppy from jumping on the cake.

> ### Skill Points
> ✓ A **plot** includes (1) a problem or goal, (2) rising action, as a character tries to solve the problem or meet the goal, (3) a climax, when the character meets the problem or goal, and (4) a resolution.
>
> ✓ A hint of something that will happen later in the story is called **foreshadowing.**

Look at the picture. **Read** the paragraph.

• What problem does the puppy almost cause? **Write** your answer in the *Problem* box.

• What does Jason do to solve the problem? **Write** your answer in the *Solution* box.

• Is there a sentence at the beginning of the story that foreshadows what happens later? **Write** the sentence in the *Foreshadowing* box.

Saving the Cake

Bringing a puppy to the wedding was a big mistake. As soon as the puppy saw the cake, she jumped for it. Fortunately, Jason saw what was going to happen. He grabbed the puppy just in time and carried her outside. The cake was safe and everyone enjoyed the wedding.

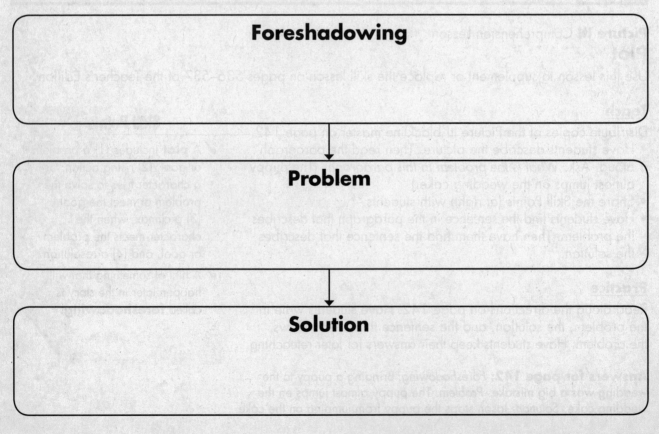

Foreshadowing

↓

Problem

↓

Solution

Vocabulary Activities and Word Cards

Copy the Word Cards on page 144 as needed for the following activities.
Use the blank cards for additional words that you want to teach.
Also see suggestions for teaching vocabulary in the ELL and Transition Handbook.

Antonym Hunt	Poster Game	Riddle Game
• Give each student a set of Word Cards for an antonym hunt. • Have students place the cards face up on their desk or table. • Remind students that antonyms are words with opposite meanings. Then say the following antonyms or near antonyms for the words: *absence, improvement, future, with others, not used to.* • Ask students to select the vocabulary word that means the opposite of each word or phrase you say.	• Reproduce one set of Word Cards for students to use in a poster game. • Have students take turns choosing a Word Card without letting others see it. • On their turn, ask students to point to a scene or detail on the ELL Poster, and then give clues about their word without saying it until other students guess the word. • Repeat the process until all students have participated in the activity.	• Divide students into pairs or small groups to play a riddle game. Give each group a set of Word Cards. • Have students place the cards face down in a pile and take turns choosing a card and making up a riddle about the word for others to solve. • Provide a model for the riddle, such as: *This word starts with the letter _____. It ends with the letter _____. It means _____.*

accustomed

decline

former

presence

unaccompanied

Multilingual Summaries

English

The View from Saturday

Noah spends the summer with his grandparents. Noah's mother wants him to write them a thank you letter. He thinks about all he did over the summer. Noah helped organize a wedding.

Two friends of his grandparents were to be married. Someone had taught Noah how to do calligraphy. He helped to make wedding invitations. He made deliveries with the wagon that his grandfather had bought him. Noah also helped to shop for food. Then the groom's best man was hurt. Noah took his place in the wedding.

Noah spilled ink on five invitations. Noah said he would give prizes to the people who received those invitations. He gave four things for the prizes. Everyone offered to do something in return. The wedding was a success. Noah writes to his grandparents with his new calligraphy pen.

Spanish

La vista desde el sábado

Noah pasa el verano con sus abuelos. La madre de Noah quiere que él le escriba una carta de agradecimiento a sus abuelos. Él piensa en todo lo que hizo durante el verano. Noah ayudó a organizar una boda.

Dos amigos de sus abuelos se iban a casar. Alguien le había enseñado a Noah cómo escribir en caligrafía. Así, él ayudó a hacer las invitaciones de boda. Hizo repartos con el vagoneta que su abuelo le había comprado. Noah también ayudó a comprar comida. Luego, el padrino del novio se hizo daño. Noah tomó su lugar en la boda.

Noah derramó tinta en cinco invitaciones. Noah dijo que les daría premios a aquellos que habían recibido esas invitaciones. Él dio cuatro premios. Todos ofrecieron algo a cambio. La boda fue un éxito. Noah les escribe a sus abuelos con su nueva pluma de caligrafía.

Multilingual Summaries

星期六的故事

夏天裏，諾亞與爺爺奶奶住在一起。回家後，媽媽讓諾亞寫一封信感謝他們。諾亞回想夏天裏做的所有事情，最難忘的是幫著籌辦婚禮。

爺爺奶奶有兩個朋友要結婚。諾亞因為學習過書法，所以幫著寫邀請信，然後坐著爺爺買給他的馬車送給大家。他還幫忙去買食物。原來的伴郎受傷不能來，讓諾亞代替他。

在其中五封邀請信裏，諾亞特意滴上了墨汁。誰有幸收到就能獲得禮品。諾亞把禮品分為四樣，收到的人都幫忙做事以表謝意。整個婚禮辦得非常成功。這回給爺爺奶奶寫信，諾亞用的是新的書法鋼筆。

Tầm Nhìn Từ Ngày Thứ Bảy

Noah trải qua mùa hè với ông bà. Mẹ của Noah muốn cậu viết một lá thư cám ơn ông bà. Cậu nghĩ về mọi điều cậu đã làm trong mùa hè. Noah đã giúp tổ chức một lễ cưới.

Hai người bạn của ông bà cậu sắp làm đám cưới. Có người đã dạy Noah cách viết thư pháp. Vì thế cậu giúp viết thiệp cưới. Cậu đi phát thiệp cưới bằng chiếc xe kéo mà ông đã mua cho cậu. Noah cũng còn giúp đi mua thức ăn. Rồi chú rể phụ bị đau. Noah làm thế rể phụ ở lễ cưới.

Noah làm đổ mực trên năm tấm thiệp mời. Noah nói là cậu sẽ trao phần thưởng cho ai nhận được những tấm thiệp này. Cậu trao bốn vật trong các phần thưởng. Mọi người đều muốn làm gì đó để đền đáp. Lễ cưới thành công. Noah viết thư cho ông bà với cây viết thư pháp mới của mình.

Multilingual Summaries

토요일의 광경

노아는 조부모님들과 함께 여름을 보낸다. 노아의 어머니는 노아가 조부모님들께 감사의 편지를 쓰기를 바란다. 그는 여름 동안 그가 한 모든 일에 대해 생각하고 결혼식 준비하는 것을 도운 것을 떠올린다.

노아 조부모님의 친구 두 분이 결혼식을 올릴 참이었다. 노아는 예전에 누군가에게 서법을 배워 결혼식 초대장을 쓰는 것을 도왔고 그의 할아버지가 사 주신 마차를 타고 초대장을 전달했다. 그는 또한 음식을 사러 다니는 것도 도왔다. 신랑의 들러리가 다치자 그를 대신해 들러리도 섰다.

노아는 초대장 다섯 장에 잉크를 쏟아 그 초대장을 받은 사람들에게 상을 주겠다고 말했고 상으로 네 가지 물건을 주었다. 모든 사람들은 그 대신에 무언가를 하도록 요청 받았다. 결혼식은 성공적이었다. 노아는 그의 새 서예 펜으로 조부모님들께 편지를 쓴다.

Hnub Saturday Kev Ntsia

Noah nrog nws pog thiab nws yawg nkawd nyob thaum lub caij ntuj so. Noah niam xav kom nws sau ntawv mus ua nkawd tsaug. Nws xav txog txhua yam uas nws ua thaum lub caij ntuj so. Noah kuj tau pab ib lub rooj tshoob.

Nws pog thiab yawg nkawd muaj ob tug phoojywg uas yuav sib yuav. Noah tau kawm sau cov maum ntawv zoo zoo nkauj los ntawm ib tug uas txawm sau yam maum ntawv no. Ces nws pab sau cov ntawv caw cov qhua tuaj rau lub rooj tshoob. Nws muab lub tsheb cab thauj khoom uas nws yawg yuav rau nws xa cov ntawv no. Noah kuj pab mus yuav cov khoom noj rau rooj tshoob. Ces tus phij laj tau raug mob. Noah thiaj li mus nyob nws qhov chaw ua tus phij laj rau rooj tshoob.

Noah ua cov kua hauv tus cwj mem nrog rau tsib daim ntawv caw. Noah hais tias nws yuav muab khoom plig rau cov uas tau txais cov ntawv no. Nws tau muab plaub yam los ua khoom plig. Lub rooj tshoob mus tau zoo kawg nkaus. Noah siv tus cwj mem tshiab sau ntawv mus rau nws pog thiab yawg.

Harvesting Hope

Student Edition pages 566–577

Week at a Glance	Customize instruction every day for your English Language Learners.				
	Day 1	**Day 2**	**Day 3**	**Day 4**	**Day 5**
Teacher's Edition	Use the ELL Notes that appear throughout each day of the lesson to support instruction and reading.				
ELL Poster 22	• Assess Prior Knowledge • Develop Concepts and Vocabulary	• Preteach Tested Vocabulary	• Review Fact and Opinion	• Before, During, and After	• Monitor Progress
ELL Teaching Guide	• Picture It! Lesson, pp. 148–149 • Multilingual Summaries, pp. 152–154	• ELL Reader Lesson, pp. 254–255	• Vocabulary Activities and Word Cards, pp. 150–151 • Multilingual Summaries, pp. 152–154		
ELL Readers	• Reread *A Special Birthday in Mexico*	• Teach *Poems for César Chávez*	• Reread *Poems for César Chávez* and other texts to build fluency		
ELL and Transition Handbook	Use the following as needed to support this week's instruction and to conduct alternative assessments: • Phonics Transition Lessons • Grammar Transition Lessons • Assessment				

Picture It! Comprehension Lesson

Fact and Opinion

Use this lesson to supplement or replace the skill lesson on pages 562–563 of the Teacher's Edition.

Teach

Distribute copies of the Picture It! blackline master on page 149.
• Have students describe the picture. Then read the paragraph aloud.
• Share the Skill Points (at right) with students.
• Have students state all of the facts in the paragraph.
• Have students state all of the opinions in the paragraph.
• Ask students to explain why each statement is a fact or an opinion.

Practice

Read aloud the directions on page 149. Have students fill in the graphic organizer. Have them keep their organizers for later reteaching.

Answers for page 149: *Facts:* My father works for a moving company. He has worked there for 15 years. *Opinions:* I think his company is the best company in the world. The people who work there are very nice. The trucks are pretty too!

Skill Points

✓ **Facts** can be proven true or false.

✓ **Opinions** are a person's beliefs or ways of thinking about something. They cannot be proven, but they can be shown to be valid or faulty.

✓ Valid statements of opinion are supported by facts or experts. Faulty statements are not supported by facts.

Look at the picture. **Read** the paragraph.

• What are the facts in this paragraph? **Write** them in the *Facts* column.

• What are the opinions in this paragraph? **Write** them in the *Opinions* column.

The World's Best Moving Company

My father works for a moving company. He has worked there for fifteen years. I think his company is the best company in the world. The people who work there are very nice. The moving trucks are pretty too!

Facts	**Opinions**

Vocabulary Activities and Word Cards

Copy the Word Cards on page 151 as needed for the following activities.
Use the blank card for an additional word that you want to teach.
Also see suggestions for teaching vocabulary in the ELL and Transition Handbook.

Clue Game	Parts-of-Speech Word Sort	Home Language Clues
• Write the definition of each vocabulary word on the back of a set of Word Cards for students to use in a clue game. • Have one student read the definition and have the others guess the word. • Once students correctly identify the word, invite volunteers to create sentences using the word.	• Give each student a set of Word Cards for a word sort activity. • Have each student prepare a three-column chart with *Nouns*, *Verbs*, and *Adjectives* as the headings. • Remind students what kinds of words belong in each column. • Have students write each vocabulary word in the appropriate column. • When all students have completed the activity, ask volunteers to explain what each word means.	• Pair students who have writing proficiency in the same home language, and give each student a set of Word Cards. • Have students work together to write translations of vocabulary words in their home language on the back of each card. (See the Multilingual Lesson Vocabulary beginning on page 272 for suggested translations.) • Have partners lay out the cards with the home language sides facing up. • Have each student choose a card, read the home language translation, and then say the vocabulary word in English.

access

authority

lush

obstacle

toll

torment

wilt

Multilingual Summaries

Harvesting Hope:
The Story of Cesar Chavez

Cesar Chavez lived on a nice ranch until he was ten years old. His family had been very happy. A drought one year kept the crops from growing. The family lost their ranch. They moved to California to work on someone else's farm. They were migrants.

Cesar became unhappy with the treatment of migrant workers. He was shy, but he organized a group to fight without violence. The group marched three hundred miles to the capital to ask for help. They were met with violence at first. Soon people became aware of the cause and offered food and water to the protesters.

Cesar was called to meet officials from the grape company. They agreed to pay the workers more. A rally and parade began when Cesar announced the victory. It was the first contract ever for farm workers in America.

Cosecha de esperanza:
La historia de César Chávez

César Chávez vivió en un rancho agradable hasta que tuvo diez años. Su familia había sido muy feliz. Un año, una sequía afectó los sembrados. La familia perdió el rancho. Ellos se mudaron a California para trabajar en la granja de otra gente. Ellos eran trabajadores itinerantes.

César llegó a ser descontento con el tratamiento que recibían los trabajadores itinerantes. Él era tímido, pero organizó un grupo para luchar sin violencia. El grupo marchó trescientas millas al capitolio para pedir ayuda. Fueron recibidos con violencia al principio. Pronto, la gente comprendió la protesta y les ofreció comida y agua a los manifestantes.

César fue llamado para entrevistarse con los oficiales de la compañía de uva. Ellos estuvieron de acuerdo en pagarles más a los trabajadores. Una manifestación y un desfile comenzaron cuando César anunció la victoria. Este fue el primer contrato que se hizo a los trabajadores del campo en América.

Multilingual Summaries

收穫希望
凱薩·查維斯的故事

10歲以前，凱薩·查維斯都住在一個美麗的農場裏，一家人非常快樂。可有一次發生旱災，田裏顆粒無收，家裏因此沒了農場。只好搬到加利福尼亞州，在別人的農場裏幹活，成為季節工人。

季節工人常常遭到不公正的對待，查維斯心裏非常不滿。可他不是衝動的人，因此組織工人和平抗議。他們走了三百多公里，來到首都要求幫助。開始時受到粗暴的對待，但不久後人們知道了真相，還為他們送來食物和水。

查維斯與葡萄公司代表交涉，最後他們同意提高工資。查維斯宣佈取得勝利，人們舉行了慶祝集會與遊行。這是美國歷史上第一個為農場工人簽定的合約。

Gặt Hái Hy Vọng:
Câu Chuyện về Cesar Chavez

Cesar Chavez sinh sống ở một trang trại đẹp cho đến khi lên mười tuổi. Gia đình của ông rất hạnh phúc. Có một năm một cơn hạn hán làm cho mùa màng không tăng trưởng. Gia đình bị mất trang trại. Họ dọn đến California để làm mướn ở một nông trại của một người khác. Họ là những người di cư.

Cesar trở nên buồn bã vì sự đối đãi đối với những công nhân di cư. Ông nhút nhát, nhưng ông đã tổ chức một nhóm tranh đấu mà không cần vũ lực. Nhóm này đã tuần hành ba trăm dặm đến thủ đô để yêu cầu giúp đỡ. Đầu tiên họ đối đầu với vũ lực. Không lâu sau đó người ta biết được nguyên nhân và cho thức ăn và nước uống cho những người phản đối.

Cesar được mời đi gặp những viên chức của một hãng nho. Họ đồng ý trả thêm lương cho các công nhân. Một cuộc tập hợp và diễn hành bắt đầu khi Cesar thông báo tin thắng lợi. Đó là hợp đồng đầu tiên mà công nhân trang trại từng có được ở Hoa Kỳ.

Multilingual Summaries

희망 거두기
세사르 차베스 이야기

세사르 차베스는 열 살 때까지 근사한 농장에서 살았고 그의 가족들은 매우 행복했다. 어느 해 일년간 가뭄이 들어 농작물이 자라지 못했고 가족은 농장을 잃었다. 가족은 캘리포니아로 이주하여 다른 사람의 농장에서 일했다. 그들은 이주자였다.

세사르는 이주 노동자에 대한 처우로 불행하게 성장했다. 그는 부끄럼을 타는 성격이었으나 폭력 없이 대항할 단체를 하나 조직했다. 그 단체는 국회의사당까지 300마일을 행진해 도움을 요청했다. 맨 처음 사람들은 폭력에 부딪쳤지만 곧 그 원인을 알게 됐고 시위 참가자들에게 음식과 마실 물을 제공했다.

포도 회사 간부들로부터 만나자는 제의가 들어왔고 간부들은 노동자들에게 보다 많은 월급을 지급하는 데 동의했다. 세사르가 승리를 공표했을 때 집회와 퍼레이드가 시작되었다. 그것은 미국 역사상 최초의 농장 노동자들이 이뤄낸 협약이었다.

Kev Cia Siab Thaum Lub Caij Nruam Qoob Loo
Zag Dabneeg Txog Cesar Chavez

Cesar Chavez nyob rau ib tsev teb zoo zoo txog thaum nws muaj kaum xyoo. Nws tsevneeg muaj kev zoo siab heev. Muaj ib xyoos cia li tsis los nag ua rau cov qoob loo tsis txawj loj. Lawv tsevneeg thiaj li poob lawv lub tsev teb. Lawv thiaj li khiav los rau California los ua haujlwm rau lwm tus daim teb. Lawv yog ib co ua txawj ua liaj ua teb noj xwb.

Cesar tsis zoo siab vim muaj cov tibneeg uas saib tsis taus cov neeg ua teb. Nws yog ib tug neeg txajmuag, tiamsis nws sau ib pab los ua ke mus xuj txojkev phem no. Lawv taug kev li 300 mais kom txog pem lub nroog loj mus nrhiav kev pab. Lawv xub mus ntsib teebmeem ua ntej. Tsis ntev sawv daws paub tias lawv ua dabtsi ces lawv mam li pub zaum mov thiab dej rau lawv.

Cesar raug hu mus sib tham nrog cov ua haujlwm rau lub hoob kas ua cov txiv hmab. Lawv pom zoo thiab txaus siab them nyiaj ntiav zog kom ntau rau lawm. Lawv tau sau ua ib pawg ua ke thaum lawv hnov qhov xovxwm zoo no. Qhov no yog thawj thawj daim ntawv sau tseg rau cov tibneeg ua liaj ua teb nyob hauv tebchaws Mekas no.

The River That Went to the Sky

Week at a Glance	Customize instruction every day for your English Language Learners.				
	Day 1	**Day 2**	**Day 3**	**Day 4**	**Day 5**
Teacher's Edition	Use the ELL Notes that appear throughout each day of the lesson to support instruction and reading.				
ELL Poster 23	• Assess Prior Knowledge • Develop Concepts and Vocabulary	• Preteach Tested Vocabulary	• Review Cause and Effect	• My Own Myth	• Monitor Progress
ELL Teaching Guide	• Picture It! Lesson, pp. 155–156 • Multilingual Summaries, pp. 159–161	• ELL Reader Lesson, pp. 256–257	• Vocabulary Activities and Word Cards, pp. 157–158 • Multilingual Summaries, pp. 159–161		
ELL Readers	• Reread *Poems for César Chávez*	• Teach *African Climates and Animals*	• Reread *African Climates and Animals* and other texts to build fluency		
ELL and Transition Handbook	Use the following as needed to support this week's instruction and to conduct alternative assessments: • Phonics Transition Lessons • Grammar Transition Lessons • Assessment				

Picture It! Comprehension Lesson
Cause and Effect

Use this lesson to supplement or replace the skill lesson on pages 582–583 of the Teacher's Edition.

Teach

Distribute copies of the Picture It! blackline master on page 156.
- Have students describe the picture. Then read the paragraph aloud.
- Ask: *What happens when plates under the Earth's surface hit each other?* (Mountains are formed.)
- Share the Skill Points (at right) with students.
- Have students find the sentence in the paragraph that tells a cause. Then have them find the sentence that tells an effect.

Practice

Read aloud the directions on page 156. Have students fill in the cause and the effect in the graphic organizer. Have students keep their organizers for later reteaching.

Answers for page 156: *Clue Words:* as a result; *Cause:* Plates under the Earth's surface hit each other. *Effect:* Mountains are formed.

> ### Skill Points
> ✓ An **effect** is something that happens. A **cause** is why something happens. Clue words such as *since, thus, as a result, therefore,* and *consequently* point to cause-effect relationships.
>
> ✓ When a cause is not directly stated, you must think about why something happened.

Look at the picture. **Read** the paragraph.

- Which clue words in the paragraph tell that something is an effect? **Underline** them.
- **Write** one cause and one effect from the paragraph.

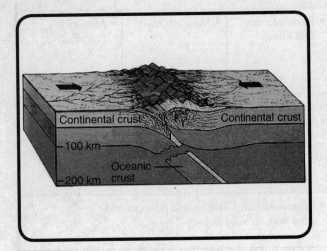

Under the Earth's Surface

Earth's crust forms large pieces called *plates*. These plates move very slowly, but they move all the time. Sometimes plates collide. The collision of plates can form mountain ranges.

Cause	**Effect**

Vocabulary Activities and Word Cards

Copy the Word Cards on page 158 as needed for the following activities.
Use the blank cards for additional words that you want to teach.
Also see suggestions for teaching vocabulary in the ELL and Transition Handbook.

Synonym Search	True or False?	Fill in the Blanks
• Give each student a set of Word Cards for a synonym search. • Have students place the cards face up on their desks or tables. • Remind students that synonyms are words that mean the same thing. Then state the following synonyms or near synonyms for some of the words: *thickest, went, wetness.* • Ask students to select the vocabulary word that is closest in meaning to each of the words you say.	• Reproduce one set of Word Cards for a true-or-false activity. • Ask a student to choose a card. • Make up a sentence using the vocabulary word and ask the student if the sentence is true or false. For example: *Plants need some moisture to live.* (true) • Ask the rest of the group whether they agree with the student's answer. • Repeat the exercise until all students have had a chance to choose a card.	• Give each student a set of Word Cards. Have students place the cards face up on their desks or tables. • Choose one vocabulary word and think of a context in which it can be used. Describe the context, omitting the vocabulary word. For example: *From the top of a mountain, I can see a large ____ of land below me.* • Have students choose the word that best fits the context. • Repeat the context clue several times as students search for the correct word.

densest

eaves

expanse

moisture

ventured

Multilingual Summaries

English

The River That Went to the Sky

In Africa, animals that live near the River have everything they need. One day the River wants to go to the sky. Everyone talks about this. Finally, the Sun hears about it.

The Sun agrees to lift the River to the sky. The River says it never wants to come down. The hot Sun draws the River into the air. The River becomes clouds. The animals and trees move away because the River is gone.

The wind pushes the clouds. The clouds do not like it. The clouds want to go back home. The wind pushes the clouds higher until they cool. The clouds turn to rain. The rain falls to the ground. The rain becomes all the lakes and rivers of Africa. No rain falls where the River had been, though. Now that place is a desert.

Spanish

El río que fue al cielo

En África, los animales que viven cerca de Río tienen todo lo que necesitan. Un día, Río quiere ir al cielo. Todos hablan de esto. Finalmente, llega a oídos del Sol.

El Sol está de acuerdo en levantar a Río al cielo. Río dice que no quiere bajar nunca. El Sol caliente atrae a Río al aire. Río se convierte en nubes. Los animales y los árboles se van porque Río se ha ido.

El viento empuja a las nubes. A las nubes no les gusta esto. Las nubes quieren regresar a casa. El viento empuja a las nubes bien alto, hasta que se enfrían. Las nubes se vuelven lluvia. La lluvia cae al suelo. La lluvia se convierte en todos los lagos y ríos de África. Sin embargo, no cae lluvia donde estuvo Río. Ahora el lugar es un desierto.

Multilingual Summaries

飛上天空的河水

在非洲，河水可以為生活在河邊的動物帶來所需要的一切。可有一天，河水突然希望能飛上天空。每個人都在議論這件事，最後讓太陽聽見了。

太陽同意把河水帶上天空，河水高興地說永遠不想回來了。熾熱的陽光將河水蒸發上升，變成了雲。沒有了河水，動物和植物只好搬到其他地方。

雲在天上總有風吹著它，它一點也不喜歡，開始想念原來的家。雲越吹越高，感到冷了，就化作雨水，落回大地，形成了非洲上的湖泊與河流。可是河水原來的家卻沒有下雨，現在那裏變成了沙漠。

Dòng Sông Chảy Đến Bầu Trời

Ở Phi Châu, thú vật nào sống gần Dòng Sông đều có được mọi thứ mà chúng cần. Một ngày kia Dòng Sông muốn đi lên bầu trời. Mọi người bàn tán về điều này. Cuối cùng, Mặt Trời nghe tin này.

Mặt Trời đồng ý nhấc Dòng Sông lên bầu trời. Dòng Sông nói là không bao giờ muốn trở xuống. Mặt Trời nóng bỏng hút Dòng Sông vào không khí. Dòng Sông trở thành những đám mây. Thú vật và cây cối dọn đi vì Dòng Sông không còn ở đó nữa.

Gió đẩy những đám mây. Các đám mây không thích. Các đám mây muốn trở về nhà. Gió đẩy những đám mây lên càng cao cho đến khi những đám mây này mát lạnh. Những đám mây trở thành mưa. Mưa rơi xuống đất. Mưa trở thành ao hồ và sông ở Phi Châu. Dù vậy, không có mưa rơi ở nơi Dòng Sông đã từng ở. Bây giờ nơi đó là một sa mạc.

Multilingual Summaries

하늘로 간 강

아프리카에서 강 근처에 사는 동물들은 필요한 모든 것들을 갖고 있다. 어느 날 강은 하늘로 올라가고 싶어한다. 모두가 이것에 관해 얘기하고 마침내 태양이 이 얘기를 듣게 된다.

태양은 강을 하늘까지 올려 주기로 하지만 강은 결코 땅으로 내려오고 싶지 않다고 얘기한다. 뜨거운 태양이 공기 중으로 강을 잡아 당기자 강은 구름이 된다. 강이 없어지자 동물들과 나무들은 떠나 버린다.

구름은 자기를 미는 바람이 싫다. 구름은 다시 집으로 가고 싶어한다. 바람은 구름이 차가워질 때까지 바람을 더 높이 밀어 올린다. 그러자 구름은 비로 바뀌어 땅에 떨어진다. 비는 아프리카의 모든 호수와 강이 된다. 하지만 어떤 비도 전에 강이었던 곳엔 내리지 않는다. 그 곳은 이제 사막이다.

Tus Dej Uas Mus Rau Saum Ntuj

Nyob rau hauv tebchaws Africa, cov tsiaj nyob ze ntawm tus Dej uas muaj ib puas tsav yam lawv xav tau. Muaj ib hnub tus Dej xav mus rau saum ntuj. Txhua tus tham txog zaj no. Txog thaum kawg, lub Hnub mam li hnov txog zaj no.

Lub Hnub pom zoo pab tsa tus Dej mus rau saum ntuj. Tus Dej hais tias nws yeej tsis xav rov qab los lawm. Lub Hnub uas kub kub tau coj tus Dej mus txog rau saum cov cua. Tus Dej cia li hloov mus ua tej tauv huab. Cov tsiaj thiab cov ntoo khiav mus lawm vim tus Dej tsis nyob lawm.

Cov cua tshuab thiab thawb tej tauv huab. Tauv huab tsis nyiam li. Tauv huab xav rov qab los tsev. Cov cua tshuab tshuab cov tauv huab mus siab zuj zus kom txog thaum nws txias hlo. Cov tauv huab mam li hloov ua cov nag los. Cov nag no mam li poob rau hauv daim av. Cov nag no thiaj li los koom nrog cov pas dej thiab cov pas zaj nyob rau hauv Africa. Tsis muaj nag los rau thaj av uas thauv tus Dej nyob. Ziag no qhov chaw ntawm yog ib lub toj roob qhua lawm xwb.

Week at a Glance	Customize instruction every day for your English Language Learners.				
	Day 1	**Day 2**	**Day 3**	**Day 4**	**Day 5**
Teacher's Edition	Use the ELL Notes that appear throughout each day of the lesson to support instruction and reading.				
ELL Poster 24	• Assess Prior Knowledge • Develop Concepts and Vocabulary	• Preteach Tested Vocabulary	• Review Main Idea	• My Favorite Things	• Monitor Progress
ELL Teaching Guide	• Picture It! Lesson, pp. 162–163 • Multilingual Summaries, pp. 166–168	• ELL Reader Lesson, pp. 258–259	• Vocabulary Activities and Word Cards, pp. 164–165 • Multilingual Summaries, pp. 166–168		
ELL Readers	• Reread *American Climates and Animals*	• Teach *The History of Metals*	• Reread *The History of Metals* and other texts to build fluency		
ELL and Transition Handbook	Use the following as needed to support this week's instruction and to conduct alternative assessments: • Phonics Transition Lessons • Grammar Transition Lessons • Assessment				

Picture It! Comprehension Lesson

Main Idea and Details

Use this lesson to supplement or replace the skill lesson on pages 600–601 of the Teacher's Edition.

Teach

Distribute copies of the Picture It! blackline master on page 163.
• Have students describe the picture. Then read the paragraph aloud. Ask: *What is this paragraph mostly about?* (why gold is valuable)
• Share the Skill Points (at right) with students.
• Have students find the sentence in the paragraph that tells the main idea. Then have them find sentences that give details.

Practice

Read aloud the directions on page 163. Have students write the main idea and supporting details in the graphic organizer. Have them keep their organizers for later reteaching.

Answers for page 163: *Main Idea:* Gold has many qualities that make it valuable. *Supporting Details:* Many people think it is a beautiful metal. It is soft enough to be made into jewelry. It can be stretched and bent. It is very rare.

Skill Points

✓ The topic is what a paragraph is about. The topic can usually be stated in one or two words.

✓ To find the **main idea** of a paragraph, think about all of the important information the paragraph gives about the topic.

✓ Supporting **details** tell more about the topic. They are less important pieces of information that support the main idea.

Name _____

Look at the picture. **Read** the paragraph.

- What is the main idea of this paragraph? **Write** it in the *Main Idea* box.
- Which sentences give supporting details? **Write** them in the *Detail* boxes.

What's So Great About Gold?

Gold has many qualities that make it valuable. Many people think it is a beautiful metal. It is soft enough to be made into jewelry. It can be stretched and bent. It is very rare.

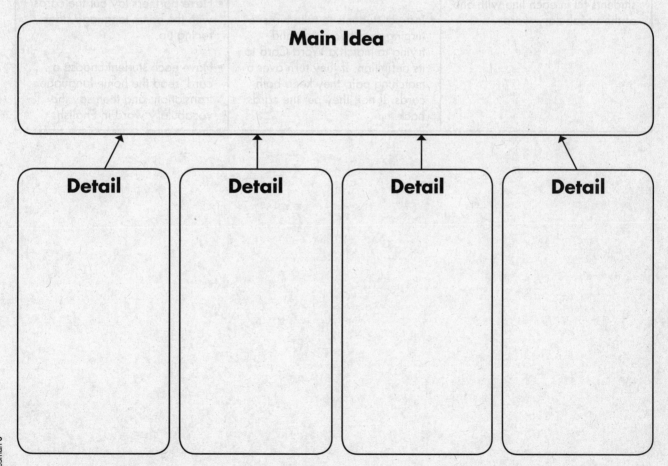

Main Idea

Detail

Detail

Detail

Detail

© Scott Foresman 6

Vocabulary Activities and Word Cards

Copy the Word Cards on page 165 as needed for the following activities.
Use the blank cards for additional words that you want to teach.
Also see suggestions for teaching vocabulary in the ELL and Transition Handbook.

Cloze Sentences	Definition Concentration	Home Language Clues
• Give each student a set of Word Cards and a piece of paper. • Have students write one sentence for each vocabulary word. • Then instruct them to rewrite the sentences, deleting the vocabulary word and replacing it with a blank line. • Have students exchange their sentences with a partner. Have students fill in each line with one of the vocabulary words.	• On blank cards, write the definition of each word. Divide students into pairs to play Definition Concentration. • Reproduce a set of Word Cards and a set of definition cards for each student pair. • Have students place the two sets of cards in rows face down on the desk or table in no particular order. • Instruct students to take turns turning over two cards and trying to match a Word Card to its definition. If they turn over a matching pair, they keep both cards. If not, they put the cards back.	• Pair students who have writing proficiency in the same home language, and give each student a set of Word Cards. • Have students work together to write translations of the vocabulary words in their home language on the back of each card. (See the Multilingual Lesson Vocabulary beginning on page 272 for suggested translations.) • Have partners lay out the cards with the home language sides facing up. • Have each student choose a card, read the home language translation, and then say the vocabulary word in English.

characteristic

corrode

engulfed

exploit

extract

hoard

Multilingual Summaries

Gold

Gold is a rare metal. People around the world value gold. Gold's shine never fades.

Gold is solid at room temperature. It melts when heated to 1,943 degrees Fahrenheit. Then it can be poured into molds.

Miners usually find tiny crystals of gold. Larger lumps, called nuggets, are rare. Gold is most often found in rocks. Sometimes gold is found in sand. The biggest gold mining area in the world is in South Africa. There is gold in the ocean floor, but it would cost too much to mine it.

Gold has been used since ancient times. Long ago people probably panned for gold. Later, people learned how to dig gold out of rocks. Today, new technology helps gold miners find gold.

Pure gold is soft enough to form into many different shapes. Gold can be used in many ways.

Spanish

El oro

El oro es un metal difícil de encontrar. Todo el mundo valora el oro. El brillo del oro nunca se desvanece.

El oro es sólido a la temperatura ambiental. Se derrite cuando está a 1,943 grados Fahrenheit. Luego puede verterse dentro de los moldes.

Los mineros con frecuencia encuentran pequeños cristales de oro. Terrones más grandes, llamados pepitas, son raros. La mayoría del tiempo el oro se encuentra en las rocas. A veces, se puede encontrar oro en la arena. La mayor mina de oro del mundo está en África del Sur. Hay oro en el fondo del océano, pero costaría demasiado sacarlo de allí.

El oro ha sido usado desde tiempos remotos. Hace muchos años la gente probablemente filtraba el oro. Después, la gente aprendió a cavar las rocas para sacar el oro. Hoy, la nueva tecnología ayuda a los mineros a encontrar el oro.

El oro puro es suficientemente blando para tomar diferentes formas. El oro se puede usar de muchas maneras.

Multilingual Summaries

Chinese

金子

金子是珍貴的金屬，世界各地的人都喜歡它。金子永遠閃耀著光芒。

常溫下金子是固體，加熱到華氏1,943度，就熔化為液體，可以鑄成各種形狀。

礦工一般只能找到細小的金粒，大的金塊非常罕見。通常金子蘊藏在金礦石中，有時也會藏在金沙裏。世界上最大的金礦在南非。海底也有金礦，但開採起來費用很大。

古代時人們就使用金子。以前人們用淘洗的方法獲取金子，慢慢地才知道怎樣開採金礦，現在礦工用新技術尋找金礦。

純金非常柔軟，可以方便地做成各種形狀。金子的用途非常廣泛。

Vietnamese

Vàng

Vàng là một kim loại hiếm có. Người ta trên khắp thế giới quý trọng vàng. Độ bóng của vàng không bao giờ phai mờ.

Vàng đặc ở nhiệt độ phòng thông thường. Vàng chảy khi nung nóng đến 1,943 độ Fahrenheit. Rồi vàng được đổ vào khuôn.

Những người thợ hầm mỏ thường tìm thấy những tinh thể vàng. Những miếng to hơn, được gọi là vàng cục (nuggets), là hiếm có. Vàng thường được tìm thấy nhất trong đá. Thỉnh thoảng vàng được tìm thấy trong cát. Khu mỏ vàng lớn nhất trên thế giới là ở Nam Phi Châu. Có vàng ở dưới đáy đại dương, nhưng quá tốn kém để khai thác.

Vàng đã được sử dụng từ thời cổ xưa. Cách đây đã lâu người ta có thể đã tìm vàng bằng cách đãi vàng. Sau này, người ta học được cách đào vàng từ đá. Ngày nay, kỹ thuật mới giúp những thợ hầm mỏ tìm được vàng.

Vàng nguyên chất mềm đến mức có thể tạo thành nhiều hình dạng khác nhau. Vàng được dùng qua nhiều cách.

Multilingual Summaries

Korean

금

금은 세상 사람들이 귀중히 여기는 희귀한 금속이다. 금의 광택은 결코 바래지 않는다.

금은 실온에서 고형이지만 화씨 1,943도로 가열하면 녹는다. 그러면 틀 안에 부어 형태를 만들 수 있다.

광부들은 흔히 작은 결정체의 금을 찾곤 하는데 너겟이라고 불리는 좀 더 큰 덩어리는 흔치 않다. 금은 보통 바위에서 발견되지만 가끔은 모래에서도 발견된다. 세계에서 가장 큰 금광은 남아프리카에 있다. 대양 밑바닥에도 금이 있으나 그것을 채굴해 내는 데는 비용이 너무 많이 든다.

금은 고대로부터 사용되어 왔다. 아주 옛날, 아마도 사람들은 흙, 모래를 일어 금을 가려냈을 것이다. 이후 사람들은 바위에서 금을 파내는 법을 배우게 됐고 오늘날에는 신기술이 광부들의 금 발굴 작업을 돕고 있다.

순금은 여러 다른 모양으로 만들어질 만큼 부드러우며 금은 현재 여러 방법으로 사용되고 있다.

Hmong

Kub

Kub yog ib yam hlau uas txawv txawv. Tibneeg nyob thoob plaws hauv ntiajteb no saib kub muaj nuj nqe heev. Cov kub yeej ci thiab tsis txawj qub.

Kub yeej nyob ruaj ruaj yog tias nws nyob rau hauv hoob uas tsis txias tsis kub. Nws txawj yaj thaum nyob kub txog li 1,943. Ces thaum ntawd yuav muab cov kub no ncuav rau cov pwm.

Cov ua haujlwm nrhiav nyiaj nrhiav kub yeej ib txwm nrhiav tau cov kub no tsuas tiam nws me me xwb. Cov kub ua ib thooj yeej tsis tshua muaj. Cov pobzeb feem coob yeej muaj kub nyob rau hauv. Muaj tej zaum, kub kuj nyob rau hauv cov xuab zeb. Qhov ua loj tshaj plaws nyob rau hauv lub ntiajteb no rau neeg nrhiav nyiaj nrhiab kub yog nyob rau hauv Africa sab qab teb. Muaj kub nyob rau hauv qab pag hiavtxwv, tiamsis yuav siv nyiaj txiag ntau thiaj li mus nrhiav tau.

Kub tau raug siv los ntawm ntau tiav neeg los mus. Puag thaum ub, tibneeg muab laujkaub nrhiav kub. Tsis ntev tom qab, tibneeg mam li kawm khawb qhov hauv tej pobzeb nrhiav kub. Hnub no, muaj ntau yam txujci pab cov tibneeg no nrhiav kub.

Tseem tseem kub yeej mos mos thiab muab puab tau ntau yam. Kub yeej siv tau ntau yam txoj hau kev.

© Scott Foresman 6

The House of Wisdom
Student Edition pages 624–637

Week at a Glance	Customize instruction every day for your English Language Learners.				
	Day 1	**Day 2**	**Day 3**	**Day 4**	**Day 5**
Teacher's Edition	Use the ELL Notes that appear throughout each day of the lesson to support instruction and reading.				
ELL Poster 25	• Assess Prior Knowledge • Develop Concepts and Vocabulary	• Preteach Tested Vocabulary	• The Student I Am	• Reading Words	• Monitor Progress
ELL Teaching Guide	• Picture It! Lesson, pp. 169–170 • Multilingual Summaries, pp. 173–175	• ELL Reader Lesson, pp. 260–261	• Vocabulary Activities and Word Cards, pp. 171–172 • Multilingual Summaries, pp. 173–175		
ELL Readers	• Reread *The History of Metals*	• Teach *Ancient Libraries*	• Reread *Ancient Libraries* and other texts to build fluency		
ELL and Transition Handbook	Use the following as needed to support this week's instruction and to conduct alternative assessments: • Phonics Transition Lessons • Grammar Transition Lessons • Assessment				

Picture It! Comprehension Lesson
Sequence
Use this lesson to supplement or replace the skill lesson on pages 620–621 of the Teacher's Edition.

Teach
Distribute copies of the Picture It! blackline master on page 170.
• Have students describe the picture. Then read the paragraph aloud. Ask: *What is the first thing that happens in the story?*
• Share the Skill Points (at right) with students.
• Have students describe the entire sequence of events that occur in the story.

Practice
Read aloud the directions on page 170. Have students fill in the graphic organizer. Have students keep their organizers for later reteaching.

Answers for page 170: *Event 1:* Rachel smelled something delicious. *Event 2:* She went to the kitchen to see what it was. *Event 3:* She looked into the oven and saw two loaves of bread. *Event 4:* Her mother walked in and told her that the bread would be ready soon. *Event 5:* Rachel went back to her room and got ready for school.

> **Skill Points**
> ✓ **Sequence** refers to the order of events or the steps of a process.
> ✓ Dates and times can help you determine the order of events.
> ✓ Clue words such as *first, next, then,* and *last* can also help you determine the order of events.

Name _____

Look at the picture. **Read** the paragraph.

• **Write** five things that happen in the story. Be sure to write them in the order in which they occur in the story.

Bread in the Morning

Rachel smelled something delicious. She jumped out of bed and ran to the kitchen to see what it was. When she looked into the oven, she saw two golden loaves of bread. Just then, her mother walked into the kitchen. "The bread will be ready in about five minutes," she said. Rachel rushed back to her room and got ready for school. She wanted to be ready for breakfast when the bread came out of the oven.

Event 1

Event 2

Event 3

Event 4

Event 5

Vocabulary Activities and Word Cards

Copy the Word Cards on page 172 as needed for the following activities.
Use the blank card for an additional word that you want to teach.
Also see suggestions for teaching vocabulary in the ELL and Transition Handbook.

Picture This	Can You Guess?	Poster Game
• Reproduce one set of Word Cards and select the vocabulary words that can be illustrated. • Have students take turns choosing a card and drawing a simple picture on the board to illustrate the word. For example, students might draw a telescope pointing out of a window for the word *observatory*. • Ask the other students to guess which vocabulary word the illustration depicts. Let the first student who guesses correctly have the next turn.	• Place a set of Word Cards face down in a pile. • Have one student choose a card and give verbal or visual clues that will help the rest of the group guess the word. • Repeat the process until all students have had a chance to provide clues.	• Reproduce one set of Word Cards for students to use in a poster game. • Have students take turns choosing a Word Card without letting others see it. • On their turn, ask students to point to a scene or detail on the ELL Poster, and then give clues about the word without saying it until other students guess the word. • Repeat the process until all students have participated in the activity.

beacon

caravans

legacy

manuscripts

medieval

observatory

patron

Multilingual Summaries

The House of Wisdom

Many years ago, people from around the world came to Baghdad. They brought goods from their homelands. They brought books and treasures too. The books excited the ruler of Baghdad.

The ruler built a library in the center of the city. The library was called the House of Wisdom. People came to the library to learn from the books.

A boy named Ishaq lived in the House of Wisdom with his parents. He wanted to be a man of learning like his father. He studied many subjects all day long.

The ruler chose Ishaq to lead a search across the world for books. Ishaq traveled through the world. He learned from everyone and everything he saw. He collected thousands of books to bring home. When he returned, Ishaq became a great scholar.

Spanish

La Casa de la Sabiduría

Hace muchos años, gente de todo el mundo vino a Bagdad. Trajeron productos de sus tierras. También trajeron libros y tesoros. Los libros entusiasmaron al gobernante de Bagdad.

El gobernante construyó una biblioteca en el centro de la ciudad. La biblioteca se llamó La Casa de la Sabiduría. La gente venía a la biblioteca a aprender de los libros.

Un niño llamado Ishaq vivía en La Casa de la Sabiduría con sus padres. Él quería ser un hombre de conocimiento como su padre. Él estudiaba diferentes materiales todo el día.

El gobernante eligió a Ishaq para dirigir una búsqueda de libros alrededor del mundo. Ishaq viajó por muchos lugares. Aprendió de todos y de cada cosa que vio. Recolectó miles de libros para llevar a casa. Cuando regresó, Ishaq se convirtió en un gran sabio.

Multilingual Summaries

智慧之屋

很久以前，世界各地的人們來到巴格達。他們帶來家鄉的貨物，也帶來書籍與珍寶。巴格達國王最喜歡那些書籍。

國王在市中心建立圖書館，把它叫做"智慧之屋"，讓人們來這裏學習知識。

有個男孩叫伊薩克，跟父母一起住在"智慧之屋"。他的願望是成為和父親一樣有學問的人，因此整天都努力學習。

後來國王讓伊薩克帶領一隊人，到世界各地尋找好書。伊薩克周遊各國，碰到許多人，看過許多事，學到很多知識。他把收集到的幾萬本書帶回家，成為了一名偉大的學者。

Vietnamese

Tòa Nhà Thông Thái

Cách đây nhiều năm, người từ khắp thế giới đi đến Baghdad. Họ mang sản vật từ quê hương của họ. Họ mang sách vở và của quý đến nữa. Các quyển sách làm người cai trị Baghdad hứng thú.

Người cai trị xây lên một thư viện ở trung tâm thành phố. Thư viện này được gọi là Tòa Nhà Thông Thái. Người ta đến thư viện để học hỏi từ các quyển sách.

Một cậu bé tên Ishaq sống trong Tòa Nhà Thông Thái với ba mẹ của cậu. Cậu bé muốn được là một học giả như ba của mình. Suốt ngày cậu nghiên cứu nhiều chủ đề.

Người cai trị chọn Ishaq dẫn đầu một cuộc tìm kiếm sách trên khắp thế giới. Ishaq du lịch khắp nơi trên thế giới. Cậu học hỏi từ mọi người và mọi thứ mà cậu thấy. Cậu thu thập hàng ngàn quyển sách để mang về nước. Khi cậu trở về, Ishaq trở thành một học giả tài ba.

Multilingual Summaries

지혜의 집

아주 오래 전 세계 각지의 사람들이 바그다드로 모여들었다. 그들은 자신들의 고국에서 물건을 가져왔는데 거기엔 서적과 보물도 포함되었다. 바그다드의 통치자는 그 중 서적에 큰 관심을 보였다.

통치자는 도시의 중앙에 도서관을 세우고 그것을 지혜의 집이라고 불렀다. 사람들은 도서관에 와서 책을 통해 배움을 알게 되었다.

이샤크란 이름의 한 소년이 부모님과 함께 지혜의 집에 살고 있었다. 소년은 자신의 아버지처럼 학식 있는 사람이 되고 싶어 하루 종일 여러 과목 공부에 매달렸다.

통치자는 책을 찾아 세상 전역을 수색하는 임무의 지휘권을 이샤크에게 주었다. 이샤크는 세계를 여행하며 그가 만나고 보는 모든 사람들과 사물들로부터 배웠다. 그는 고국으로 가져올 수천 권의 책을 모았고 고국에 돌아왔을 때 이샤크는 위대한 학자가 되어 있었다.

Lub Tsev Uas Muaj Tswvyim

Ntau xyoo dhau los, tibneeg thoob plaws lub ntiajteb no tuaj rau hauv Baghdad. Lawv nqa tau ntau yam khoom zoo hauv lawv lub tebchaws nrog lawv tuaj. Lawv nqa tej phau ntawv thiab tej nyiaj tej kub nrog lawv ib yam. Tej phau ntawv no txawm ua rau tus nom tswv kav tebchaws Baghdad zoo siab.

Tus nom tswv txawm txua tau ib lub tsev rau cov phau ntawv no nyob nruab nrab hauv lub nroog ntawm. Lub tsev no txawm raug hu tias Lub Tsev Uas Muaj Tswvyim. Tibneeg tuaj rau hauv lub tsev no tuaj kawm los ntawm cov phau ntawv no.

Ib tug tub npe hu ua Ishaq nyob rau hauv Lub Tsev Ua Muaj Tswvyim no nrog nws niam thiab nws txiv. Nws xav hlob los ua ib tug txivneej nyiam kawm ntawv ib yam li nws txiv. Nws niaj hnub kawm txog ntau yam ib hnub nkaus.

Tus nom tswv thiab txib kom Ishaq mus thoob plaws hauv lub ntiajteb no mus nrhiav tej phau ntawv los ntxiv. Ishaq tau mus thoob plaws lub ntiajteb no. Nws kawm los ntawm txhua tus thiab txhua yam uas nws mus pom. Nws mus sau tau txhiab txhiab pua pua phau ntawv coj nrog nws rov qab los mus tsev. Nws thiaj li los mus ua ib tug tub txawj ntse heev.

Don Quixote and the Windmills
Student Edition pages 656–667

Week at a Glance	Customize instruction every day for your English Language Learners.				
	Day 1	Day 2	Day 3	Day 4	Day 5
Teacher's Edition	Use the ELL Notes that appear throughout each day of the lesson to support instruction and reading.				
ELL Poster 26	• Assess Prior Knowledge • Develop Concepts and Vocabulary	• Preteach Tested Vocabulary	• And the Quest Continues	• Ride into Action	• Monitor Progress
ELL Teaching Guide	• Picture It! Lesson, pp. 176–177 • Multilingual Summaries, pp. 180–182	• ELL Reader Lesson, pp. 262–263	• Vocabulary Activities and Word Cards, pp. 178–179 • Multilingual Summaries, pp. 180–182		
ELL Readers	• Reread Ancient Libraries	• Teach Cervantes and Don Quixote	• Reread Cervantes and Don Quixote and other texts to build fluency		
ELL and Transition Handbook	Use the following as needed to support this week's instruction and to conduct alternative assessments: • Phonics Transition Lessons • Grammar Transition Lessons • Assessment				

Picture It! Comprehension Lesson
Author's Purpose

Use this lesson to supplement or replace the skill lesson on pages 652–653 of the Teacher's Edition.

Teach

Distribute copies of the Picture It! blackline master on page 177.
• Have students describe the picture. Then read the paragraph aloud. Ask: *Why did the author write this paragraph?* (to tell people about the Ufizzi Gallery)
• Share the Skill Points (at right) with students.
• Have students identify the author's purpose in writing. Then have them identify the facts the author uses to achieve this purpose.

Practice

Read aloud the directions on page 177. Have students fill in the graphic organizer. Have them keep their organizers for later reteaching.

Answers for page 177: *Purpose:* To inform. *Facts:* The Uffizi has been used as a public art gallery since 1591. The museum has more than 45 rooms holding about 1,700 paintings, 300 sculptures, and other pieces of art. People from all over the world travel to Florence to visit the Uffizi Gallery.

> ### Skill Points
>
> ✓ Authors have different reasons for writing. They may write to persuade, inform, entertain, or express thoughts and feelings.
>
> ✓ You may have to draw conclusions from what the author writes to determine the purpose for writing.
>
> ✓ If the **author's purpose** is to entertain, you may want to read faster. If the author's purpose is to inform, you may want to read more slowly.

Look at the picture. **Read** the paragraph.

- What is the author's purpose in writing this paragraph? **Write** the purpose in the graphic organizer.

- What facts from text help the author meet this purpose? **Write** the facts in the graphic organizer.

The Uffizi Gallery

One of the greatest art museums in the world is in Florence, Italy. The Uffizi has been used as a public art gallery since 1591. This makes it the oldest museum in the world. The museum has more than 45 rooms. These rooms contain about 1,700 paintings, 300 sculptures, and many other pieces of art. People from all over the world travel to Florence to visit the Uffizi.

Vocabulary Activities and Word Cards

Copy the Word Cards on page 179 as needed for the following activities.
Use the blank card for an additional word that you want to teach.
Also see suggestions for teaching vocabulary in the ELL and Transition Handbook.

Find the Prefix	Fill in the Blanks	Home Language Clues
• Give each student a set of Word Cards to play Find the Prefix. Have them lay the cards face up on their desks or tables.	• Give each student a set of Word Cards. Have students place the cards face up on their desk or table.	• Pair students who have writing proficiency in the same home language, and give each student a set of Word Cards.
• Write the prefixes *re-* and *mis-* on the board, and explain what they mean.	• Choose one vocabulary word and think of a context in which it can be used. Describe the context, omitting the vocabulary word. For example: *The _____ is a type of weapon.*	• Have students work together to write translations of the vocabulary words in their home language on the back of each card. (See the Multilingual Lesson Vocabulary beginning on page 272 for suggested translations.)
• Have all students identify the vocabulary words that include these prefixes.	• Have students choose the word that best fits the context.	• Have partners lay out the cards with the home language sides facing up.
• Ask volunteers to tell what each word means.	• Repeat the context clue several times as students search for the correct word.	• Have each student choose a card, read the home language translation, and then say the vocabulary word in English.

lance

misfortune

quests

renewed

renowned

resound

squire

Multilingual Summaries

Don Quixote and the Windmills

Señor Quexada reads stories of knights. He decides to be the knight Don Quixote. He finds an old suit of armor. He has an old horse. He asks his neighbor Sancho Panza to be his squire. He chooses a pretty farm girl to be his fair lady.

One night Don Quixote and Sancho ride away to find adventure. In the morning, Don Quixote thinks he sees giants. Sancho says that they are only windmills. Don Quixote decides to fight them.

Don Quixote rides his horse toward a windmill. His lance sticks in an arm of the windmill. The arm lifts him in the air. Sancho tries to save Don Quixote. He is lifted in the air too. Don Quixote cuts the windmill's ropes. When he cuts the ropes, both men fall. Don Quixote gets back on his horse. Sancho gets back on his donkey. They ride away to another adventure.

Don Quijote y los molinos de viento

El Señor Quijano lee historias de caballería. Decide ser el caballero Don Quijote. Él encuentra una vieja armadura. Tiene un viejo caballo. Le pide a su vecino Sancho Panza que sea su escudero. Eligea una bella aldeana para que sea su dama.

Una noche, Don Quijote y Sancho se van en busca de aventuras. Por la mañana, Don Quijote piensa que ve gigantes. Sancho le dice que son sólo molinos de viento. Pero Don Quijote decide luchar contra ellos.

Don Quijote dirige su caballo hacia un molino de viento. Su lanza se traba en una de las astas del molino de viento. El asta lo eleva por el aire. Sancho trata de salvar a Don Quijote. Él también es levantado por el aire. Don Quijote corta las cuerdas del molino de viento. Cuando corta las cuerdas los dos hombres se caen. Don Quijote se sube de nuevo a su caballo. Sancho se sube a su burro. Ellos se van en busca de otra aventura.

Multilingual Summaries

堂吉珂德與風車

堂吉珂德很喜歡讀騎士傳奇，決心要當勇敢的騎士。於是找來破舊的盔甲與老馬，慫恿鄰居桑科作隨從，將漂亮的農村姑娘當作他的情人。

一天晚上，堂吉珂德與桑科離開家去冒險。早上，堂吉珂德說他看見了巨人，桑科說那只不過是普通的風車。堂吉珂德不相信，他要與巨人大戰。

他騎著馬沖向風車，舉起長矛刺向它，風車把堂吉珂德掀到半空中。桑科想去營救，也被帶到半空中。一陣慌亂，堂吉珂德切斷了風車繩子，兩人摔落下來，回到地面。堂吉珂德又跨上老馬，桑科也騎上毛驢，開始新的冒險。

Don Quixote và Những Cối Xay Gió

Ông Quexada đọc chuyện về các hiệp sĩ. Ông quyết định mình sẽ là Hiệp Sĩ Don Quixote. Ông tìm gặp một bộ áo giáp cũ. Ông có một con ngựa già. Ông rủ người láng giềng của mình là Sancho Panza làm cận vệ. Ông chọn một thôn nữ xinh xắn làm nàng tiểu thơ để ông bảo vệ.

Một buổi tối nọ Don Quixote và Sancho cưỡi ngựa đi tìm phiêu lưu mạo hiểm. Vào buổi sáng, Don Quixote nghĩ là mình thấy những người khổng lồ. Sancho nói đó chỉ là những cối xay gió. Don Quixote quyết định chiến đấu với chúng.

Don Quixote cưỡi ngựa chạy đến một cối xay gió. Ngọn giáo của ông đâm dính vào một cánh của cối xay gió. Cánh cối xay nhấc bổng ông lên. Sancho cố gắng cứu Don Quixote. Ông này cũng bị nhấc bổng lên nữa. Don Quixote cắt những sợi dây thừng của cái cối xay gió. Khi ông cắt những sợi dây, cả hai người đều rơi xuống. Don Quixote leo lên lưng ngựa của mình. Sancho leo lên lưng lừa của mình. Họ chạy đến một cuộc phiêu lưu khác.

Multilingual Summaries

돈키호테와 풍차

케사다씨는 기사들에 관한 이야기를 읽고 기사 돈키호테가 되기로 결심한다. 그는 낡은 갑옷과 투구를 찾아낸다. 그는 늙은 말을 갖고 있다. 그는 이웃에 사는 산초 판자에게 자신의 종자가 되어달라고 부탁한다. 그는 사랑하는 연인이 되어줄 한 예쁜 시골 처녀를 선택한다.

어느 날 밤 돈키호테와 산초는 말을 타고 모험을 찾아 나선다. 아침에 돈키호테는 그가 거인을 보고 있다고 생각한다. 산초는 그것이 단지 풍차일 뿐이라고 말하지만 돈키호테는 그들과 싸우기로 결심한다.

돈키호테는 말을 타고 풍차로 달려간다. 그의 창이 풍차의 날개를 찌르자 날개가 그를 공중으로 들어올린다. 산초는 돈키호테를 구하려고 애쓰지만 그도 역시 공중으로 들어올려진다. 돈키호테는 풍차의 밧줄을 끊고 산초와 함께 땅에 떨어진다. 돈키호테는 다시 말을 타고 산초는 당나귀를 탄다. 그들은 또 다른 모험을 찾아 떠난다.

Don Quixote thiab Tej Dig Huab

Senor Quexada nyeem ib zaj txog cov thaj ham qub tuav rab ntaj. Nws txiav txim siab ua tus thaj ham qub muaj npe Don Quixote. Nws nrhiav khaub ncaws hlau qub. Nws muaj nees qub. Nws noog nws kwv tij Sancho Panza ua nws tus pab cuam. Nws hos xaiv ib tug hluas nkauj txawj ua teb los ua nws tus pojniam.

Muaj Ib Hmo Don Quixote thiab Sancho caij nees mus nkaum nrhiav kev lom zem. Thaum sawv ntxov, Don xav tias nws pom cov neeg loj loj heev. Sancho hais tias cov neeg ntawd yog tej dig huab xwb. Don Quixote txiav txim siab nws mam mus tom lawv ua rog.

Don Quixote caij nws tus nees txog ib lub dig huab. Nws tus hlau ntev ntev ntse txawm khuam rau ntawm lub dig huab caj npab. Caj npab ntawd txhawv nws mus pem huab cua. Sancho sim pab Don Quixote. Nws kuj los mus txhawv pem huab cua thiab. Don Quixote muab tej txoj hlua ntawm lub dig huab hlaiv kiag. Thaum nws muab txoj hlua hlaiv kiag ob txiv neej ntawd txawm poob lawm. Don Quixote rov qab nce mus saum nws tus nees. Sancho rov qab nce mus saum nws tus luav. Lawv hos caij mus lwm qhov nrhiav kev lom zem ntxiv.

Ancient Greece   Student Edition pages 676–691

 Week at a Glance	Customize instruction every day for your English Language Learners.				
	Day 1	**Day 2**	**Day 3**	**Day 4**	**Day 5**
Teacher's Edition	Use the ELL Notes that appear throughout each day of the lesson to support instruction and reading.				
ELL Poster 27	• Assess Prior Knowledge • Develop Concepts and Vocabulary	• Preteach Tested Vocabulary	• My Myth	• Democracy in Action	• Monitor Progress
ELL Teaching Guide	• Picture It! Lesson, pp. 183–184 • Multilingual Summaries, pp. 187–189	• ELL Reader Lesson, pp. 264–265	• Vocabulary Activities and Word Cards, pp. 185–186 • Multilingual Summaries, pp. 187–189		
ELL Readers	• Reread *Cervantes and Don Quixote*	• Teach *Ancient Cultures and Our Culture*	• Reread *Ancient Cultures and Our Culture* and other texts to build fluency		
ELL and Transition Handbook	Use the following as needed to support this week's instruction and to conduct alternative assessments: • Phonics Transition Lessons • Grammar Transition Lessons • Assessment				

Picture It! Comprehension Lesson
Graphic Sources

Use this lesson to supplement or replace the skill lesson on pages 672–673 of the Teacher's Edition.

Teach

Distribute copies of the Picture It! blackline master on page 184.
- Have students describe what they see in the chart. Then read the paragraph aloud.
- Ask: *Why did the author include a chart?* (to provide specific information about average temperatures)
- Share the Skill Points (at right) with students.
- Have students study the graphic. Ask them which months are hottest in Greece and which are coldest.

Practice

Read aloud the directions on page 184. Have students answer the questions at the bottom of the page. Have them keep their answers for later reteaching.

Answers for page 184: 1. average monthly temperatures in Greece **2.** Yes, because it shows what the climate is like each month. **3.** 54°F or 12°C

> ### Skill Points
>
> ✓ **Graphic sources** include maps, charts, diagrams, and other illustrations.
>
> ✓ While reading, study the information in the graphics and ask: *What does this information tell me about this topic? How does this graphic connect to what I am reading in the text?*

Name _____

Look at the picture and the chart. **Read** the paragraph. **Write** the answers to the questions below.

Planning a Trip to Greece

Month	Average Temp. in Degrees Fahrenheit	Average Temp. in Degrees Centigrade
January	50	10
February	50	10
March	54	12
April	49	15
May	67	19
June	75	24
July	81	27
August	81	27
September	75	24
October	67	19
November	59	15
December	53	12

Greece has a mild climate. The coldest part of year is December through April. The average temperature then is 51°F (10°C). July and August are the hottest months of year. The average temperature during these months is 81°F (27°C). Many people think the late spring and early fall are the nicest months to visit Greece, because it is not too hot and not too cold.

1. What does the graphic show?

_____

2. Would the graphic help you decide when to visit Greece? Explain.

_____

_____

3. What is the average temperature in Greece in March?

_____

Vocabulary Activities and Word Cards

Copy the Word Cards on page 186 as needed for the following activities.
Use the blank cards for additional words that you want to teach.
Also see suggestions for teaching vocabulary in the ELL and Transition Handbook.

Clue Game	True or False?	Poster Game
• Write the definition of each vocabulary word on the back of a set of Word Cards. • Have one student choose a card and read the definition, and have the others guess the word. • Once students correctly identify the word, invite volunteers to create sentences using the word.	• Reproduce one set of Word Cards for a true-or-false activity. • Ask a student to choose a card. • Make up a sentence using the vocabulary word, and ask the student if the sentence is true or false. For example: *The United States is a democracy.* (true) • Ask the rest of the group whether they agree with the student's answer. • Repeat the activity until all students have had a chance to choose a card.	• Reproduce one set of Word Cards for students to use in a poster game. • Have students take turns choosing a Word Card without letting others see it. • On their turn, ask students to point to a scene or detail on the ELL Poster, and then give clues about their word without saying it until other students guess the word. • Repeat the process until all students have participated in the activity.

architecture

democracy

empire

ideal

mythology

Multilingual Summaries

Ancient Greece

The Greeks first held the Olympic Games in 776 B.C. in the town of Olympia. The Minoans and Mycenaeans were the first civilizations in Greece. They built cities, ports, and palaces.

1100 B.C. to 800 B.C. saw a Dark Age of Greek history. Little is known about this period. Greek city-states rose at the end of the Dark Age. A Greek Golden Age followed. Greeks achieved much during this period in science, the arts, philosophy, and government. Many Greek ideas from this age underlie modern systems of government and education.

The Greeks' power began to fade. The Roman Empire grew. Romans copied Greek culture and ideas. Today we copy the style of Greek buildings. We study their art, poetry, and philosophy. We use their scientific ideas. We read their plays and stories.

Life in ancient Greece was very different from life today, but we still use ancient Greek ideas.

La Grecia antigua

Los griegos tuvieron los primeros Juegos Olímpicos en 776 a.C., en la ciudad de Olimpia. Las primeras civilizaciones de Grecia fueron la micénica y la minoica. Ellos construyeron ciudades, puertos y palacios.

Desde 1100 a.C. a 800 a.C. ocurrió una Edad Oscura en la historia de Grecia. Se conoce muy poco sobre ese período. Las ciudades-estados griegas emergieron al final de la Edad Oscura. A esta edad le siguió una gran Edad de Oro. Los griegos lograron mucho durante ese período en las ciencias, las artes, la filosofía y el gobierno. Muchas de las grandes ideas griegas de esa edad sentaron las bases de los sistemas modernos del gobierno y de la educación.

El poder de los griegos comenzó a decaer. El Imperio Romano creció. Los romanos copiaron de los griegos su cultura e ideas. Hoy copiamos el estilo de los edificios griegos. Estudiamos su arte, poesía y filosofía. Usamos sus ideas científicas. Leemos sus obras y sus historias.

La vida en la Grecia antigua fue muy diferente a la vida actual, pero nosotros todavía usamos las ideas antiguas griegas.

Multilingual Summaries

古希臘

西元前776年，希臘人在奧林匹亞城，舉行奧林匹克運動會。克裏特與邁錫尼是希臘文明的發源地。他們建造了許多宏偉的城邦、港口與宮殿。

西元前1100至800年，是希臘歷史上的黑暗時代。這段歷史人們知之甚少。黑暗時代後期出現了許多城邦國家。接著是黃金時代，這期間希臘科學、藝術、哲學與政治取得很高的成就。源於那時的偉大思想，為現代政治與教育奠定了基礎。

後來，希臘勢力衰弱了，羅馬帝國崛起，但他們完全採納了希臘的文化與思想。今天的人們也借鑒希臘建築風格，研究他們的藝術、詩歌與哲學，學習希臘的科學思想，喜歡希臘的戲劇與故事。

雖然古希臘的生活與現在的大不相同，但是他們的思想我們沿用至今。

Hy Lạp Cổ Xưa

Người Hy Lạp lần đầu tiên tổ chức Thế Vận Hội vào năm 776 BC (Trước Công Nguyên) tại thành phố Olympia. Người Minoan và người Mycenaean là những người lập nền văn minh đầu tiên ở Hy Lạp. Họ đã dựng nên thành phố, hải cảng, và lâu đài.

Những năm 1100 BC đến 800 BC là Thời Đại Đen Tối của lịch sử Hy Lạp. Có ít điều được biết đến ở giai đoạn này. Các bang đô thị mọc lên vào cuối Thời Đại Đen Tối. Thời Đại Hoàng Kim của Hy Lạp theo sau đó. Ở giai đoạn này, người Hy Lạp đạt được nhiều thành tựu về khoa học, nghệ thuật, triết học, và chính phủ. Nhiều ý tưởng Hy Lạp từ thời đại này là cơ sở cho hệ thống chính phủ và giáo dục ngày nay.

Thế lực của Hy Lạp bắt đầu suy yếu. Đế Quốc La Mã phát triển. Người La Mã đã bắt chước nền văn hóa và những ý tưởng của Hy Lạp. Ngày nay chúng ta bắt chước kiểu của các tòa nhà Hy Lạp. Chúng ta học nghệ thuật, văn thơ, và triết lý của họ. Chúng ta dùng những ý tưởng khoa học của họ. Chúng ta đọc chuyện và các vở kịch của họ.

Đời sống ở Hy Lạp cổ xưa thì rất khác biệt với đời sống ngày nay, nhưng chúng ta vẫn còn dùng những ý tưởng của Hy Lạp cổ xưa.

Multilingual Summaries

고대 그리스

그리스인은 기원전 776년 올림피아라는 마을에서 처음으로 올림픽을 열었다. 크레타인과 미케네인이 그리스 최초의 문명인으로 이들은 도시와 항구 그리고 궁전을 지었다.

기원전 1100년과 800년 사이는 그리스 역사에 있어서 암흑기로 이 시기에 대해 알려진 것은 별로 없다. 그리스의 도시 국가들은 이 암흑기의 말엽에 생겨났고 그리스의 황금기가 뒤를 이었다. 그리스인은 이 기간 동안 과학, 예술, 철학, 그리고 행정 분야에 있어서 많은 업적을 이루었는데 이 시기의 많은 그리스 사상들은 현대의 행정과 교육 시스템의 기초가 되고 있다.

후에 그리스의 세력이 쇠퇴하기 시작했고 로마 제국이 성장했다. 로마인은 그리스의 문화와 사상을 모방했고 오늘날 우리들은 그리스의 건축 스타일을 모방한다. 우리는 또한 그들의 예술, 시 및 철학을 공부하고 그들의 과학 사상을 활용하며 그들의 희곡과 이야기를 읽는다.

고대 그리스의 삶은 오늘날의 그것과는 매우 달랐으나 우리는 여전히 그리스식 사고방식을 이용하고 있다.

Greece Puag Thaum Ub

Cov neeg Greeks xub ua qhov ua si Olympic Games thaum xyoo 776 BC hauv cheeb tsam ntawm Olympia. Cov neeg Minoans thiab Mycenaeans yog thawj thawj neeg hauv Greece. Lawv txhim tsa tej nroog, tej nres nkoj, thiab tej tsev loj loj zoo nkauj.

Xyoo 1100 BC mus txog xyoo 800 BC muaj kev tsau ntuj nti kev txom nyem ntawm cov Greek keeb kwm. Neeg niaj hnub nim no paub me me txog lub caij ntawd. Greek tej nroog-xeeb kov yeej lub caij muaj kev tsau ntuj nti kev txom nyem thaum kawg lub caij ntawd. Ib lub caij zoo heev hos tawm tuaj tom qab hu ua lub caij kub kub. Greeks ua ntau yam zoo xws li txawj kawm txuj ci, txawj teev duab, thiab txoj kev xav, thiab kev tsoom fwv. Muaj ntau yam kev tswv yim ntawm lub caij ntawd uas pab pub tswv yim ntawm txoj kev peb ua tsoom ua fwv kawm ntaub kawm ntawv niaj hnub nim no.

Cov Greeks qaug zog zuj zu mus. Cov Roman teb chaws loj tsim txiaj loj hlob tuaj mus. Cov Roman muaj txoj kev xav thiaj ua txuj ci ib yam nkau li cov Greek. Niaj hnub nim no peb ua vaj ua tsev zoo li cov Greek. Peb kawm lawv txoj kev teev duab, paj lug, thiab txoj kev xav. Peb siv lawv txoj kev xav txog tej txuj ci. Peb nyeem lawv tej zag yeeb yam thiab tej zag dab neeg.

Greece txoj kev ua neeg nyob puag thaum ub yeej txawv kev ua neeg nyob niaj hnub no, tiam si peb tseem siv cov greek puag thaum ub txoj kev xav.

The All-American Slurp

Week at a Glance	Customize instruction every day for your English Language Learners.				
	Day 1	**Day 2**	**Day 3**	**Day 4**	**Day 5**
Teacher's Edition	Use the ELL Notes that appear throughout each day of the lesson to support instruction and reading.				
ELL Poster 28	• Assess Prior Knowledge • Develop Concepts and Vocabulary	• Preteach Tested Vocabulary	• Review Compare and Contrast	• Everyone's a Critic	• Monitor Progress
ELL Teaching Guide	• Picture It! Lesson, pp. 190–191 • Multilingual Summaries, pp. 194–196	• ELL Reader Lesson, pp. 266–267	• Vocabulary Activities and Word Cards, pp. 192–193 • Multilingual Summaries, pp. 194–196		
ELL Readers	• Reread *Ancient Cultures and Our Culture*	• Teach *The Homework Club*	• Reread *The Homework Club* and other texts to build fluency		
ELL and Transition Handbook	Use the following as needed to support this week's instruction and to conduct alternative assessments: • Phonics Transition Lessons • Grammar Transition Lessons • Assessment				

Picture It! Comprehension Lesson
Compare and Contrast
Use this lesson to supplement or replace the skill lesson on pages 698–699 of the Teacher's Edition.

Teach
Distribute copies of the Picture It! blackline master on page 191.
• Have students describe the picture. Then read the paragraph aloud. Ask: *How are Simon and the author alike?*
• Share the skill points (at right) with students.
• Have students fill in the Venn diagram to show how the boys are alike and how they are different.

Practice
Read aloud the directions on page 191. Have students fill in the graphic organizer. Have them keep their organizers for later reteaching.

Answers for page 191: *Simon:* freckles, messy hair, not good at math; *Author:* no freckles, neat hair, good at math; *Both:* same height, love to play soccer, like pizza more than any other food

Skill Points
✓ When you **compare**, you tell how two or more things are alike. When you **contrast**, you tell how two or more things are different.

✓ Clue words such as *like*, *similarly*, and *both* can show comparison. Clue words such as *unlike*, *on the other hand*, and *however* can indicate contrast.

Look at the picture. **Read** the paragraph.

- What traits does Simon have that the author does not? **Write** them in the circle labeled *Simon*.

- What traits does the author have that Simon does not? **Write** them in the circle labeled *Author*.

- In what ways are the author and Simon similar? **Write** the traits they share in the section labeled *Both*.

My Best Friend

In many ways, my best friend, Simon, is very different from me. He has a lot of freckles, but I don't have any. His hair is always messy, but mine is always neat. Unlike me, he is not very good at math. We are different in all of these ways. But in other ways, we are the same. We are almost exactly the same height. We both love to play soccer. And both of us like pizza more than any other food.

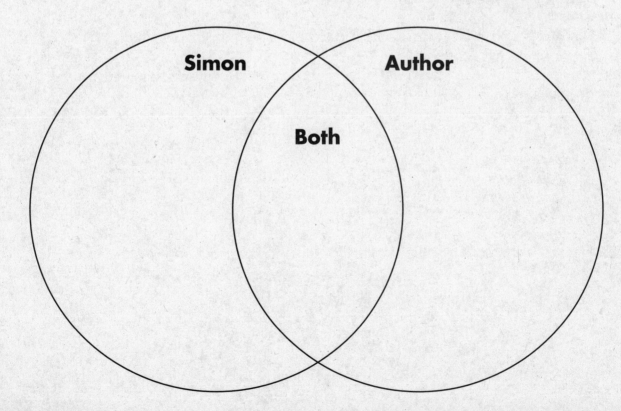

Simon   Author

Both

Vocabulary Activities and Word Cards

Copy the Word Cards on page 193 as needed for the following activities.
Use the blank card for an additional word that you want to teach.
Also see suggestions for teaching vocabulary in the ELL and Transition Handbook.

Parts-of-Speech Word Sort	Synonym Search	Can You Guess?
• Give each student a set of Word Cards for a word sort activity.	• Give each student a set of Word Cards for a synonym search.	• Reproduce one set of Word Cards for a guessing game.
• Have each student prepare a three-column chart with *Nouns, Verbs,* and *Adjectives* as the column headings.	• Have students place the cards face up on their desks or tables.	• Place all of the Word Cards face down in a pile.
• Remind students what kinds of words belong in each column.	• Remind students that synonyms are words that mean the same or almost the same thing. Then say the following synonyms or near synonyms for the words: *raw vegetables; disgusting, return, embarrassed; advancement; agreement; advanced.*	• Have one student choose a card and give verbal or visual clues that will help the rest of the group guess the word.
• Have students write each vocabulary word in the appropriate column.		• Repeat the process until all students have had a chance to provide clues.
• When all students have completed the activity, ask volunteers to explain what each word means.	• Ask students to select the vocabulary word that is closest in meaning to each word or phrase you say.	

disgraced

progress

promoted

relish

retreat

revolting

unison

Multilingual Summaries

English

The All-American Slurp

The Lin family recently moved to America from China. Many American customs are new to them. The Gleasons and the Lins are neighbors. The Gleasons invite the Lins to dinner. The Lins have never been to a buffet dinner. They do their best.

The Lins' daughter must wear skirts to school. The other girls may wear jeans. Mrs. Lin sees that jeans are practical. She buys jeans for her daughter.

Mr. Lin receives a promotion at work. The family goes to a fine restaurant. The family slurps their soup. Other diners stare. The daughter is embarrassed. She hides in the bathroom.

Then, the Lins invite the Gleasons to dinner. The Gleasons do not know how to eat Chinese food. They do their best.

The two girls go to an ice cream shop. Meg slurps her milkshake. The Lins' daughter is surprised. Meg tells her friend that all Americans slurp.

Spanish

Todos los estadounidenses sorben ruidosamente

La familia Lin se mudó recientemente de China a Estados Unidos. Muchas costumbres estadounidenses son nuevas para ellos. Los Gleason y los Lin son vecinos. Los Gleason invitan a los Lin a cenar. Los Lin nunca habían estado en una cena buffet. Hacen lo que pueden.

La hija de los Lin tiene que usar faldas para la escuela. Las otras niñas usan *jeans*. La Sra. Lin se da cuenta que los *jeans* son prácticos. Ella le compra *jeans* a su hija.

El Sr. Lin tuvo una promoción esta semana. La familia va a un distinguido restaurante. La familia sorben la sopa ruidosamente. Los demás comensales los miran fijo. La hija tiene vergüenza. Se esconde en el baño.

Luego, los Lin invitan a los Gleason a cenar. Los Gleason no saben cómo comer la comida china. Hacen lo que pueden.

Las dos niñas van a comprar un helado. Meg sorbe ruidosamente su batido. La hija de los Lin está sorprendida. Meg le dice a su amiga que todos los americanos sorben ruidosamente.

Multilingual Summaries

美國人也唏哩呼嚕

林先生一家剛從中國搬到美國，不熟悉美國的風俗習慣。鄰居家叫格裏森，邀請林先生一家參加宴會。雖然一家人從未吃過自助晚餐，他們還是努力做到得體大方。

林家女兒一直都穿裙子去上學，其他美國女孩卻可以穿牛仔褲。林太太看牛仔褲方便實用，也買了讓女兒穿。

林先生工作出色被提升，家人去高級餐廳慶祝一番。喝湯時唏哩呼嚕的聲音，惹得他人盯著看。女兒覺得很尷尬，連忙躲進洗手間。

林家回請格裏森一家來赴宴。雖然格裏森不知道怎麼用中餐，他們還是努力做到得體大方。

兩家的女孩去霜淇淋店。梅格喝奶昔時，也是唏哩呼嚕。林家女兒很驚訝，梅格說所有美國人都這樣。

Húp Sùm Sụp Kiểu Mỹ

Gia đình họ Lin vừa dọn đến Hoa Kỳ từ Trung Quốc. Nhiều phong tục của Hoa Kỳ còn rất mới lạ đối với họ. Gia đình họ Gleason và họ Lin là láng giềng. Gia đình Gleason mời gia đình họ Lin đi ăn tối. Gia đình họ Lin chưa bao giờ ăn tối ở một tiệm ăn tự phục vụ. Họ cố làm cho giống mọi người.

Cô con gái nhà họ Lin phải mặc váy đi học. Các cô gái khác được mặc quần jean đi học. Bà Lin thấy là quần jean thì thiết thực hơn. Bà đi mua quần jean cho con gái.

Ông Lin được lên chức ở sở. Gia đình đi đến một nhà hàng thanh lịch. Gia đình húp sùm sụp món canh của mình. Các thực khách khác nhìn họ chằm chằm. Cô con gái ngượng ngùng. Cô đi trốn trong phòng vệ sinh.

Kế đến, nhà họ Lin mời gia đình họ Gleason đến ăn tối. Gia đình Gleason không biết cách ăn thức ăn Trung Hoa. Họ cố làm giống mọi người.

Hai cô gái đi đến một tiệm bán kem. Meg húp sùm sụp ly sinh tố của mình. Cô con gái nhà họ Lin ngạc nhiên. Meg nói với cô ấy là người Hoa Kỳ ai cũng húp sùm sụp cả.

Multilingual Summaries

모든 미국인들이 소리를 내며 먹는다

린 가족은 최근 중국에서 미국으로 이주했다. 미국의 많은 관습이 그들에겐 새로워 보인다. 글리슨 가족과 린 가족은 이웃이다. 글리슨 가족이 린 가족을 저녁 식사에 초대한다. 린 가족은 뷔페 식사를 한 적이 없었지만 최선을 다해 식사한다.

린 가족의 딸은 학교에 갈 때 치마를 입어야만 한다. 다른 소녀들은 아마 청바지를 입을 것이다. 린 아주머니는 청바지가 실용적이라는 것을 알게 되고 딸에게 청바지를 사 준다.

린 아저씨가 직장에서 승진을 하여 가족들과 근사한 식당에 간다. 가족들이 후루룩 소리를 내며 수프를 먹자 다른 사람들이 쳐다본다. 딸은 무안해져 화장실로 숨는다.

며칠 후 린 가족이 글리슨 가족을 저녁에 초대한다. 글리슨 가족은 중국 음식을 어떻게 먹는지 모르지만 최선을 다해 식사한다.

두 소녀가 아이스크림 가게에 간다. 메그가 밀크쉐이크를 소리를 내며 먹자 린씨네 딸은 놀란다. 메그는 모든 미국인들이 소리를 내며 음식을 먹는다고 얘기해 준다.

Kev Nqus Mikas

Tsev neeg Lin los tsiv rau tebchaws Ameslikas, lawv tuaj suav teb tuaj. Asmeslikas txoj kevcai tshiab tshiab rau lawv. Tsev neeg Gleason thiab tsev neeg Lin yog kwvtij zej zog. Tsev neeg Gleason caw tsev neeg Lin los tuaj noj hmo. Tsev neeg Lin tsis tau mus noj tom ib lub qhov chaw uas yus txais yus tus kheej cov mov xwb (buffet). Lawv sim coj lawv cwj pwm zoo.

Tsev neeg Lin ib tug ntxhais yuav tsum hnav ib daim tiab thaum mus kawm ntawv. Luag lwm cov hluas nkauj hnav tau lub ris. Niam tsev, ntawm tsev neeg Lin, saib tias hnav cov ris kuj zoo thiab. Nws mus yuav cov ris pub rau tus ntxhais hnav.

Txiv tsev, ntawm tsev neeg Lin, vam meej tom nws lub qhov chaw haujlwm. Tsev neeg mus noj mov tom ib lub qhov chaw zoo noj. Lawv haus lawv cov mov dej nrov nrov. Luag tej ntsia ntsoov. Tus ntxhais, txaj txaj muag. Nws mus zais nws tus kheej tom lub hoob nab.

Ces, tsev neeg Lin caw tsev neeg Gleason los tuaj noj hmo. Tsev neeg Gleason tsis paub noj mov suav licas. Lawv sim coj lawv cwj pwm zoo.

Ob tug ntxhais mus tom lub khw ice cream. Meg haus nws cov milkshake nrov nrov. Tsev neeg Lin ib tug ntxhais xav tsis thoob li. Meg qhia nws tias txhua neeg Ameslikas haus los yog noj cov mov nrov nrov zoo li ntawd.

The Aztec News

Student Edition pages 728–743

Week at a Glance	Customize instruction every day for your English Language Learners.				
	Day 1	**Day 2**	**Day 3**	**Day 4**	**Day 5**
Teacher's Edition	Use the ELL Notes that appear throughout each day of the lesson to support instruction and reading.				
ELL Poster 29	• Assess Prior Knowledge • Develop Concepts and Vocabulary	• Preteach Tested Vocabulary	• You Are What You Throw Away?	• Finding Solutions	• Monitor Progress
ELL Teaching Guide	• Picture It! Lesson, pp. 197–198 • Multilingual Summaries, pp. 201–203	• ELL Reader Lesson, pp. 268–269	• Vocabulary Activities and Word Cards, pp. 199–200 • Multilingual Summaries, pp. 201–203		
ELL Readers	• Reread *The Homework Club*	• Teach *Letters from New Spain*	• Reread *Letters from New Spain* and other texts to build fluency		
ELL and Transition Handbook	Use the following as needed to support this week's instruction and to conduct alternative assessments: • Phonics Transition Lessons • Grammar Transition Lessons • Assessment				

Picture It! Comprehension Lesson
Draw Conclusions

Use this lesson to supplement or replace the skill lesson on pages 724–725 of the Teacher's Edition.

Teach

Distribute copies of the Picture It! blackline master on page 198.
• Have students describe the illustration. Then read the paragraph aloud.
• Ask: *What can you conclude about Pizarro from the fact that he kept trying to reach Peru?* (that he was determined to conquer it)
• Share the Skill Points (at right) with students.
• Have students identify all of the facts in the paragraph. Then have them tell what conclusions they can draw from the facts.

Practice

Read aloud the directions on page 198. Have students fill in the graphic organizer. Have them keep their organizers for later reteaching.

Answers for page 198: *Conclusion:* Pizarro was a determined man who wanted to conquer Peru. *Facts:* He tried in 1524 and 1525 to reach Peru but failed. He tried and failed again two years later. He traveled to Spain to get the king's support. He finally conquered Peru.

Skill Points

✓ When you **draw a conclusion,** you form a reasonable opinion about something you have read.

✓ Evaluate whether your conclusions are valid. Ask yourself: *Do the facts and details in the text support my conclusion? Is my conclusion valid, based on logical thinking and common sense?*

Look at the picture. **Read** the paragraph.

- What facts are in the paragraph? **Write** them in the graphic organizer.
- What conclusion can you draw from these facts? **Write** it in the graphic organizer.

King
Crown

Conquering Peru

The Incan Empire was a rich civilization in Peru. A Spanish explorer named Francisco Pizarro had heard about this empire. He wanted to find it. In 1524 and 1525, he tried to reach Peru. He failed. Two years later, he tried again. Once again, he was unable to reach Peru. In 1528, Pizarro went to Spain. He convinced the king to give him permission to conquer Peru for Spain. In 1531, Pizarro finally succeeded. He reached the Inca city of Tumbes.

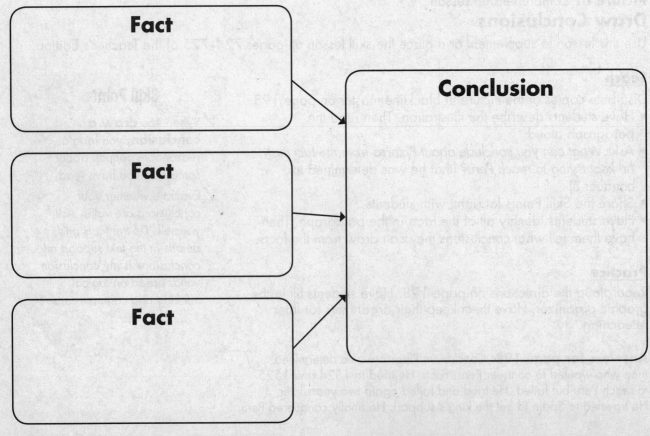

Fact

Fact

Fact

Conclusion

Vocabulary Activities and Word Cards

Copy the Word Cards on page 200 as needed for the following activities.
Use the blank cards for additional words that you want to teach.
Also see suggestions for teaching vocabulary in the ELL and Transition Handbook.

Clue Game	True or False?	Home Language Clues
• Write the definition of each vocabulary word on the back of a set of Word Cards. • Have one student choose a card and read the definition, and have the others guess the word. • Once students correctly identify the word, invite volunteers to create sentences using the word.	• Reproduce one set of Word Cards for a true-or-false activity. • Ask a student to choose a card. • Make up a sentence using the vocabulary word and ask the student if the sentence is true or false. For example: *Enemies are the same as comrades.* (false) • Ask the rest of the group whether they agree with the student's answer. • Repeat the activity until all students have had a chance to choose a card.	• Pair students who have writing proficiency in the same home language, and give each student a set of Word Cards. • Have students work together to write translations of the vocabulary words in their home language on the back of each card. (See the Multilingual Lesson Vocabulary beginning on page 272 for suggested translations.) • Have partners lay out the cards with the home language sides facing up. • Have each student choose a card, read the home language translation, and then say the vocabulary word in English.

benefits

campaigns

comrades

enrich

foreigners

invaders

Multilingual Summaries

The Aztec News

In 1458, the Aztecs defeated the Mixtecs. The Aztec leader, Montezuma, was pleased. The Mixtecs were required to send Montezuma goods and money. Many years later, the Aztecs found themselves at war again—with the Spaniards.

The Spanish took Montezuma prisoner and killed him. The Aztecs fought back. They attacked the Spaniards and killed more than two thirds of them.

Nobles received a share of the nation's wealth. They were allowed to wear cotton clothes and gold jewelry. These were forbidden to commoners. Nobles and commoners attended different schools.

Tenochtitlán was the capital of the Aztec empire. It had a busy market place and festivals. Pochtecas, or merchants, traded in faraway cities. They traveled at night to avoid attacks.

People in the city liked to give parties. Dancers, singers, and musicians entertained the guests. Hosts gave a present to each guest.

Noticias aztecas

En 1458, los aztecas vencieron a los mixtecas. El líder azteca, Moctezuma, estaba satisfecho. Los mixtecas debían enviar a Moctezuma productos y dinero. Muchos años después, los aztecas se encontraron en guerra otra vez, esta vez con los españoles.

Los españoles tomaron prisionero a Moctezuma y lo mataron. Los aztecas lucharon contra ellos. Atacaron a los españoles y mataron más de dos tercios de ellos.

Los nobles recibían y compartían las riquezas de la nación. Se les permitía usar ropas de algodón y joyas de oro. Esto era prohibido a los plebeyos. Los nobles y los plebeyos iban a diferentes escuelas.

Tenochtitlán era la capital del Imperio Azteca. Tenía un mercado concurrido y festivales. Los pochtecas, o mercaderes, comerciaban con ciudades lejanas. Viajaban de noche para evitar ser atacados.

A la gente de la ciudad le gustaban las fiestas. Bailarines, cantantes y músicos entretenían a los invitados. Los anfitriones le daban regalos a los invitados.

Multilingual Summaries

Chinese

阿茲特克

1458年，阿茲特克打敗米斯克。國王蒙地祖馬非常高興，強迫米斯克上貢禮品與金錢。後來，阿茲特克又與西班牙打仗。

西班牙人抓住蒙地祖馬，把他殺了。阿茲特克人英勇地反擊，殺了三分之二以上的西班牙人。

阿茲特克的貴族掌握國家的財富，可以穿棉布衣服、戴黃金珠寶。平民百姓不可能有這些，他們去的學校也與貴族的不一樣。

阿茲特克帝國的首都叫特諾茲提朗。那裏有繁榮的市集與盛大的節日。商人叫做波切特克斯，會將貨物運到遙遠的他鄉。他們都在晚上趕路，以避免遭到打劫。

城裏的阿茲特克人喜歡舉辦晚會。客人可以觀看跳舞、唱歌與音樂表演，並且每人都會收到主人贈送的禮物。

Vietnamese

Tin Aztec

Vào năm 1458, người Aztec đánh bại người Mixtec. Thủ lĩnh của Aztec, Montezuma, rất hài lòng. Người Mixtec bị quy định phải gởi cho Montezuma tiền bạc và sản vật. Nhiều năm sau đó, người Aztec lại có chiến tranh nữa — với người Tây Ban Nha.

Người Tây Ban Nha bắt Montezuma làm tù binh và giết ông ấy. Dân Aztec chống lại. Họ tấn công quân Tây Ban Nha và giết hơn hai phần ba quân này.

Những nhà quý tộc nhận lãnh một phần tài sản của quốc gia. Họ được phép mặc áo quần làm bằng vải và mang nữ trang bằng vàng. Những điều này bị cấm đối với dân thường. Những người quý tộc và dân thường học ở những trường riêng biệt.

Tenochtitlán là thủ đô của đế quốc Aztec. Thủ đô này có khu chợ nhộn nhịp và có các lễ hội. Những thương gia, hay còn gọi là "pochtecas", buôn bán ở những thành phố xa xôi. Họ du hành vào ban đêm để tránh bị tấn công.

Dân ở thành phố thích mở tiệc tùng. Các vũ nhân, ca sĩ, và nhạc sĩ giải trí quan khách. Chủ nhà trao quà cho từng quan khách.

Multilingual Summaries

아즈텍 뉴스

1458년 아즈텍이 믹스텍을 무찔렀고 아즈텍의 우두머리인 몬테주마는 기뻐했다. 믹스텍은 몬테주마에게 재화를 보내야만 했다. 수년 후 아즈텍은 다시 전쟁을 하게 되었는데 상대는 바로 스페인 사람이었다.

스페인사람들은 몬테주마를 감옥에 넣고 죽여버렸다. 아즈텍은 이에 저항하며 스페인사람을 공격해 그들의 3분의 2 이상을 죽였다.

귀족들은 국가 부의 일정 부분을 할당받았고 그들은 면으로 된 옷과 금 장식을 걸치는 것이 허용되었는데 이것은 평민에게는 금지된 것이었다. 귀족과 평민은 다른 학교에 다녔다.

테노치티뜰란은 아즈텍 제국의 수도였다. 그곳에는 번화한 시장과 축제가 가득했다. 포츠떼까라고 하는 상인들은 머나먼 도시에서 교역했고 습격을 피하기 위해 밤에 이동했다.

도시 사람들은 파티 여는 것을 좋아했고 무희, 가수, 그리고 음악가가 손님을 즐겁게 했다. 파티의 주인은 손님들 각자에게 선물을 증정했다.

Txoj Xov Ntawm Cov Neeg Aztec

Thaum xyoo 1458, Cov neeg Aztec yeej cov neeg Mixtecs. Tus thawj coj ntawm cov neeg Aztec, Montezuma, muaj kev siab nqis. Cov neeg Mixtecs yuav tsum xa Montezuma tej khoom tej nyiaj tuag nthi. Ntau ntau xyoo tom qab, cov neeg Aztecs txawm muaj kev ua tsov ua rog dua nrog cov neeg Spaniards.

Cov Spaniards txom Montezuma cab nws mus kaw muab nws tuag. Cov neeg Aztecs rov qab ua tsov rog. Lawv ntau kiag cov Spaniards thiab muab ob feem peb tawm ntawm lawv tuag.

Cov neeg siab siab ho txais ib feem ntawm lub teb chaw tej nyiaj txiag. Lawv muaj cai hnav khaub ncaws zoo zoo thiab coj tej kub. Cov neeg dog dig tsis muaj cai hnav los coj tej ntawd. Cov neeg siab siab thiab cov neeg dog dig nyias mus nyias hoob kawm.

Tenochtitlan yog lub plawv nroog ntawm Aztec teb chaws tsim txiaj. Nws muaj muaj kev muab ub muab no thiab kev lom zem heev. Pochtecas, los yog cov neeg muaj khoom, sib pauv hauv tej nroog deb deb. Lawv mus kev thaum tsau ntuj xwv kom zam tau cov tub sab.

Cov neeg hauv nroog nyiam ua kev lom zem. Cov txawj seem cev, los hu nkauj, los ntau ub ntau no tau mus mus los los kom neeg muaj tau kev lom zem. Cov zov tej kev lom zem no yuav tsum pub khoom plig rau txhua tus uas tuaj.

Where Opportunity Awaits
Student Edition pages 754–761

Week at a Glance	Customize instruction every day for your English Language Learners.				
	Day 1	**Day 2**	**Day 3**	**Day 4**	**Day 5**
Teacher's Edition	Use the ELL Notes that appear throughout each day of the lesson to support instruction and reading.				
ELL Poster 30	• Assess Prior Knowledge • Develop Concepts and Vocabulary	• Preteach Tested Vocabulary	• Dream Job	• Words of Migration	• Monitor Progress
ELL Teaching Guide	• Picture It! Lesson, pp. 204–205 • Multilingual Summaries, pp. 208–210	• ELL Reader Lesson, pp. 270–271	• Vocabulary Activities and Word Cards, pp. 206–207 • Multilingual Summaries, pp. 208–210		
ELL Readers	• Reread *Letters from New Spain*	• Teach *Moving North*	• Reread *Moving North* and other texts to build fluency		
ELL and Transition Handbook	Use the following as needed to support this week's instruction and to conduct alternative assessments: • Phonics Transition Lessons • Grammar Transition Lessons • Assessment				

Picture It! Comprehension Lesson
Generalize

Use this lesson to supplement or replace the skill lesson on pages 750–751 of the Teacher's Edition.

Teach

Distribute copies of the Picture It! blackline master on page 205.
• Have students describe the picture. Then read the paragraph aloud.
• Ask: *What kind of jobs did most African Americans do when they moved north during and after World War I?*
• Have students identify the generalization in the paragraph. Then have them identify the facts that support the generalization.

Practice

Read aloud the directions on page 205. Have students fill in the graphic organizer. Have them keep their organizers for later reteaching.

Answers for page 205: *Generalization:* Most African Americans who went north during and after World War I worked in hard, low-paying jobs. *Supporting Facts:* African Americans worked in steel mills; African Americans worked in factories; African Americans worked in meat-packing houses. They worked long hours.

Skill Points

✓ A **generalization** is a rule that fits many examples. Authors sometimes make generalizations about a group of things or people to make a point.

✓ You can often recognize a generalization by clue words, such as *most, all, always,* or *never.*

✓ Generalizations should be supported by examples, facts, or logical thinking.

© Scott Foresman 6

Look at the picture. **Read** the paragraph.

- What generalization is made in this paragraph? **Write** it in the large box below.

- What facts support the generalization? **Write** them in the smaller boxes below.

Moving North

During and after World War I, millions of African Americans left the South to move north. They took hard jobs that did not pay very much money. Some made steel in hot steel mills. Some made cars in noisy factories. Others packed meat in smelly meat-packing houses. They all worked long hours at hard jobs. Most of these people were happy to work hard, however. They knew that their children would have a better life in the North than they had had in the South.

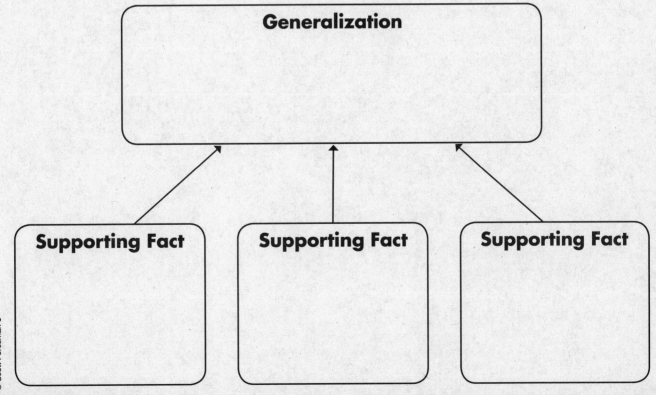

Generalization

Supporting Fact

Supporting Fact

Supporting Fact

Vocabulary Activities and Word Cards

Copy the Word Cards on page 207 as needed for the following activities.
Use the blank card for an additional word that you want to teach.
Also see suggestions for teaching vocabulary in the ELL and Transition Handbook.

Riddle Game	Synonym Search	Secret Word
• Divide students into pairs or small groups to play a riddle game. Give each group a set of Word Cards. • Have students place the cards face down in a pile and take turns choosing a card and making up a riddle about the word for others to guess. • Provide a model for the riddle, such as: *This word starts with the letter _____. It ends with the letter _____. It means _____.*	• Give each student a set of Word Cards for a synonym search. • Have students place the cards face up on their desks or tables. • Remind students that synonyms are words that mean the same or almost the same thing. Then state the following synonyms or near synonyms for some of the words: *free time, country, city, enough.* • Ask students to select the vocabulary word that is closest in meaning to each word or phrase you say.	• Divide students into pairs for a Secret Word activity. Give each pair a set of Word Cards. • Have students place the Word Cards face up on a desk or table so that both students can see them. • Have one student secretly choose a word and give verbal and visual clues that will help the other student guess the word. Have the student pause after each clue so that his or her partner can guess the word. • Have students take turns giving clues and guessing words.

burden

conformed

leisure

maintenance

rural

sufficient

urban

Multilingual Summaries

Where Opportunity Awaits

In the early 1900s, many African Americans moved from the South to the North. This was called the Great Migration. People moved to find better pay and living conditions. They often moved to places where they had friends or relatives.

Life was not easy for those who moved. Rents in black neighborhoods were often high. Landlords did not repair buildings. Tenants who complained could be replaced. Workdays in stockyards, factories and on railroads were long. Strict bosses kept tight schedules.

People migrated despite these hardships. There were rewards for their struggle. Their children could go to school. Black people could vote. The pay was better than in the South. These benefits made people want to come North.

Donde hay oportunidad

A inicios del siglo XX, muchos afroamericanos se mudaron del Sur al Norte. A esto se le llamó La Gran Migración. La gente se mudó para encontrar mejor sueldo y condiciones de vida. Ellos, a menudo, se mudaban a lugares donde tenían amigos o parientes.

La vida no era fácil para aquellos que se mudaban. Los alquileres en los barrios negros eran, muchas veces, altas. Los dueños no reparaban los edificios. Los inquilinos que se quejaban podían ser reemplazados. Las jornadas en los corrales, las fábricas y el ferrocarril eran largas. Jefes rectos mantenían horarios estrictos.

La gente emigraba a pesar de estos inconvenientes. Ellos tuvieron recompensas por sus esfuerzos. Sus hijos pudieron ir a la escuela. Las personas negras pudieron votar. El sueldo era mejor que en el Sur. Esos beneficios hicieron que la gente quisiera venir al Norte.

Multilingual Summaries

機遇在哪兒

二十世紀初的時候，許多美國黑人從南方遷移到北方，歷史上稱為 "大遷徙"。人們為了尋找好工作和改善生活條件，常常遷到北方已有親戚或朋友的地方。

人們剛遷到北方時，生活非常艱難。黑人區的房子租金很貴，壞了房東也不修。誰要抱怨，就會被趕走。他們常常在畜牧場、工廠和鐵路裏工作到很晚。刻薄的老闆很少讓他們休息。

儘管生活這麼艱苦，人們還是不斷地遷往北方。他們的努力最終也獲得回報：孩子們可以上學，黑人也能參與選舉，工資要比南方高。這些好處吸引了更多人遷移到北方。

Nơi Cơ Hội Đang Chờ Đón

Vào những thập niên đầu của 1900, nhiều người Mỹ gốc Phi Châu rời Miền Nam để dọn đến Miền Bắc. Việc này được gọi là Cuộc Di Cư Vĩ Đại. Người ta dọn đi để tìm lương cao hơn và điều kiện sinh sống tốt hơn. Họ thường dọn đến những nơi nào họ có bạn bè hoặc thân nhân ở đó.

Đời sống không dễ dàng gì cho những người dọn đi. Tiền thuê nhà ở khu phố người da đen thường đắt đỏ. Chủ nhà không sửa chữa các tòa nhà. Người thuê nhà nào than phiền thì bị đuổi ra. Ngày làm việc ở các chuồng nhốt gia súc, phân xưởng và trên các tuyến đường xe lửa thì dài. Các ông chủ khắc nghiệt giữ lịch trình làm việc gấp rút.

Người ta vẫn di cư cho dù có những vất vả này. Họ nhận được phần thưởng cho sự gian lao của mình. Con cái của họ được đi học. Người da đen được đi bầu. Tiền lương khá hơn là ở miền Nam. Những quyền lợi này làm cho người ta muốn dọn lên phía bắc.

Multilingual Summaries

기회의 땅으로

1900년대 초기에 많은 흑인들이 남부에서 북부로 이주했고 이것을 '흑인들의 대이주'라고 불렀다. 사람들은 더 나은 임금과 생활 여건을 찾아 이주했는데 그들은 종종 친구나 친척들이 사는 곳으로 이주하기도 했다.

이주자들의 삶은 그리 쉽지 않았다. 흑인 거주지의 집세는 대부분 비쌌고 집주인들은 건물을 수리하지도 않았으며 불평을 하는 세입자들은 쫓겨날 수도 있었다. 그들에겐 가축 사육장, 공장, 그리고 철도 공사장에서의 하루 일과가 길기만 했고 엄격한 상관은 빡빡한 일정을 강요했다.

사람들은 이런 고생을 하면서도 이주를 했지만 그들의 노력에는 그만한 보상이 따랐다. 그들의 아이들이 학교에 다닐 수 있었고 흑인들도 투표를 할 수 있었으며 급료는 남부에서보다 나았다. 이러한 장점들은 사람들을 북부로 오고 싶게 만들었다.

Qhov Chaw uas ib lub Cib Fim Nyob Nyob

Nyuam qhuav tom qab xyoo ib txhiab cuaj puas, cov neeg African American tsiv ntawm sab qab teb mus txog sab qaum tebv. Txoj kev khiav rau lwm qhov no, hu ua Txoj Kev Tsiv Tsev Loj. Cov neeg xav khiav vim rau qhov lawv xav nrhiav txoj hauhlwm them zoo thiab tej chaw zoo zoo nyob. Ntau zaus lawv tsiv tsev mus nyob ze ze lawv cov phoojywg los yog lawv cov kwvtij thiab neej tsa.

Ua neej nyob twb tsis yoojyim rau cov uas tau khiav mus. Tej nqi tsev kim heev nyob rau lub thaj tsam muaj neeg mecha dub nyob. Cov Tswv tsev tsis kho lawv tej lub tsev hlo li. Yog cov neeg uas xauj tsev yws yws, ces cov tsev tsev kom cov no khiav. Sijawm ntev ntev thaum ua haulwm tom tej thaj tsam txhab khoom, tej tsev ua khoom ub no, thiab ua tshev nqaj. Cov nais kom cov ua haulwm siv sijhawm nruj.

Txawm yog muaj tej kev nyuaj siab li no, cov neeg tseem tsiv tsev mus. Muaj tej nqi zog thaum lawv ntsiv kev ny7uaj siab li no. Lawv cov menyuam muaj peevxwm muskawm ntawv. Neeg khej dub muaj peevxwm xaiv cov thawj cov. Cov nyiaj haujlwm lawv txais haj yam ntxiv thaum muab pib rau sab qab teb. Tej yam zoo li no, caw kom cov neeg khiav mus pev qaum teb.

ELL Reader Lessons and Study Guides

Ranches of the American West

by Carmelo Campos

ELL Reader 6.1.1   Expository Nonfiction

INTRODUCE THE BOOK

Activate Prior Knowledge/Build Background Read the title, and show the cover photo. Invite students to share what they know about the American West.

Preview/Use Text Features Preview the reader by talking about the illustrations together, naming the labeled items, and reading the captions. Point out the map on page 2 and the *Extend Language* feature on page 3.

Preteach Vocabulary Review the tested vocabulary words that appear in this book: **romping** and **rowdy**. Introduce these key words from the book: **mission** (p. 2), **beef** (p. 4), **freeze** (p. 6), and **economy** (p. 7). Discuss these words and add them to a Word Wall.

READ THE BOOK

Choose among these options for reading to support students at all English proficiency levels.

Read Aloud Read the book aloud as students follow along. Pause to verify comprehension and to explain unfamiliar concepts.

Monitored Reading Have students silently read a few pages at a time. Use the following questions to support comprehension:
- **Pages 2–3** Who first brought cattle and horses to the American West? (Spanish explorers)
- **Pages 4–7** How did ranchers get their cattle to cities to be sold and transported? (They hired cowboys to drive the cattle to cities that had trains.)
- **Pages 8–10** How is ranching today different from the 1800s? (Ranchers now have machines to help with the work; they don't depend on wild grasses and plants to feed the animals because they grow hay and other foods themselves.)
- **Pages 11–12** What important jobs are done during spring roundup? (Calves are branded, tagged, and immunized.)

Reread Have students reread the book with a partner, in small groups, or independently. Have them complete the Study Guide on page 213.

RESPOND

Answers to the Reader's Inside Back Cover:

Talk About It
1. They must keep cattle from freezing; make sure they have enough to eat and drink; brand, tag, and immunize calves; cut wood; grow hay and other crops; fix machinery; take care of other animals. (Main Idea and Details)
2. Answers will vary. Students may say that riding horses, taking care of animals, and riding on tractors would be different experiences for them. (Compare and Contrast)

Write About It
3. *Cattle:* keep cattle warm; make sure they have enough to eat and drink; brand, tag, and immunize calves; *Ranch:* grow vegetables and fruits, preserve food, cut wood, make clothes, grow hay, fix machinery (Categorize)
Support writers at various English proficiency levels.
   Beginning Let students dictate their ideas for someone else to record.
   Intermediate Have students brainstorm a list of words they can use when writing about ranching.
   Advanced Have students include at least four items on each side of their graphic organizers.

Extend Language *dancer;* Invite students to give other examples of words that end in *-er.*

Answers to page 213:
Drawings and captions will vary but should be consistent with description of spring roundup on page 11 of the reader.

Family Link Read aloud the Family Link activity on page 213 before sending copies of the Study Guide home with students. Later, invite students to share what their families say about ranches and about the advantages and disadvantages of ranching as a way of life.

Name _____

- **Read** *Ranches of the American West* again.
- **Draw** two pictures illustrating the spring roundup. In the first box, show ranchers doing their work. In the second box, show ranchers and their families celebrating after the work is done.
- **Write** a sentence below each picture telling what your drawing shows.

_____

_____

Family Link

Ask family members whether they have ever worked on or visited a ranch. Find out what they think would be the best and the worst parts of being a rancher.

Birds of a Feather

by Linda Lara Puente

ELL Reader 6.1.2   Realistic Fiction

INTRODUCE THE BOOK

Activate Prior Knowledge/Build Background Read the title, and discuss what it means. Ask students if they have ever had a friend from a place other than their home country or the United States.

Preview/Use Text Features Preview the reader by talking about the illustrations together and naming the labeled items. Point out the *Extend Language* feature on page 12.

Preteach Vocabulary Review the tested vocabulary words that appear in this book: **apparently** and **survive**. Introduce these key words from the book: **moved** (p. 2), **neighborhood** (p. 5), and **curious** (p. 6). Discuss these words and add them to a Word Wall.

READ THE BOOK

Choose among these options for reading to support students at all English proficiency levels.

Read Aloud Read the book aloud as students follow along. Pause to verify comprehension and to explain unfamiliar concepts.

Monitored Reading Have students silently read a few pages at a time. Use the following questions to support comprehension:
- **Pages 2–4** Who is Helen? (a new neighbor who seems angry and unfriendly)
- **Pages 5–8** What is Mami like? (She is friendly; she gets along well with people.)
- **Pages 9–11** Why did Helen invite Adriana and her mom to come to her house? (to see her parakeet, Sammy)

Reread Have students reread the book with a partner, in small groups, or independently. Have them complete the Study Guide on page 215.

RESPOND

Answers to the Reader's Inside Back Cover:

Talk About It
1. Possible response: Helen is 75 years old, wears braids on top of her head, is strong looking, does not seem very friendly. (Character)
2. Helen is lonely. She realizes they all like birds. (Draw Conclusions)

Write About It
3. *Helen:* Ukrainian, retired, not friendly to strangers, lives alone
Mami: Guatemalan, friendly, lives with her daughter
Both: immigrants, widows, like birds, work(ed) cleaning offices, live in Chicago
Support writers at various English proficiency levels.

Beginning Provide a copy of the Venn diagram for students to fill in. Review how a Venn diagram works.

Intermediate Have students look through the reader to find the information they need to complete their Venn diagrams.

Advanced Tell students to include at least three points in each section of their Venn diagrams.

Extend Language *mother*

Answers to page 215:
Pages 2–5: Adriana and Mami meet their new neighbor, Helen. She is unfriendly to them and to others in the neighborhood.
Pages 6–8: Adriana hangs a bird feeder because she is studying birds in school. She hopes to see monk parakeets.
Pages 9–11: Helen invites Adriana and her mother over to see her parakeet. They become friends.

Family Link Read aloud the Family Link activity on page 215 before sending copies of the Study Guide home with students. Later, have students share what family members said about their friendships with people from other countries.

Name _____

- **Read** *Birds of a Feather* again.
- Use the graphic organizer below. **Write** the events that happen in the story, in order. Use as many sentences as you need to describe the events in each part of the story.

Beginning (pages 2–5)

Middle (pages 6–8)

End (pages 9–11)

Family Link
Has anyone in your family made friends with someone from a different country? Ask family members to share their experiences.

American Immigrants

by Slava Petrovsky

ELL Reader 6.1.3   Expository Nonfiction

INTRODUCE THE BOOK

Activate Prior Knowledge/Build Background Read the title, and explain that immigrants are people who leave their homeland to live in a new country. Ask students if they know of any famous Americans who were born in other countries.

Preview/Use Text Features Preview the reader by talking about the photographs together, naming the labeled items, and reading the captions. Point out the map on pages 2 and 3 and the *Extend Language* feature on page 4.

Preteach Vocabulary Review the tested vocabulary words that appear in this book: **destination** and **menacing**. Introduce these key words from the book: **immigrants** (p. 1), **recognize** (p. 7), and **celebrate** (p. 11). Discuss these words and add them to a Word Wall.

READ THE BOOK

Choose among these options for reading to support students at all English proficiency levels.

Read Aloud Read the book aloud as students follow along. Pause to verify comprehension and to explain unfamiliar concepts.

Monitored Reading Have students take turns reading a page aloud. Use the following questions to support comprehension:

- **Pages 2–3** Why is the United States considered a land of immigrants? (Millions of people from all over the world have come to live in the United States; even the ancestors of the Native Americans may have originally come from Asia.)
- **Pages 4–5** How did the early immigrants reach the United States? (by sea)
- **Pages 6–8** Who are some immigrants to the United States who became famous for their accomplishments? (Albert Einstein, Irving Berlin, Madeline Albright)
- **Pages 9–12** How do immigrant groups show pride in their cultures? (traditional holiday celebrations; parades)

Reread Have students reread the book with a partner, in small groups, or independently. Have them complete the Study Guide on page 217.

RESPOND

Answers to the Reader's Inside Back Cover:

Talk About It

1. for better lives; to live in a free country; for good education for their children; to practice their religion without fear; to escape wars and famines; in search of jobs; to take advantage of the opportunities the United States offers (Main Idea and Details)

2. Today we have planes, phones, and e-mail.

Write About It

3. Answers will vary.

Support writers at various English proficiency levels.

Beginning Have less-proficient speakers dictate their ideas to more-proficient speakers. Then have them read their ideas aloud.

Intermediate Have students tell partners what they want to say before writing it down.

Advanced Have more-proficient speakers write down the ideas dictated to them by less-proficient speakers.

Extend Language to become part of a culture

Answers to page 217:

Albert Einstein: physicist; born in Germany; immigrated in 1933; won Nobel Prize in physics
Irving Berlin: songwriter; born in Russia; immigrated in 1893; wrote "God Bless America"
Madeleine Albright: former secretary of state; born in Czechoslovakia; immigrated in 1950

Family Link Read aloud the Family Link activity on page 217 before sending copies of the Study Guide home with students. Later, have students share what they learned from their families, friends, or neighbors about customs, foods, and holidays in other countries.

- **Read** *American Immigrants* again.
- **Look** through the book to find examples of famous Americans who were immigrants. In each *Supporting Detail* box, **write** the person's name and as many details about the person as you can.

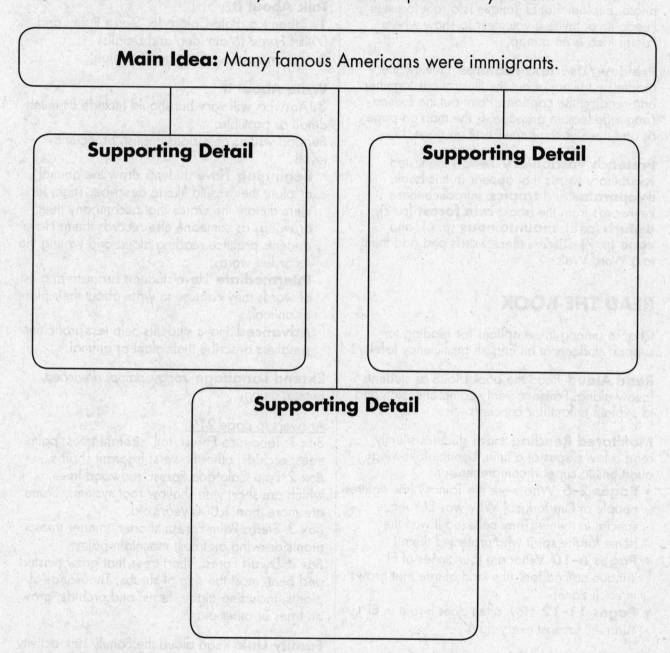

Main Idea: Many famous Americans were immigrants.

Supporting Detail

Supporting Detail

Supporting Detail

Family Link

Ask family members, friends, or neighbors who have come to the United States from other countries to tell you about their favorite customs. Ask them to describe their favorite foods and to tell you about their favorite holidays.

A Visit to El Yunque

by Hugo Acevedo

ELL Reader 6.1.4   Expository Nonfiction

INTRODUCE THE BOOK

Activate Prior Knowledge/Build Background Read the title, and show the cover photo. Explain that El Yunque is a rain forest in Puerto Rico. Invite a volunteer to show where Puerto Rico is on a map.

Preview/Use Text Features Preview the reader by talking about the illustrations together and reading the captions. Point out the *Extend Language* feature on page 4, the map on page 6, and the *Did You Know?* box on page 12.

Preteach Vocabulary Review the tested vocabulary words that appear in this book: **evaporates** and **tropics**. Introduce these key words from the book: **rain forest** (p. 2), **disturb** (p. 3), **mountainous** (p. 6), and **zone** (p. 7). Discuss these words and add them to a Word Wall.

READ THE BOOK

Choose among these options for reading to support students at all English proficiency levels.

Read Aloud Read the book aloud as students follow along. Pause to verify comprehension and to explain unfamiliar concepts.

Monitored Reading Have students silently read a few pages at a time. Use the following questions to support comprehension:

- **Pages 2–6** Who were the Tainos? (the native people of Puerto Rico) Why was El Yunque special to them? (They believed it was the home for the spirit who protected them.)
- **Pages 6–10** What are four zones of El Yunque named for? (the kind of tree that grows in each zone)
- **Pages 11–12** How often does it rain in El Yunque? (almost every day)

Reread Have students reread the book with a partner, in small groups, or independently. Have them complete the Study Guide on page 219.

RESPOND

Answers to the Reader's Inside Back Cover:

Talk About It
1. Tabonuco, Palo Colorado, Sierra Palm, and Dwarf Forest (Main Idea and Details)
2. It is an opinion. (Fact and Opinion)

Write About It
3. Answers will vary but should include as much detail as possible.
Support writers at various English proficiency levels.

> **Beginning** Have students draw the animal or plant they would like to describe. Then, let them dictate the words that accompany their drawings as someone else records them. Have students practice reading aloud and writing the recorded words.
> **Intermediate** Have students brainstorm a list of words they can use to write about their plant or animal.
> **Advanced** Have students help less-proficient speakers describe their plant or animal.

Extend Language *soggy, damp, drenched, humid, muggy*

Answers to page 219:
Box 1: Tabonuco Forest: tall, straight trees; palm trees; orchids; other flowers; fragrant shrubs
Box 2: Palo Colorado Forest: redwood trees, which are short with shallow root systems; Some are more than 1,000 years old.
Box 3: Sierra Palm Forest: shorter, thinner trees; plants growing on trees; mountain palms
Box 4: Dwarf Forest: short trees that grow twisted and bent, most the size of shrubs; Thousands of plants, including algae, ferns, and orchids, grow on trees or other plants.

Family Link Read aloud the Family Link activity on page 219 before sending copies of the Study Guide home with students. Later, have students discuss what their families know or would like to know about rain forests.

- **Read** *A Visit to El Yunque* again.
- Use the book to find the details that support the main idea shown below. **Write** the details in the boxes.

> **Main Idea:** Each zone in the El Yunque rain forest has different types of plants and trees.

Detail	**Detail**	**Detail**	**Detail**

Family Link

Has anyone in your family ever been to a rain forest? Would anyone in your family like to go? Ask family members to tell you about what they have seen or would like to see.

Horses and Their Trainers

by Joe Alvear

ELL Reader 6.1.5 Expository Nonfiction

INTRODUCE THE BOOK

Activate Prior Knowledge/Build Background Read the title, and ask students if they know what a trainer is. Ask them to share any experiences with horses. Then tell them that this is a story about people who help riders and horses to understand each other.

Preview/Use Text Features Preview the reader by talking about the photographs together and reading the captions. Point out the *Did You Know?* box on page 4 and the *Extend Language* feature on page 11.

Preteach Vocabulary Review the tested vocabulary words that appear in this book: **aggressive** and **detected**. Introduce these key words from the book: **communicate** (p. 2), **rider** (p. 3), and **tamed** (p. 4). Discuss these words and add them to a Word Wall.

READ THE BOOK

Choose among these options for reading to support students at all English proficiency levels.

Read Aloud Read the book aloud as students follow along. Pause to verify comprehension and to explain unfamiliar concepts.

Monitored Reading Have students silently read a few pages at a time. Use the following questions to support comprehension:

- **Pages 2–3** What is a horse whisperer? (someone who helps riders and horses understand each other)
- **Pages 4–5** How did the untamed horse behave when Alexander tried to ride him? (The horse became calm.)
- **Pages 6–11** What does it mean to groom a horse? (to comb and clean the mane, brush the coat, and clean the hooves)

Reread Have students reread the book with a partner, in small groups, or independently. Have students complete the Study Guide on page 221.

RESPOND

Answers to the Reader's Inside Back Cover:

Talk About It
1. A trainer teaches horses and riders to trust one another, teaches riders what signals to give the horse, and shows riders how to care for their horses. (Main Idea and Supporting Details)
2. They were used to take soldiers into battle; to do farm work; for transportation; to help ranchers herd cattle. (Draw Conclusions)

Write About It
3. Answers will vary but could involve talking quietly to it, touching it gently, and feeding it treats. (Generalize)
Support writers at various English proficiency levels.
　Beginning Display the following sentence frame: *I could teach a(n) [animal name] to trust me. I would ___.* Have students dictate their ideas to complete the sentence.
　Intermediate Provide the same sentence frame, but have students copy and complete it.
　Advanced Have students write a short paragraph about how they would teach an animal to trust them.

Extend Language The clearest word is *groom*. Guide students in making a list of the different forms of *groom* on pages 10 and 11.

Answers to page 221:
1. Horses are powerful. They can hurt riders who don't know what to do.
2. He was able to calm an un tamed, aggressive horse.
3. by talking to them, touching them, giving them treats, or using other tricks
4. a famous trainer from England
5. Possible question: How can a rider communicate with a horse? Possible response: by pressing the horse with his or her legs

Family Link Read aloud the Family Link activity on page 221 before sending copies of the Study Guide home with students. Later, have students share their families' experiences with horses.

- **Read** *Horses and Their Trainers* again.
- Use the information in the book to **answer** these questions.
- Then, **write** your own question and answer it.

pages 2–3

1. Why is it important for a horse and a rider to understand each other?

_____

_____

pages 4–5

2. Why do people think Alexander the Great was a horse whisperer?

_____

_____

pages 6–7

3. How do trainers help a horse to calm down?

_____

_____

pages 8–9

4. Who is Sandie Chambers?

_____

_____

pages 10–12

(Write your own question here.)

5. _____

_____

_____

Family Link

Has anyone in your family ever ridden a horse?
Ask family members to share what they know about horses.

Eyes in the Skies

by Yolanda Williams

ELL Reader 6.2.1   Expository Nonfiction

INTRODUCE THE BOOK

Activate Prior Knowledge/Build Background Read the title and ask students what they think the cover picture shows. Ask if they have ever seen or used a telescope.

Preview/Use Text Features Preview the reader by talking about the photographs together and reading the captions. Point out the *Extend Language* feature on page 6 and the *Did You Know?* box on page 7.

Preteach Vocabulary Review the tested vocabulary words that appear in this book: **galaxy** and **astronomer**. Introduce these key words from the book: **universe** (p. 2), **telescope** (p. 3), and **space** (p. 3). Discuss these words and add them to a Word Wall.

READ THE BOOK

Choose among these options for reading to support students at all English proficiency levels.

Read Aloud Read the book aloud as students follow along. Pause to verify comprehension and to explain unfamiliar concepts.

Monitored Reading Have students read aloud a few pages at a time. Use the following questions to support comprehension:
- **Pages 2–5** Why are large telescopes built away from cities? (Light and pollution make it hard to see the skies clearly.)
- **Pages 6–9** Why were the first pictures from Hubble fuzzy? (There was a problem with one of the mirrors.)
- **Pages 10–12** What did astronauts add to Hubble in 2002? (a new camera and other instruments)

Reread Have students reread the book with a partner, in small groups, or independently. Have them complete the Study Guide on page 223.

RESPOND

Answers to the Reader's Inside Back Cover:

Talk About It
1. Astronomers study events in the skies. (Main Idea and Details)
2. to let astronomers view the universe from beyond Earth's atmosphere (Cause and Effect)

Write About It
3. 1990: carried into space aboard the space shuttle *Discovery*. 1993: Crew from the space shuttle *Endeavour* corrects the defect in the primary mirror. 2001: takes image of spiral galaxy NGC 3949. 2002: Shuttle astronauts install a new camera and other scientific instruments. 2004: plan formed to have robots do maintenance work.

Support writers at various English proficiency levels.

Beginning Provide a copy of the time line for students to fill in. Pair students with more-proficient speakers to complete their time lines.
Intermediate Let students copy and complete the sample time line. Remind them that their time lines should include all of the important dates mentioned in the reading selection.
Advanced Have students help less-proficient speakers complete their time lines.

Extend Language A telephone lets you talk to someone far away. A television lets you see things that happen far away.

Answers to page 223:
Detail (page 5): The Keck telescopes are on top of a high mountain.
Detail (page 5): The Hubble telescope is in outer space.
Detail (page 10): Hubble sent back images of spiral galaxy NGC 3949.
Detail (page 11): It viewed galaxies in the oldest area of the universe.

Family Link Read aloud the Family Link activity on page 223 before sending copies of the Study Guide home with students. Later, have students share what they learned from their families about the night sky.

- **Read** *Eyes in the Skies* again.
- Find and **write** details that support the important ideas.

Important Ideas

Telescopes work best when they are above the dirt and moisture in Earth's atmosphere.

The Hubble Space Telescope has helped astronomers learn about other galaxies.

Supporting Details

Detail (page 5)

_____

_____

Detail (page 5)

_____

_____

Detail (page 10)

_____

_____

Detail (page 11)

_____

_____

Family Link

Does anyone in your family know the names of any of the stars or constellations? Ask family members to share what they know about the stars and the night sky.

The Story of Sue

by Curtis Washington

ELL Reader 6.2.2   Expository Nonfiction

INTRODUCE THE BOOK

Activate Prior Knowledge/Build Background Read the title, and ask students what they think the cover picture shows. Ask them if they think Sue is a person or a dinosaur. Then ask them if they have ever seen dinosaurs in museums or the movies.

Preview/Use Text Features Preview the reader by talking about the photographs together and reading the captions. Point out the *Did You Know?* box on page 12 and the *Extend Language* features on pages 11 and 12.

Preteach Vocabulary Review the tested vocabulary words that appear in this book: **fragile** and **prey**. Introduce these key words from the book: **skeleton** (p. 2), **dinosaur** (p. 2), **fossil** (p. 3), and **bone** (p. 6). Discuss these words and add them to a Word Wall.

READ THE BOOK

Choose among these options for reading to support students at all English proficiency levels.

Read Aloud Read the book aloud as students follow along. Pause to verify comprehension and to explain unfamiliar concepts.

Monitored Reading Have students take turns reading aloud. Use the following questions to support comprehension:

- **Pages 2–4** Who is Peter Larson? (the head bone hunter with the Black Hills Institute)
- **Pages 5–7** Why did Peter Larson name the tyrannosaurus his team found Sue? (for Susan Hendrickson, the woman who discovered it)
- **Pages 8–11** How much did a dinosaur such as Sue weigh? (about 14,000 pounds)

Reread Have students reread the book with a partner, in small groups, or independently. Have them complete the Study Guide on page 225.

RESPOND

Answers to the Reader's Inside Back Cover:

Talk About It

1. Susan Hendrickson found them in a cliff in South Dakota. (Main Idea and Details)

2. Answers will vary but could include the following: Tyrannosaurus babies may have been covered with feathers; dinosaurs may be related to birds of prey.

Write About It

3. Like *T. rex*, eagles are meat eaters and good hunters. There is evidence that a feathered theropod has been found, and that *T. rex* babies were cared for like bird babies. Dinosaur and bird skeletons are similar. Both have hollow bones and wishbones.

Support writers at various English proficiency levels.

   Beginning Have students reread page 10 to find the information they need. Then have them dictate their answer as someone else records their words. Have them practice reading aloud and writing the recorded words.

   Intermediate Have students reread the book to find the information they need.

   Advanced Have students help less-proficient speakers generate a list of words they can use to answer the question.

Answers to page 225:

1. the largest, most complete, and best-preserved tyrannosaurus skeleton ever found

2. She was a diver, she hunted for amber on tropical islands, and she hunted for meteorites in Peru.

3. He was surprised. He knew right away that they came from *T. rex*.

4. 58

5. about 30 years old

Family Link Read aloud the Family Link activity on page 225 before sending copies of the Study Guide home with students. Later, have students share what their families know and want to know about dinosaurs.

Name _____

- **Read** *The Story of Sue* again.
- Use the information in the book to **answer** the questions.

Pages	Question	Answer
2–3	**1.** What did Susan Hendrickson discover in 1990?	
4–5	**2.** What are some of the things Susan Hendrickson did before she began hunting for dinosaurs?	
6–7	**3.** What was Peter Larson's reaction when Susan showed him the bone fragments?	
8–9	**4.** How many teeth did a tyrannosaurus such as Sue have?	
10–11	**5.** How old was Sue when she died?	

Family Link

Has anyone in your family ever visited a museum with dinosaur skeletons or seen a movie about dinosaurs? Talk about dinosaurs with your family. Ask family members to share what they know and what they would like to find out about dinosaurs.

The Corbin Farm
by William Schick

INTRODUCE THE BOOK

Activate Prior Knowledge/Build Background Read the title, and explain that this story takes place over a period of more than 100 years. Ask students how they think life has changed since 1852, when the story begins. Explain that this story about real people includes fictional scenes; this is what makes it historical fiction.

Preview/Use Text Features Preview the reader by talking about the photographs together and reading the captions.

Preteach Vocabulary Review the tested vocabulary words that appear in this book: **technology**, **identity**, and **physical**. Introduce these key words from the book: **change** (p. 5), **married** (p. 8), and **factories** (p. 10). Discuss these words and add them to a Word Wall.

READ THE BOOK

Choose among these options for reading to support students at all English proficiency levels.

Read Aloud Read the book aloud as students follow along. Pause to verify comprehension and to explain unfamiliar concepts.

Monitored Reading Have students take turns reading aloud. Use the following questions to support comprehension:
- **Pages 2–6** Where did old William Corbin spend most of his life? (on a farm in Pennsylvania) How was life starting to change before his death in 1852? (Railroad tracks were laid nearby and trains were starting to run in the area.)
- **Pages 7–8** Which of William's sons fought in the Civil War? (Mathew and George) What happened to them? (They both survived, but Mathew was wounded.)
- **Pages 9–12** Who was Charles Corbin? (the son of George Washington Corbin and the grandson of Mathew Corbin; the last of the Corbin family to be born in Pennsylvania)

Reread Have students reread the book with a partner, in small groups, or independently. Have them complete the Study Guide on page 227.

RESPOND

Answers to the Reader's Inside Back Cover:

Talk About It
1. exploring the hills; climbing rocks and trees; swimming and fishing; helping his father; enjoying the animals, birds, and mountains (Main Idea and Details)
2. It polluted the air; it started a long series of changes that completely changed the Corbin family's way of life. (Draw Conclusions)

Write About It
3. Answers will vary but could include electric lights, telephones, modern appliances, and computers. (Generalize)
Support writers at various English proficiency levels.
  Beginning Let students dictate their list for someone else to record.
  Intermediate Have students tell partners what they want to say before writing it down.
  Advanced Have students help less-proficient speakers complete their lists.

Extend Language
birth/day; horse/back; news/paper

Answers to page 227:
1. seeing his father on horseback, exploring the hills, climbing rocks and trees, swimming and fishing, doing chores on the farm
2. Pennsylvania Railroad laid tracks across from William's boyhood home.
3. Charles stayed home to run the farm. George joined the army and fought in many battles, including the Battle of Gettysburg.
4. The Pennsylvania Railroad built huge factories there, where it built train cars and repaired locomotives.
5. none

Family Link Read aloud the Family Link activity on page 227 before sending copies of the Study Guide home with students. Later, have students share what their family members say about the changes they have experienced in their lifetimes.

- **Read** *The Corbin Farm* again.
- Use the book to **answer** the questions below.

---

pages 2–6

1. What are some of the things William Corbin remembers about his childhood?

_____

_____

2. How did things change when William was older?

_____

_____

---

pages 7–9

3. What did Charles and George Corbin do during the Civil War?

_____

_____

---

pages 10–12

4. Why did people move to Altoona, Pennsylvania?

_____

_____

5. How many of Mathew and Elizabeth Corbin's children stayed on the family farm?

_____

Family Link

Ask friends, neighbors, or people in your family to tell you about changes they have seen in their lifetimes. Ask them how talking on the phone was different when they were young. Ask them how watching a movie was different. Ask them whether they think they have seen more changes than their own parents did in their lifetimes.

The Day the Earthmen Came

by Elizabeth Franco   ELL Reader 6.2.4   Science Fiction Drama

INTRODUCE THE BOOK

Activate Prior Knowledge/Build Background Read the title, and ask students what they think the story is about. Help them make a web of what they know about the exploration of the Moon. Ask them if they know the names of any astronauts who landed on the Moon.

Preview/Use Text Features Preview the reader by talking about the photographs and illustrations together and reading the captions. Point out the list of characters on page 2.

Preteach Vocabulary Review the tested vocabulary words that appear in this book: **lunar** and **traversed**. Introduce these key words from the book: **museum** (p. 2), **recreation** (p. 3), **replica** (p. 10), and **mission** (p. 11). Discuss these words and add them to a Word Wall.

READ THE BOOK

Choose among these options for reading to support students at all English proficiency levels.

Read Aloud Read the book aloud as students follow along. Pause to verify comprehension and to explain unfamiliar concepts.

Monitored Reading Assign roles to students, and have them read the play aloud. Use the following questions to support comprehension:
- **Pages 2–5** Where do the characters in this play live? (on the Moon) What kind of museum are they visiting? (a museum about people from Earth who visited the Moon)
- **Pages 6–9** What happens when visitors to the museum put on Transporter Caps? (They seem to experience what is happening in a photograph.)
- **Page 10–12** What was *Apollo 11*? (the first manned mission to land on the Moon)

Reread Have students reread the book with a partner, in small groups, or independently. Have them complete the Study Guide on page 229.

RESPOND

Answers to the Reader's Inside Back Cover:

Talk About It
1. It was the first mission to land a man on the Moon. (Draw Conclusions)
2. They stayed twenty-one hours, took many photos, and collected Moon rocks and Moon dust to take back to Earth. (Main Idea and Details)

Write About It
3. Answers will vary.
Support writers at various English proficiency levels.

   Beginning Let students dictate their descriptions as someone else records their words. Have them practice reading aloud and writing the recorded words.
   Intermediate Have students look through the book to find words, details, and ideas they can use in their writing
   Advanced Have students state at least three specific ways they think life on the Moon would be different from life on Earth.

Extend Language In this book, the word *space* means above the Earth's atmosphere.

Answers to page 229:
1. the first men landed on the Moon
2. Neil Armstrong
3. so that scientists could study what the Moon is made of
4. 17
5. Alarms went off, and Armstrong manually steered the spacecraft to the Moon's surface.

Family Link Read aloud the Family Link activity on page 229 before sending copies of the Study Guide home with students. Later, have students discuss what their families say about traveling to the Moon.

- **Read** *The Day the Earthmen Came* again.
- Use the information in the book to **answer** the questions below.

Pages	Question	Answer
2–3	**1.** What happened on July 20, 1969?	
4–5	**2.** Who was the first person from Earth to stand on the Moon?	
6–7	**3.** Why did the *Apollo 11* astronauts collect rocks and dust?	
8–9	**4.** How many *Apollo* missions were there?	
10–12	**5.** What happened just before *Apollo 11* landed on the Moon?	

Family Link
Would anyone in your family like to travel to the Moon? Find out why or why not.

The Art of Making Mummies

by Rene Laplace

ELL Reader 6.2.5   Expository Nonfiction

INTRODUCE THE BOOK

Activate Prior Knowledge/Build Background Read the title, and ask students if they know what a mummy is. Show them the picture of the mummy on the cover of the reader.

Preview/Use Text Features Preview the reader by talking about the photographs together, naming the labeled items, and reading the captions. Point out the map on page 5 and the *Did You Know?* box on page 8.

Preteach Vocabulary Review the tested vocabulary words that appear in this book: **abundant** and **eternity**. Introduce these key words from the book: **ancient** (p. 2), **layers** (p. 6), and **servants** (p. 11). Discuss these words and add them to a Word Wall.

READ THE BOOK

Choose among these options for reading to support students at all English proficiency levels.

Read Aloud Read the book aloud as students follow along. Pause to verify comprehension and to explain unfamiliar concepts.

Monitored Reading Have students take turns reading aloud. Use the following questions to support comprehension:

- **Pages 2–3** What is a mummy? (a preserved body)
- **Pages 4–5** What did the Egyptians do with the internal organs? (put them in jars)
- **Pages 6–8** What did they wrap the bodies with? (strips of linen)
- **Pages 9–12** Besides people, what else did the Egyptians mummify? (animals, such as cats, monkeys, ducks, falcons, and crocodiles)

Reread Have students reread the book with a partner, in small groups, or independently. Have them complete the Study Guide on page 231.

RESPOND

Answers to the Reader's Inside Back Cover:

Talk About It
1. to preserve them forever (Main Idea and Details)
2. food, tools, clothing, games, furniture, household items, and shabtis; The Egyptians thought that the dead would need these items in the next world. (Cause and Effect)

Write About It
3. Answers will vary, but will probably include current popular board games.
Support writers at various English proficiency levels.

Beginning Have less-proficient speakers dictate their ideas to more-proficient speakers. Then have them read their ideas aloud.
Intermediate Tell students to describe the games they like in as much detail as possible.
Advanced Encourage students to tell why they like the games in addition to describing them.

Extend Language
strong (full of power); Invite students to think of other words with the suffix *-ful*, such as *wonderful, meaningful,* and *helpful.*

Answers to page 231:
Step 1: removing the internal organs
Step 2: cleaning and drying the body
Step 3: wrapping the body
Step 4: putting the body in a tomb or coffin

Family Link Read aloud the Family Link activity on page 231 before sending copies of the Study Guide home with students. Later, have students share what their families know about mummies.

- **Read** *The Art of Making Mummies* again.
- **Look** through the book to find all the steps involved in making a mummy. Then **complete** the graphic organizer below.

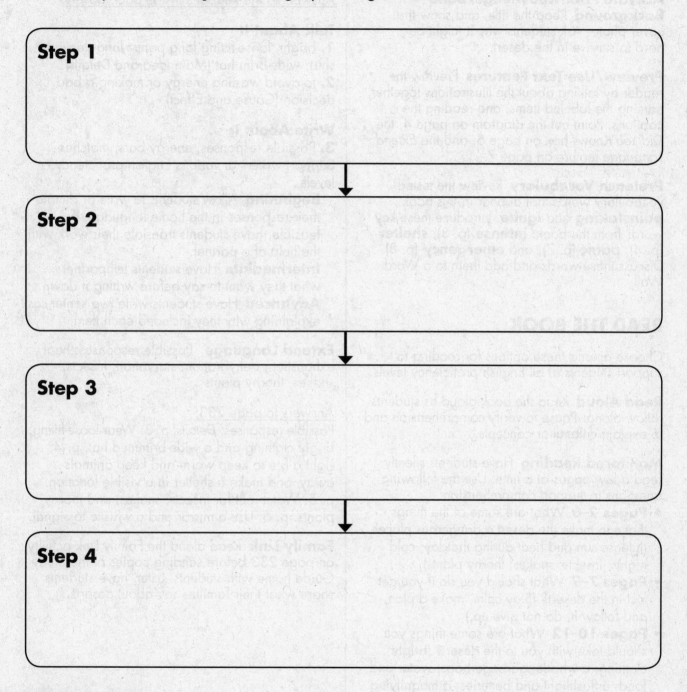

Step 1

Step 2

Step 3

Step 4

Family Link

Ask your family members whether they have ever heard of or seen pictures of mummies. Ask them if they have ever seen a mummy or a decorated coffin in a museum or on television.

How to Survive in the Desert
by Antonio Kennedy

ELL Reader 6.3.1   Nonfiction

INTRODUCE THE BOOK

Activate Prior Knowledge/Build Background Read the title, and show the cover photo. Ask students why it might be hard to survive in the desert.

Preview/Use Text Features Preview the reader by talking about the illustrations together, naming the labeled items, and reading the captions. Point out the diagram on page 4, the *Did You Know?* box on page 6, and the *Extend Language* feature on page 7.

Preteach Vocabulary Review the tested vocabulary words that appear in this book: **painstaking** and **ignite**. Introduce these key words from the book: **intense** (p. 3), **shelter** (p. 4), **panic** (p. 7), and **emergency** (p. 8). Discuss these words and add them to a Word Wall.

READ THE BOOK

Choose among these options for reading to support students at all English proficiency levels.

Read Aloud Read the book aloud as students follow along. Pause to verify comprehension and to explain unfamiliar concepts.

Monitored Reading Have students silently read a few pages at a time. Use the following questions to support comprehension:
- **Pages 2–6** What are some of the things that can make the desert a dangerous place? (intense sun and heat during the day; cold nights; insects; snakes; thorny plants)
- **Pages 7–9** What should you do if you get lost in the desert? (Stay calm, make a plan, and follow it; do not give up.)
- **Pages 10–12** What are some things you should take with you to the desert? (bright clothing; a whistle; garbage bags; water and food; a flashlight and batteries; a magnifying glass; a mirror; identification)

Reread Have students reread the book with a partner, in small groups, or independently. Have them complete the Study Guide on page 233.

RESPOND

Answers to the Reader's Inside Back Cover:

Talk About It
1. bright, loose-fitting long pants; long-sleeved shirt; wide-brim hat (Main Idea and Details)
2. to avoid wasting energy or making a bad decision (Cause and Effect)

Write About It
3. Possible responses: energy bars, matches Support writers at various English proficiency levels.
   Beginning Allow students to write or dictate their responses in the home language. If feasible, have students translate their work with the help of a partner.
   Intermediate Have students tell partners what they want to say before writing it down.
   Advanced Have students write two sentences explaining why they included each item.

Extend Language Possible responses: heat exhaustion, dehydration, starvation, insects, snakes, thorny plants

Answers to page 233:
Possible responses: *Details:* p. 3: Wear loose-fitting, bright clothing and a wide-brimmed hat. p. 4: Light a fire to keep warm and keep animals away, and make a shelter in a visible location. p. 5: Watch out for insects, snakes, and thorny plants. p. 6: Use a mirror and a whistle to signal.

Family Link Read aloud the Family Link activity on page 233 before sending copies of the Study Guide home with students. Later, have students share what their families say about deserts.

Name _____

- **Read** *How to Survive in the Desert* again.
- Use the book to find details that support the main idea. **Write** the details in the boxes below.

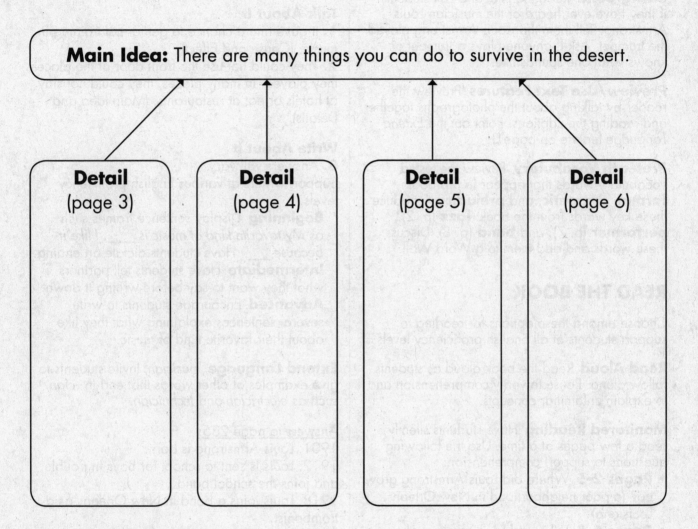

Main Idea: There are many things you can do to survive in the desert.

Detail (page 3)

Detail (page 4)

Detail (page 5)

Detail (page 6)

Family Link

Are there deserts in your family's country of origin? Has anyone in your family ever visited a desert? Ask family members to tell you what they know about surviving in the desert.

Louis Armstrong, Jazz Artist

by Maya Davis

ELL Reader 6.3.2 Biography

INTRODUCE THE BOOK

Activate Prior Knowledge/Build Background Read the title, and ask students if they have ever heard of the musician Louis Armstrong. Tell them that Louis Armstrong played the trumpet. Ask if anyone plays a trumpet or knows what one sounds like.

Preview/Use Text Features Preview the reader by talking about the photographs together and reading the captions. Point out the *Extend Language* feature on page 3.

Preteach Vocabulary Review the tested vocabulary words that appear in this book: **formal**, **dramatic**, and **prejudice**. Introduce these key words from the book: **jazz** (p. 2), **performer** (p. 7), and **band** (p. 8). Discuss these words and add them to a Word Wall.

READ THE BOOK

Choose among these options for reading to support students at all English proficiency levels.

Read Aloud Read the book aloud as students follow along. Pause to verify comprehension and to explain unfamiliar concepts.

Monitored Reading Have students silently read a few pages at a time. Use the following questions to support comprehension:
- **Pages 2–5** Where did Louis Armstrong grow up? (a poor neighborhood in New Orleans, Louisiana)
- **Pages 6–8** What did Louis like best about the strict school he attended? (It had a band.)
- **Pages 9–10** Why did Louis move to New York in 1924? (to play with the top African American band, the Fletcher Henderson Orchestra)
- **Pages 11–12** Why was Louis Armstrong known as "Ambassador Satch"? (He was loved by audiences all over the world.)

Reread Have students reread the book with a partner, in small groups, or independently. Have them complete the Study Guide on page 235.

RESPOND

Answers to the Reader's Inside Back Cover:

Talk About It
1. It gave him a chance to get formal training in music. (Cause and Effect)
2. They could not use the front door of the places they played. In many places, they could not stay at hotels or eat at restaurants. (Main Idea and Details)

Write About It
3. Answers will vary.
Support writers at various English proficiency levels.
> **Beginning** Display sentence frames such as *My favorite kind of music is ____. I like it because ___.* Have students dictate an ending.
> **Intermediate** Have students tell partners what they want to say before writing it down.
> **Advanced** Encourage students to write several sentences explaining what they like about their favorite kind of music.

Extend Language *musician;* Invite students to give examples of other words that end in *-cian,* such as *electrician* and *technician.*

Answers to page 235:
1901: Louis Armstrong is born.
1912: Louis is sent to school for boys in trouble, and joins the school band.
1918: Louis joins a band in New Orleans as a trombonist.
1922: Louis moves to Chicago.
1924: Louis moves to New York.
1971: Louis dies.

Family Link Read aloud the Family Link activity on page 235 before sending copies of the Study Guide home with students. Later, have students share their families' experiences with jazz or other music.

- **Read** *Louis Armstrong, Jazz Artist* again.
- On the line above each year, **write** an important event in Louis Armstrong's life that happened in that year.

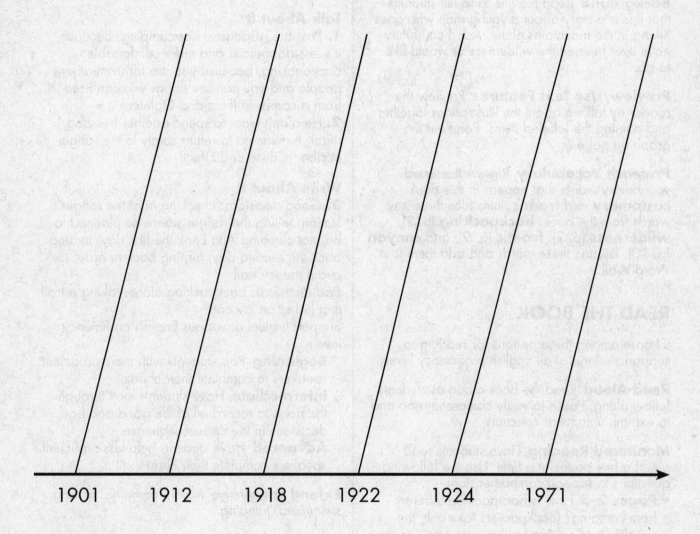

1901   1912   1918   1922   1924   1971

Family Link

Does anyone in your family play a musical instrument or listen to jazz? Ask them if they can name any other jazz musicians.

Alta Peak

by Richard Culver

ELL Reader 6.3.3   Realistic Fiction

INTRODUCE THE BOOK

Activate Prior Knowledge/Build Background Read the title, and tell students that this is a story about a young man who goes hiking in the mountains alone. Ask them if they have ever been in the wilderness or would like to go.

Preview/Use Text Features Preview the reader by talking about the illustrations together and naming the labeled items. Point out the graph on page 6.

Preteach Vocabulary Review the tested vocabulary words that appear in this book: **customary** and **frantic**. Introduce these key words from the book: **backpacking** (p. 2), **wilderness** (p. 2), **frantic** (p. 9), and **canyon** (p. 10). Discuss these words and add them to a Word Wall.

READ THE BOOK

Choose among these options for reading to support students at all English proficiency levels.

Read Aloud Read the book aloud as students follow along. Pause to verify comprehension and to explain unfamiliar concepts.

Monitored Reading Have students read aloud a few pages at a time. Use the following questions to support comprehension:
- **Pages 2–5** How is backpacking different from camping? (Backpackers take only the supplies and equipment they can carry on their backs.) Who went on the backpacking trip to Alta Peak? (just the narrator)
- **Pages 6–9** Where did the narrator plan on spending the night? (at a campsite near Moose Lake)
- **Pages 10–12** What did the narrator do when he realized the trail he wanted to take was covered with ice and snow? (He went back and took a different trail.)

Reread Have students reread the book with a partner, in small groups, or independently. Have them complete the Study Guide on page 237.

RESPOND

Answers to the Reader's Inside Back Cover:

Talk About It
1. Possible responses: car camping, because it's less dangerous and more comfortable; backpacking, because you are far from other people and you can see things you can't see from a campsite (Fact and Opinion)
2. He didn't want to spend another freezing night; he wanted to return safely to the ranger station. (Cause and Effect)

Write About It
3. *Good decisions:* checking in at the ranger's station; telling the ranger where he planned to be; not climbing Alta Peak the first day; turning back the second day; turning back in order to avoid the icy trail
Bad decisions: backpacking alone; taking a trail that led to an icy one
Support writers at various English proficiency levels.
   Beginning Pair students with more-proficient speakers to complete their charts.
   Intermediate Have students look through the book to record all of the good and bad decisions in the correct sequence.
   Advanced Have students help less-proficient speakers complete their charts.

Extend Language *hiking, camping, driving, swimming, jumping*

Answers to page 237:
Characters: the narrator, the park ranger
Setting: wilderness of California
Important Events: The narrator gets lost while backpacking alone.
Ending: The narrator returns safely after some scary moments.

Family Link Read aloud the Family Link activity on page 237 before sending copies of the Study Guide home with students. Later, have students talk about their families' experiences camping or backpacking.

Name _____

- **Read** *Alta Peak* again.
- **Write** the characters, setting, important events, and the ending of the story in the chart below.

Characters

Setting

Important Events

Ending

Family Link

Has anyone in your family ever gone camping or backpacking? Is this something your family would like to do? Talk to family members about their experiences in the wilderness. Ask them where they might like to go on a camping or backpacking trip.

Golden Sea Farm
by Luther Torgersen

ELL Reader 6.3.4   Realistic Fiction

INTRODUCE THE BOOK

Activate Prior Knowledge/Build Background Read the title, and ask students if they have ever been on a farm. Ask them to name things they might find on a farm.

Preview/Use Text Features Preview the reader by talking about the illustrations together and naming the labeled items. Point out the *Extend Language* feature on page 12.

Preteach Vocabulary Review the tested vocabulary words that appear in this book: **distressed** and **vigorously**. Introduce these key words from the book: **farm** (p. 2), **dozen** (p. 5), **barking** (p. 7), and **memories** (p. 10). Discuss these words and add them to a Word Wall.

READ THE BOOK

Choose among these options for reading to support students at all English proficiency levels.

Read Aloud Read the book aloud as students follow along. Pause to verify comprehension and to explain unfamiliar concepts.

Monitored Reading Have students silently read a few pages at a time. Use the following questions to support comprehension:
- **Pages 2–3** Where did the author grow up? (on a farm in Iowa) Where did his great grandmother come from? (Sweden)
- **Pages 4–6** What is Golden Sea Farm? (the name of the farm where the author grew up) Where did he and his brother take the children from the city? (to the farm)
- **Pages 7–9** Who lives on the farm now? (a Mexican American family)
- **Page 10** What did the children do at the farm? (climbed the hayloft, ran through the cornfields, met a goat)

Reread Have students reread the book with a partner, in small groups, or independently. Have them complete the Study Guide on page 239.

RESPOND

Answers to the Reader's Inside Back Cover:

Talk About It
1. He felt uncomfortable asking a stranger to let a dozen children play on his farm. (Cause and Effect)
2. Answers may include ideas about how people can be friendly to strangers or can pleasantly surprise you.

Write About It
3. *Eric:* friendly, outgoing, adventurous, talkative; *Luther:* serious, reserved, cautious, quiet; Answers will vary.
Support writers at various English proficiency levels.
   Beginning Allow students to write their response in the home language.
   Intermediate Have students tell partners what they want to say before writing it down.
   Advanced Encourage students to write two paragraphs about the person they know.

Extend Language Answers will vary. Extend the activity by inviting students to share names of farm animals and the sounds they make in their home languages.

Answers to page 239:
Possible responses: *First,* Luther and Eric drove the children to the farm. *Next,* they asked the owner of the farm if the children could visit. *Then,* the children had fun playing on the farm. *Last,* everyone drove back to the city.

Family Link Read aloud the Family Link activity on page 239 before sending copies of the Study Guide home with students. Later, have students share their families' ideas about city and country living.

- **Read** *Golden Sea Farm* again.
- **Write** what happened in each part of the story next to each picture.
  Write the names of any of the people from the story you see.

1.	**First,** _____ _____ _____
2.	**Next,** _____ _____ _____
3.	**Then,** _____ _____ _____
4.	**Last,** _____ _____ _____

Family Link
Ask family members whether they grew up in a city or in the country.
Ask whether they have ever been to a farm. Find out what they like
most and least about country life and city life.

Alice Hamilton: A Worker's Best Friend

by Ruth Cohen

ELL Reader 6.3.5   Expository Nonfiction

INTRODUCE THE BOOK

Activate Prior Knowledge/Build Background Read the title, and explain to students that this story is about a woman doctor who helped improve the health and working conditions of workers about 100 years ago. Ask students what risks they think factory workers may have faced at that time.

Preview/Use Text Features Preview the reader by talking about the photographs together and reading the captions. Point out the *Did You Know?* box on page 11.

Preteach Vocabulary Review the tested vocabulary words that appear in this book: **diploma** and **reject**. Introduce these key words from the book: **diseases** (p. 4), **hospital** (p. 4), **conditions** (p. 7), and **factories** (p. 7). Discuss these words and add them to a Word Wall.

READ THE BOOK

Choose among these options for reading to support students at all English proficiency levels.

Read Aloud Read the book aloud as students follow along. Pause to verify comprehension and to explain unfamiliar concepts.

Monitored Reading Have students silently read a few pages at a time. Use the following questions to support comprehension:
- **Pages 2–5** Where did Alice get her education? (Her mother taught her at home; then she went to Miss Porter's School for Girls; then she went to the University of Michigan Medical School.)
- **Pages 6–9** Why didn't most factory owners let Alice into their factories? (They didn't care about protecting workers, and they didn't want her telling them what to do.)
- **Pages 10–12** What is OSHA? (the Occupational Safety and Health Administration) What does it do? (It makes sure people have safe working conditions.)

Reread Have students reread the book with a partner, in small groups, or independently. Have them complete the Study Guide on page 241.

RESPOND

Answers to the Reader's Inside Back Cover:

Talk About It
1. safe work habits, safety glasses, steel-toed shoes, the Occupational Safety and Health Administration, worker safety laws (Main Idea and Details)
2. Possible responses: Workers might still be suffering from industrial diseases; other people might have worked to improve worker safety. (Draw Conclusions)

Write About It
3. Answers will vary but should mention some of the dangerous conditions and diseases cited in the book.
Support writers at various English proficiency levels.
   Beginning Let students work with partners to create a bilingual letter in English and the home language.
   Intermediate Have students look through the book to find words, details, and ideas they can use in their writing.
   Advanced Have students also write about what they would do to improve conditions.

Extend Language
Dr. (pages 4 and 8), *USA* (on stamp on page 12); Discuss other acronyms students may be familiar with.

Answers to page 241:
1. marry a man with a promising future
2. They were poor and lacked formal educations.
3. skin rashes, bad coughs, injuries to teeth and jawbones, paralysis, and insanity
4. safety glasses, steel-toed shoes, safe working conditions

Family Link Read aloud the Family Link activity on page 241 before sending copies of the Study Guide home with students. Later, have students share what family members, friends, or neighbors said about safe practices in their workplaces.

- **Read** *Alice Hamilton: A Worker's Best Friend* again.
- Use the book to **answer** the questions below.

Page	Question	Answer
2	**1.** What did most mothers in the 1870s want their daughters to do?	
5	**2.** How were the people Alice took care of different from her?	
7	**3.** What kinds of diseases did Alice see?	
11	**4.** What are some of the things that OSHA requires?	

Family Link

Ask family members, friends, or neighbors to tell you about things they are supposed to do at work to protect themselves from getting hurt.

Matthew Henson's Story

by Kenneth Neal Parker

ELL Reader 6.4.1 Biography

INTRODUCE THE BOOK

Activate Prior Knowledge/Build Background Read the title, and ask students to look at the cover illustration. Ask them who they think Matthew Henson was. Help them make a web of what they know about the North Pole and polar exploration. Post the web where students can see it as you read the book together.

Preview/Use Text Features Preview the reader by talking about the photographs together and reading the captions. Point out the map on page 6.

Preteach Vocabulary Review the tested vocabulary words that appear in this book: **expedition** and **isolation**. Introduce these key words from the book: **journeys** (p. 2), **adventure** (p. 4), **assistant** (p. 4), and **Eskimos** (p. 8). Discuss these words and add them to a Word Wall.

READ THE BOOK

Choose among these options for reading to support students at all English proficiency levels.

Read Aloud Read the book aloud as students follow along. Pause to verify comprehension and to explain unfamiliar concepts.

Monitored Reading Have students silently read a few pages at a time. Use the following questions to support comprehension:
- **Pages 2–5** Who are the first people known to have reached the North Pole? (Peary and Henson) What did Matthew Henson do as a teenager? (He worked on ships and traveled around the world. He worked in a fur shop.)
- **Pages 6–9** What were some of Henson's jobs on the expedition? (fixing things; trading; hunting; finding Eskimos to join the expedition; training dogs; building sledges)
- **Page 10–12** Why did Henson and the other explorers have to wait until March to begin their trip to the North Pole? (During the winter it is dark all day near the Pole.)

Reread Have students reread the book with a partner, in small groups, or independently. Have them complete the Study Guide on page 243.

RESPOND

Answers to the Reader's Inside Back Cover:

Talk About It
1. It is dark the entire winter; it is very cold; sometimes huge ridges of ice stand in the way. (Cause and Effect)
2. Possible responses: scary, lonely, sad (Fact and Opinion)

Write About It
3. Letters should mention Henson's love of travel and adventure and his experience working as a cabin boy and sailor.
Support writers at various English proficiency levels.
> **Beginning** Display a sentence frame such as *Henson would be a good person to have on an expedition because he _____.* Have students dictate an ending.
> **Intermediate** Provide the same sentence frame, but have students copy it and write their own endings.
> **Advanced** Have students include at least five sentences in their letters.

Extend Language He meant *we were on our way. Offshore* means *away from the coast.*

Answers to page 243:
1866: Matthew Henson is born in Maryland.
1891: Henson makes first trip to the Arctic.
1908: Henson sets off for the North Pole with Robert E. Peary.
1909: Henson reaches the North Pole.

Family Link Read aloud the Family Link activity on page 243 before sending copies of the Study Guide home with students. Later, have students share their families' ideas about cold climates and the North Pole.

- **Read** *Matthew Henson's Story* again.
- Use the book to **find** four important events in the life of Matthew Henson. **Write** the events on the lines above the years on the time line below.

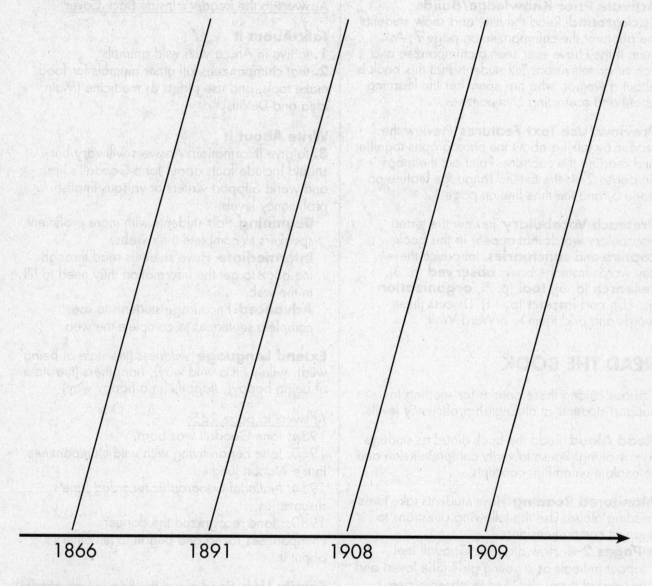

1866   1891   1908   1909

Family Link

Ask members of your family to describe the coldest place they have ever been. Find out if they would be interested in traveling to a cold and dangerous place like the North Pole.

Jane Goodall: Scientist and Protector of Chimpanzees

by Asher Jonic

ELL Reader 6.4.2   Biography

INTRODUCE THE BOOK

Activate Prior Knowledge/Build Background Read the title, and show students the photo of the chimpanzee on page 7. Ask them if they have ever seen a chimpanzee at a zoo or on television. Tell students that this book is about a woman who has spent her life learning about and protecting chimpanzees.

Preview/Use Text Features Preview the reader by talking about the photographs together and reading the captions. Point out the maps on pages 2–4, the *Extend Language* feature on page 5, and the time line on page 12.

Preteach Vocabulary Review the tested vocabulary words that appear in this book: **captive** and **sanctuaries**. Introduce these key words from the book: **observed** (p. 3), **research** (p. 5), **tool** (p. 7), **organization** (p. 10), and **impact** (p. 11). Discuss these words and add them to a Word Wall.

READ THE BOOK

Choose among these options for reading to support students at all English proficiency levels.

Read Aloud Read the book aloud as students follow along. Pause to verify comprehension and to explain unfamiliar concepts.

Monitored Reading Have students take turns reading aloud. Use the following questions to support comprehension:
- **Pages 2–4** How did Jane Goodall feel about animals as a young girl? (She loved and respected them; she liked to observe them.)
- **Pages 5–7** How old was Jane when she first went to Africa? (23) What did she use to get closer to the chimpanzees and gain their trust? (patience and bananas)
- **Pages 8–11** Why did Jane leave the jungle? (She felt she needed to tell the world about the problems chimpanzees faced.)

Reread Have students reread the book with a partner, in small groups, or independently. Have them complete the Study Guide on page 245.

RESPOND

Answers to the Reader's Inside Back Cover:

Talk About It
1. to live in Africa with wild animals
2. that chimpanzees kill other animals for food, make tools, and use plants as medicine (Main Idea and Details)

Write About It
3. to give information; Answers will vary but should include facts about Jane Goodall's life and work. Support writers at various English proficiency levels.
   Beginning Pair students with more proficient speakers to complete their webs.
   Intermediate Have students read through the book to get the information they need to fill in the web.
   Advanced Encourage students to use complete sentences to complete the web.

Extend Language *wildness* (the state of being wild), *wildly* (in a wild way), *happiness* (the state of being happy), *happily* (in a happy way)

Answers to page 245:
1934: Jane Goodall was born.
1960: Jane began living with wild chimpanzees in the African jungle.
1964: *National Geographic* recorded Jane's discoveries.
1980s: Jane recognized the danger chimpanzees faced and began to tell others about it.

Family Link Read aloud the Family Link activity on page 245 before sending copies of the Study Guide home with students. Later, have students share their families' experiences with wild animals.

Name _____

- **Read** *Jane Goodall: Scientist and Protector of Chimpanzees* again.
- Use the book. **Write** the events that took place during the years shown on the time line.

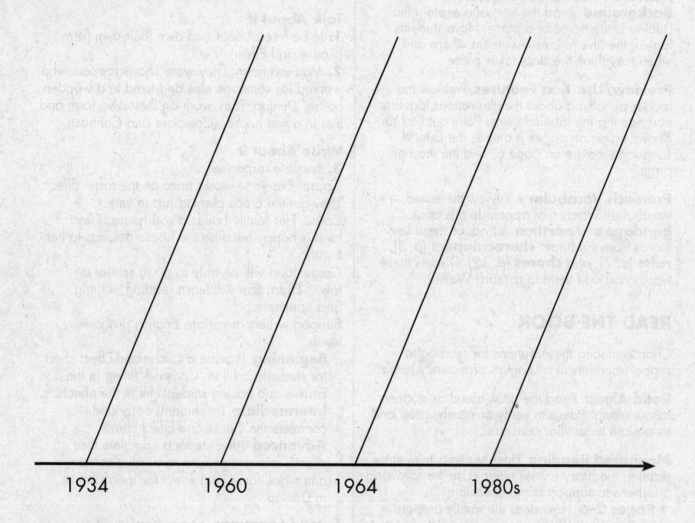

1934   1960   1964   1980s

Family Link

Has anyone in your family ever visited a jungle or other area where wild animals roam free? Ask family members to share any experiences they have had with wild animals

Dunlap, Here We Come!

by Caleb Lee

ELL Reader 6.4.3　Historical Fiction

INTRODUCE THE BOOK

Activate Prior Knowledge/Build Background Read the title, and explain that Dunlap is the name of a place. Have students look at the illustrations. Ask them where and when they think the story takes place.

Preview/Use Text Features Preview the reader by talking about the illustrations together and naming the labeled items. Point out *Did You Know?* boxes on pages 3 and 8, the *Extend Language* feature on page 6, and the map on page 9.

Preteach Vocabulary Review the tested vocabulary words that appear in this book: **bondage** and **earthen**. Introduce these key words from the book: **sharecroppers** (p. 3), **rafts** (p. 7), and **chores** (p. 12). Discuss these words and add them to a Word Wall.

READ THE BOOK

Choose among these options for reading to support students at all English proficiency levels.

Read Aloud Read the book aloud as students follow along. Pause to verify comprehension and to explain unfamiliar concepts.

Monitored Reading Have students take turns reading the diary entries aloud. Use the following questions to support comprehension:

- **Pages 2–6** How does the family prepare for their trip? (They sell everything they can't carry; Jimmy marries Sara.)
- **Pages 7–8** How does the Madison family get across the Mississippi River? (They pay someone to take them on a raft.)
- **Pages 9–11** What does Iona notice about Dunlap, Kansas, the first time she sees it? (It is very beautiful; there are sod houses and fields covered with grass.)

Reread Have students reread the book with a partner, in small groups, or independently. Have them complete the Study Guide on page 247.

RESPOND

Answers to the Reader's Inside Back Cover:

Talk About It
1. to be free of debt and own their own farm (Cause and Effect)
2. *Madison Farm:* They were sharecroppers who worked for someone else and lived in a wooden house. *Dunlap:* They work on their own farm and live in a sod house. (Compare and Contrast)

Write About It
3. Possible responses:
Cause: Everyone works hard on the farm. *Effect:* They get the crops planted just in time.
Cause: Her family builds a sod house. *Effect:* Iona is happy because the house belongs to her family.
Cause: Iona will be able to go to school in town. *Effect:* She will learn reading, writing, and arithmetic.
Support writers at various English proficiency levels.
    Beginning Provide a Cause-and-Effect chart for students to fill in. Consider filling in the causes and having students fill in the effects.
    Intermediate Let students copy and complete the Cause-and-Effect chart.
    Advanced After students complete their charts, encourage them to predict at least one more cause and effect for Iona's future in Dunlap.

Extend Language *somewhere* (p. 2), *sharecropper* (p. 3), *themselves* (p. 7), *alongside* (p. 10), *breakfast* (p. 12)

Answers to page 247:
1. It is too far; they are too poor.
2. $15
3. parents; brother Jimmy; brother's wife, Sara
4. They walked for several days, and then another family took them in a wagon for $4.
5. They feed the animals, collect the eggs, milk the goat, and get the mule ready to work in the fields.

Family Link Read aloud the Family Link activity on page 247 before sending copies of the Study Guide home with students. Later, have students share what their families say about farms.

Name _____

- **Read** *Dunlap, Here We Come!* again.
- Use the book to **answer** the questions below.

Page	Question	Answer
2	**1.** Why does Ma think the family should not move to Kansas?	
4	**2.** How much money did the family have after they sold all of their things?	
6	**3.** Who are all of the people in Iona's family who make the trip to Dunlap?	
10	**4.** After they crossed the river, how did Iona's family get to Dunlap?	
12	**5.** What chores do Iona and Sara have to do every morning?	

Family Link

Ask family members if they have ever worked on or visited a farm.
Ask them to share their experiences.

Space—and People's Ideas About Space

by Israel Walker   ELL Reader 6.4.4   Expository Nonfiction

INTRODUCE THE BOOK

Activate Prior Knowledge/Build Background Read the title, and show students the photo on page 2 to illustrate what *space* means. Ask them if they ever think about what is in outer space.

Preview/Use Text Features Preview the reader by talking about the photographs and the illustration together and reading the captions. Point out the *Extend Language* features on pages 7 and 11.

Preteach Vocabulary Review the tested vocabulary words that appear in this book: **aliens** and **version**. Introduce these key words from the book: **space** (p. 2), **astronomer** (p. 3), **spacecraft** (p. 4), and **science fiction** (p. 9). Discuss these words and add them to a Word Wall.

READ THE BOOK

Choose among these options for reading to support students at all English proficiency levels.

Read Aloud Read the book aloud as students follow along. Pause to verify comprehension and to explain unfamiliar concepts.

Monitored Reading Have students silently read a few pages at a time. Use the following questions to support comprehension:
- **Pages 2–3** Who were Copernicus and Galileo? (early astronomers)
- **Pages 4–7** What country sent the first human into space? (the Soviet Union) What country sent the first humans to the Moon? (the United States) What countries are working together to build the International Space Station? (Russia, the United States, and other countries)
- **Pages 8–11** Why did people in 1938 think the Earth was being invaded by aliens? (They didn't realize they were listening to a science fiction story on the radio.)

Reread Have students reread the book with a partner, in small groups, or independently. Have them complete the Study Guide on page 249.

RESPOND

Answers to the Reader's Inside Back Cover:

Talk About It
1. The Sun is at the center of our Solar System; there are nine planets in our Solar System.
2. stories about aliens, space travel, and life in outer space

Write About It
3. Answers will vary but could include discoveries by Copernicus, Galileo, or modern-day astronauts or astrobiologists.
Support writers at various English proficiency levels.
   Beginning Let students work together to choose one of the discoveries cited in the book and complete the web with thoughts about it. Then have pairs of students work together to write their stories. Have them read their stories aloud.
   Intermediate Have students work together to choose a discovery cited in the book and brainstorm ideas about it. Then have them work independently on their stories.
   Advanced Encourage students to write stories that include a clear beginning, middle, and end.

Extend Language the study of life

Answers to page 249:
Responses will vary. Possible responses:
1. People have always been interested in space.
2. They had the greatest scientific resources.
3. People were afraid that "Martians" might hurt them.
4. A lot of people like to think about space and the future.

Family Link Read aloud the Family Link activity on page 249 before sending copies of the Study Guide home with students. Later, have students share their families' ideas about space and space travel.

- **Read** *Space—and People's Ideas About Space* again.
- **Read** each sentence below. Under each sentence **write** a conclusion you can draw from it.

1. People have studied the skies for thousands of years.

_____

_____

2. The Soviet Union and the United States were the first countries to explore space.

_____

_____

3. Some people who listened to "The War of the Worlds" in 1938 panicked when they heard that aliens from Mars had landed on Earth.

_____

_____

4. Movies about aliens, space travel, and the future are very popular.

_____

_____

Family Link

Ask your family members if they would travel into outer space if they could. Find out if they think many people who are not astronauts will visit outer space in the future.

Inventions Through Time in Rhyme

by Hepzibah Flurge

ELL Reader 6.4.5   Nonfiction in Rhyme

INTRODUCE THE BOOK

Activate Prior Knowledge/Build Background Read the title, and ask students if they recognize the inventions shown on the book's cover. Invite students to name any inventors they can think of.

Preview/Use Text Features Preview the reader by talking about the illustrations and photographs together, naming the labeled item, and reading the captions.

Preteach Vocabulary Review the tested vocabulary words that appear in this book: **devise** and **reproduce**. Introduce these key words from the book: **inventions** (p. 2), **designed** (p. 4), **architecture** (p. 6), **ink** (p. 7), and **creative** (p. 9). Discuss these words and add them to a Word Wall.

READ THE BOOK

Choose among these options for reading to support students at all English proficiency levels.

Read Aloud Read the book aloud as students follow along. Pause to verify comprehension and to explain unfamiliar concepts.

Monitored Reading Have students take turns reading stanzas of the poem. Use the following questions to support comprehension:
- **Pages 2–5** Who were the Sumerians? (a group of people who lived in the Middle East about 6,000 years ago)
- **Pages 6–8** How did the Chinese make writing easier? (They invented paper and ink.)
- **Pages 9–12** Which inventors helped humans learn to fly? (Leonardo da Vinci and the Wright brothers)

Reread Have students reread the book with a partner, in small groups, or independently. Have them complete the Study Guide on page 251.

RESPOND

Answers to the Reader's Inside Back Cover:

Talk About It
1. the wheel; writing; farming; developments in architecture, engineering, art, literature, and government; competitive sports; ink and paper; kites; gunpowder and fireworks; chocolate (Main Idea and Details)
2. The wheel makes transportation possible; writing improves communication; crop cultivation makes it possible for people to live in settlements; paper allows us to write easily. (Cause and Effect)

Write About It
3. Answers will vary.
Support writers at various English proficiency levels.
   Beginning Pair students with more-proficient speakers to complete their graphic organizers.
   Intermediate Remind students that their graphic organizers should include as many of the inventions mentioned in the book as possible.
   Advanced Encourage students to add two or three inventions not mentioned in the book and explain how these inventions have affected them.

Extend Language y (assembly), *ea* (cheap), *ee* (keep)

Answers to page 249:
Sumerians: the wheel, writing, farming
Greeks: engineering, art, literature, sports, government
Chinese: ink, kites, silk strings, paper, gunpowder, fireworks
Olmecs: chocolate
Modern: airplane (Leonardo da Vinci and the Wright brothers); assembly line (Olds and Ford); washing machine; dryer; TV; dish washer; computer; CD

Family Link Read aloud the Family Link activity on page 251 before sending copies of the Study Guide home with students. Later, invite students to discuss their families' ideas about inventions.

© Scott Foresman 6

Name _____

- **Read** *Inventions Through Time in Rhyme* again.
- **Write** the inventions from each culture in the correct circle. If you know the inventor's name, **write** it next to the invention.

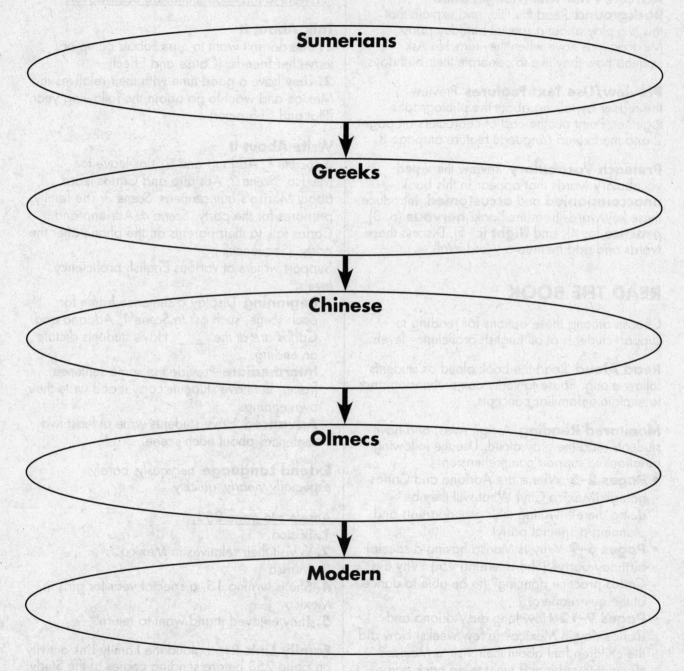

Sumerians

Greeks

Chinese

Olmecs

Modern

Family Link

Ask family members if they or anyone they know ever invented something or came up with an idea for an invention. Find out what new things they would like to see invented.

A Special Birthday in Mexico

by Pedro Gonzales

ELL Reader 6.5.1   Drama

INTRODUCE THE BOOK

Activate Prior Knowledge/Build Background Read the title, and explain that this is a play about a special birthday party Mexican girls have when they turn 15. Ask students how they like to celebrate their birthdays.

Preview/Use Text Features Preview the reader by talking about the photographs together. Point out the cast of characters on page 2 and the *Extend Language* feature on page 3.

Preteach Vocabulary Review the tested vocabulary words that appear in this book: **unaccompanied** and **accustomed**. Introduce these key words from the book: **nervous** (p. 3), **practice** (p. 4), and **flight** (p. 5). Discuss these words and add them to a Word Wall.

READ THE BOOK

Choose among these options for reading to support students at all English proficiency levels.

Read Aloud Read the book aloud as students follow along. Pause to verify comprehension and to explain unfamiliar concepts.

Monitored Reading Assign roles, and have students read the play aloud. Use the following questions to support comprehension:

- **Pages 2–5** Where are Adriana and Carlos going? (Mexico City) What will they be doing there? (visiting their grandparents and planning a special party)
- **Pages 6–9** Why is Marisa having a special birthday party? (She is turning 15.) Why did Carlos practice dancing? (to be able to dance at the *quinceañera*)
- **Pages 9–12** How long did Adriana and Carlos stay in Mexico? (a few weeks) How did the children feel about their visit to Mexico? (They enjoyed it and want to go back again next year.)

Reread Have students reread the book with a partner, in small groups, or independently. Have them complete the Study Guide on page 253.

RESPOND

Answers to the Reader's Inside Back Cover:

Talk About It

1. She doesn't want to miss soccer camp or leave her friends. (Cause and Effect)
2. They have a good time with their relatives in Mexico and want to go again the following year. (Plot and Character)

Write About It

3. *Scene 1:* Adriana and Carlos leave for Mexico. *Scene 2:* Adriana and Carlos learn about Marisa's *quinceañera. Scene 3:* The family prepares for the party. *Scene 4:* Adriana and Carlos talk to their parents on the phone after the party. (Sequence)

Support writers at various English proficiency levels.

Beginning Display a sentence frame for each scene, such as: *In Scene 1, Adriana and Carlos are at the* ____. Have students dictate an ending.
Intermediate Provide the same sentence frame, but have students copy it and write their own endings.
Advanced Have students write at least two sentences about each scene.

Extend Language *nervously, barely, especially, nearly, quickly*

Answers to page 253:
1. Boston
2. to visit their relatives in Mexico
3. Marisa
4. She is turning 15, a special year for girls in Mexico.
5. They enjoyed it and want to return.

Family Link Read aloud the Family Link activity on page 253 before sending copies of the Study Guide home with students. Later, invite students to share how their families celebrate birthdays.

- **Read** *A Special Birthday in Mexico* again.
- Use the book to **answer** the questions below.

Pages	Question	Answer
2–5	**1.** Where do Carlos and Adriana live?	
	2. Where are they going?	
6–7	**3.** Who is having a special birthday?	
	4. Why is the birthday special?	
8–12	**5.** What did Carlos and Adriana think about their visit to Mexico?	

Family Link

How does your family celebrate birthdays? Are some birthdays more important than others? Ask family members to tell you how they would like to celebrate their next birthday.

Poems for César Chávez

by Micki Shelton

INTRODUCE THE BOOK

Activate Prior Knowledge/Build Background Read the title, and explain that César Chávez was a man who helped to improve the lives of poor farm workers. Tell them that the book includes poems about Chávez's life.

Preview/Use Text Features Preview the reader by talking about the photographs and illustrations together, naming the labeled items, and reading the captions. Point out the *Extend Language* feature on page 7.

Preteach Vocabulary Review the tested vocabulary words that appear in this book: **authority**, **torment**, and **wilt**. Introduce these key words from the book: **rights** (p. 5), **crops** (p. 6), and **boycott** (p. 10). Discuss these words and add them to a Word Wall.

READ THE BOOK

Choose among these options for reading to support students at all English proficiency levels.

Read Aloud Read the book aloud as students follow along. Pause to verify comprehension and to explain unfamiliar concepts.

Monitored Reading Have students take turns reading aloud. Use the following questions to support comprehension:
- **Pages 2–5** Where did César live when he was young? (on his grandfather's ranch in Arizona) What was life like for César and his family? (They worked hard, but they were comfortable and happy.)
- **Pages 6–8** How did César's life change after 1937? (His family lost their farm. They ended up traveling all over California as farm workers.)
- **Pages 9–12** What did César Chávez hope to achieve through strikes, boycotts, and marches? (fair pay and safe working conditions for migrant farm workers)

Reread Have students reread the book with a partner, in small groups, or independently. Have them complete the Study Guide on page 255.

RESPOND

Answers to the Reader's Inside Back Cover:

Talk About It
1. He spent his childhood working on his grandfather's farm. Then he traveled from farm to farm as a migrant worker in California. (Cause and Effect)
2. Possible response: Yes, because he organized people to stand up for themselves and found ways to make his point without turning to violence. (Fact and Opinion)

Write About It
3. Possible responses: *Fact:* In 1967 he organized a boycott of grapes. *Opinion:* His parents were good people.
Support writers at various English proficiency levels.
   Beginning Display sentence frames such as: *In 1937, the Chávez family lost their ___.* Have students dictate the ending and tell you whether each sentence is a fact or opinion.
   Intermediate Provide the same sentence frames, but have students copy them and write their own endings.
   Advanced Have students write at least three facts and three opinions from the book.

Extend Language Examples include the following: *The hot sun pours hazy lines from the sky* (p. 4); *the air sizzles with the song of cicadas* (p. 4); *the desert clay fries under your feet* (p. 4); *animals travel across the heavens* (p. 5); *tiny bowls that hold the Sun* (p. 11).

Answers to page 255:
F, F, O, O, F

Family Link Read aloud the Family Link activity on page 255 before sending copies of the Study Guide home with students. Later, have students share their poems with the class.

- **Read** *Poems for César Chávez* again.
- Use the book to tell whether each sentence is a fact or an opinion.
  Write an *F* next to sentences that are facts. **Write** an *O* next to
  sentences that are opinions.

1. César Chávez was a leader of farm workers. _____

2. César spoke both Spanish and English. _____

3. César's mother was too strict. _____

4. The worst thing that ever happened to César Chávez was when his family
lost their farm in the 1930s. _____

5. César Chávez died in 1993. _____

Family Link
Read one or two of the poems from the book to a family member.
Then ask that person to help you choose an event from your
childhood to write about. Write a simple poem or story describing
the event.

African Climates and Animals

by Sidan Jono   ELL Reader 6.5.3   Expository Nonfiction

INTRODUCE THE BOOK

Activate Prior Knowledge/Build Background Read the title, and show students the cover photo. Have a volunteer show where Africa is located on a map or globe. Ask students to share what they know about the weather, landscape, and animals of Africa.

Preview/Use Text Features Preview the reader by talking about the photographs together and naming the labeled items. Point out the map on page 2, the *Did You Know?* box on page 3, and the *Extend Language* features on pages 6 and 10.

Preteach Vocabulary Review the tested vocabulary words that appear in this book: **expanse** and **densest**. Introduce these key words from the book: **climate** (p. 3), **deserts** (p. 3), **storms** (p. 5), and **mountains** (p. 11). Discuss these words and add them to a Word Wall.

READ THE BOOK

Choose among these options for reading to support students at all English proficiency levels.

Read Aloud Read the book aloud as students follow along. Pause to verify comprehension and to explain unfamiliar concepts.

Monitored Reading Have students take turns reading one page of the book aloud. Use the following questions to support comprehension:

- **Pages 2–5** What are oases? (ponds in the middle of a desert)
- **Pages 6–8** What is another name for the African grasslands? (savannahs)
- **Pages 9–11** What two tall mountains are located in Africa? (Mount Kilimanjaro and Mount Kenya)

Reread Have students reread the book with a partner, in small groups, or independently. Have them complete the Study Guide on page 257.

RESPOND

Answers to the Reader's Inside Back Cover:

Talk About It
1. deserts, grasslands, rain forests, and mountains
2. *deserts:* jerboas, fennec foxes, camels; *grasslands:* elephants, rhinos, hippos, ostriches, hyenas, lions, cheetahs; *rain forests:* chimpanzees, leopards, frogs, bees, birds, monkeys; *mountains:* mountain goats, mountain gorillas (Classify)

Write About It
3. Answers will vary.
Support writers at various English proficiency levels.
Beginning Let students work in pairs or small groups to complete their webs. Assign each pair or group a climate region.
Intermediate Have students look through the book to find the information they need to complete their webs.
Advanced After completing their webs, have students write a short paragraph telling why they would or would not like to visit the region they wrote about.

Extend Language Humans eat chicken, beef, fish, lamb, goat, pork, and other kinds of meat. They eat leafy vegetables, such as lettuce and kale. They eat roots, such as carrots and potatoes. They eat fruits, nuts, and seeds. They eat grains such as wheat and rice.

Answers to page 257:
camel, desert
elephant, grasslands
leopard, rain forest
snake, rain forest
mountain gorilla, mountains

Family Link Read aloud the Family Link activity on page 257 before sending copies of the Study Guide home with students. Later, have students share their families' experiences with climate regions and African animals.

- **Read** *African Climates and Animals* again.
- **Look** at the drawings below. Next to each one, **write** the name of the animal and the region where it lives.

	Name of animal: _____ Climate region: _____
	Name of animal: _____ Climate region: _____
	Name of animal: _____ Climate region: _____
	Name of animal: _____ Climate region: _____
	Name of animal: _____ Climate region: _____

Family Link

Ask family members if they have ever visited climate regions such as the ones described in the book. Find out if they have seen any of the animals mentioned. Make a list of the regions they have visited and animals they have seen, in the wild or in a zoo.

The History of Metals

by Benjamin Joseph Howard

ELL Reader 6.5.4   Nonfiction

INTRODUCE THE BOOK

Activate Prior Knowledge/Build Background Read the title, and show the cover photo. Ask students what kinds of metal they see in the classroom. Ask them to tell you some of the things that metal can be used for.

Preview/Use Text Features Preview the reader by talking about the photographs together and reading the captions. Point out the *Extend Language* feature on page 3.

Preteach Vocabulary Review the tested vocabulary words that appear in this book: **characteristics**, **corrode**, and **extract**. Introduce these key words from the book: **metal** (p. 2), **steel** (p. 3), **gold** (p. 4), and **silver** (p. 6). Discuss these words and add them to a Word Wall.

READ THE BOOK

Choose among these options for reading to support students at all English proficiency levels.

Read Aloud Read the book aloud as students follow along. Pause to verify comprehension and to explain unfamiliar concepts.

Monitored Reading Have students silently read a few pages at a time. Use the following questions to support comprehension:
- **Pages 2–3** Where do most metals come from? (from rocks underground)
- **Pages 4–8** What metal is reddish brown? (copper)
- **Pages 9–12** Why is steel a more useful metal than iron? (It is lighter and stronger.)

Reread Have students reread the book with a partner, in small groups, or independently. Have them complete the Study Guide on page 259.

RESPOND

Answers to the Reader's Inside Back Cover:

Talk About It
1. Possible answers: *gold:* coins, jewelry, headdresses, household decorations; *silver:* jewelry, household decorations, coins; *copper:* jewelry, spoons, knives, weapons; *bronze:* weapons, artwork, buildings; *iron:* tools and weapons; *steel:* weapons, pots and pans (Main Idea and Details)
2. Possible answers: *gold:* jewelry, household decorations, microchips, astronaut helmets; *silver:* jewelry, household decorations, medicines; *copper:* plumbing pipes, electrical wires, coins; *aluminum:* soda cans, roofs, foil, bicycle frames; *bronze:* decorations, coins, statues; *steel:* plows, pots and pans, railroads, trains, skyscrapers, bridges, parts for cars (Main Idea and Details)

Write About It
3. Answers will vary but could include the invention of household appliances, such as refrigerators and toasters, and the jobs created in producing them. (Generalize)
Support writers at various English proficiency levels.

> **Beginning** Allow students to write or dictate their answers in the home language and draw a picture to illustrate what they have written.
> **Intermediate** Have students tell partners what they want to say before writing it down.
> **Advanced** Have students respond with at least six sentences.

Extend Language Examples include *heated, valued, used, learned.*

Answers to page 259:
gold: headdresses, computer microchips, astronaut helmets
silver: medicines
both: jewelry, household decorations, coins

Family Link Read aloud the Family Link activity on page 259 before sending copies of the Study Guide home with students. Later, have students discuss the metals they found at home.

- **Read** *The History of Metals* again.
- **Complete** the graphic organizer below. In the left-hand circle, **write** the ways only gold is used. In the right-hand circle, **write** the ways only silver is used. In the middle section, **write** the ways both gold and silver are used.

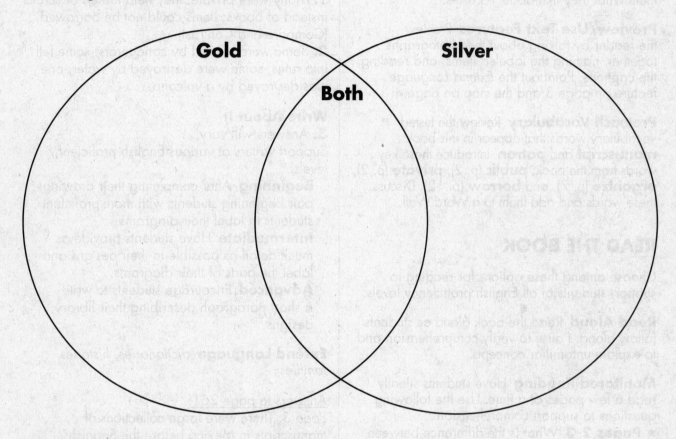

Family Link

Ask family members to help you find ways metal is used around your home. Make a list of the different objects you find that are made of metal.

Ancient Libraries

by Joelle Laliberté

ELL Reader 6.5.5   Expository Nonfiction

INTRODUCE THE BOOK

Activate Prior Knowledge/Build Background Read the title, and ask students if they have visited a library outside of school. Ask them what they like about libraries.

Preview/Use Text Features Preview the reader by talking about the photographs together, naming the labeled items, and reading the captions. Point out the *Extend Language* feature on page 3 and the map on page 4.

Preteach Vocabulary Review the tested vocabulary words that appear in this book: **manuscript** and **patron**. Introduce these key words from the book: **public** (p. 2), **private** (p. 2), **organize** (p. 7), and **borrow** (p. 12). Discuss these words and add them to a Word Wall.

READ THE BOOK

Choose among these options for reading to support students at all English proficiency levels.

Read Aloud Read the book aloud as students follow along. Pause to verify comprehension and to explain unfamiliar concepts.

Monitored Reading Have students silently read a few pages at a time. Use the following questions to support comprehension:

- **Pages 2–3** What is the difference between a public library and a private library? (Public libraries are open to everyone; a private library belongs to a person, family, or group of people.)
- **Pages 4–7** What did people read in the first known library? (clay tablets that were organized by subjects such as history, science, poetry; bilingual dictionaries)
- **Pages 8–11** Why was it hard to get books in ancient times? (There were no printing presses, so each book had to be copied by hand.)
- **Page 12** What are some of the things you can borrow from a public library today? (books, tapes, CDs, DVDs)

Reread Have students reread the book with a partner, in small groups, or independently. Have them complete the Study Guide on page 261.

RESPOND

Answers to the Reader's Inside Back Cover:

Talk About It
1. Many were private; they held tablets or scrolls instead of books; items could not be borrowed. (Compare and Contrast)
2. Some were burned by conquerors; some fell into ruins; some were destroyed by water; one was destroyed by a volcano.

Write About It
3. Answers will vary.
Support writers at various English proficiency levels.

    Beginning After completing their drawings, pair beginning students with more-proficient students to label their diagrams.
    Intermediate Have students provide as much detail as possible in their designs and label the parts of their diagrams.
    Advanced Encourage students to write a short paragraph describing their library designs.

Extend Language *dictionaries, histories, families*

Answers to page 261:
Page 3: There were large collections of manuscripts in Mexico before the Spanish conquest.
Pages 4–5: The first known library was in Assyria.
Pages 6–7: There were many private libraries in ancient Greece.
Page 8: The first public library was built in Alexandria.
Page 9: There were many private libraries in Rome.
Pages 10–11: Caeser's library and the Palatine Library were two public libraries in Rome.

Family Link Read aloud the Family Link activity on page 261 before sending copies of the Study Guide home with students. Later, have students discuss how libraries have changed since their family members were young.

- **Read** *Ancient Libraries* again.
- Use the information in the book to **complete** the web below.

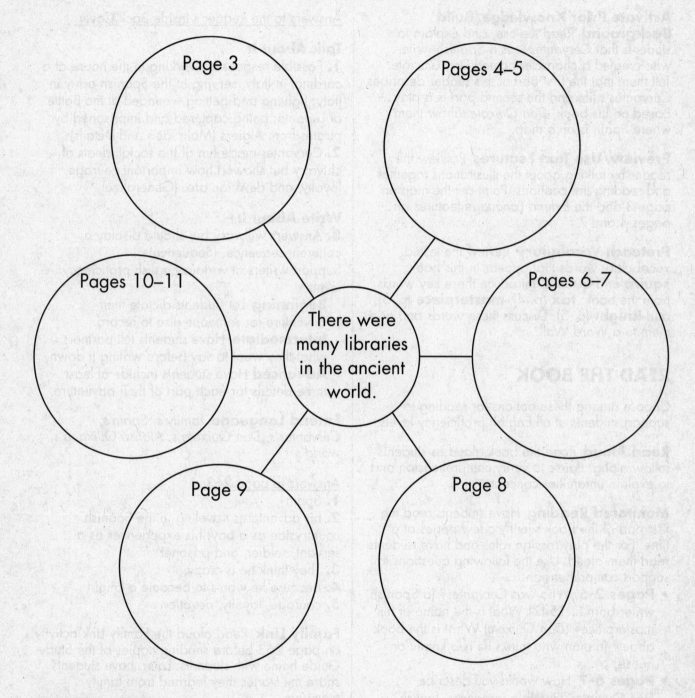

Page 3

Pages 4–5

Pages 10–11

There were many libraries in the ancient world.

Pages 6–7

Page 9

Page 8

Family Link

Ask family members if they like going to the library. Find out if they went to the library when they were your age, and ask them how libraries have changed since they were children.

Cervantes and Don Quixote Two Adventurers

by Susana Brillando   ELL Reader 6.6.1   Nonfiction, Drama

INTRODUCE THE BOOK

Activate Prior Knowledge/Build Background Read the title, and explain to students that Cervantes was a Spanish writer who created a character named Don Quixote. Tell them that the first part of this reader describes Cervantes's life and the second part is a play based on his book, *Don Quixote.* Show them where Spain is on a map.

Preview/Use Text Features Preview the reader by talking about the illustrations together and reading the captions. Point out the map on page 3 and the *Extend Language* features on pages 4 and 7.

Preteach Vocabulary Review the tested vocabulary words that appear in this book: **squire** and **quests**. Introduce these key words from the book: **tax** (p. 4), **masterpiece** (p. 5), and **knight** (p. 5). Discuss these words and add them to a Word Wall.

READ THE BOOK

Choose among these options for reading to support students at all English proficiency levels.

Read Aloud Read the book aloud as students follow along. Pause to verify comprehension and to explain unfamiliar concepts.

Monitored Reading Have students read the first part of the book silently a few pages at a time. For the play, assign roles and have students read them aloud. Use the following questions to support comprehension:

- **Pages 2–5** Who was Cervantes? (a Spanish writer born in 1547) What is the name of his masterpiece? (*Don Quixote*) What is the book about? (a man who thinks he is a knight on quests)
- **Pages 6–7** How would you describe Don Quixote? (Possible responses: foolish, chivalrous, brave, courteous, loyal)
- **Pages 8–12** Why does Don Quixote want to become a knight? (to fight evil)

Reread Have students reread the book with a partner, in small groups, or independently. Have them complete the Study Guide on page 263.

RESPOND

Answers to the Reader's Inside Back Cover:

Talk About It
1. Possible responses: working in the house of a cardinal in Italy; serving in the Spanish army in Italy; fighting and getting wounded at the Battle of Lepanto; being captured and imprisoned by pirates from Algiers (Main Idea and Details)
2. Cervantes made fun of the social ideals of chivalry but showed how important courage, loyalty, and devotion are. (Generalize)

Write About It
3. Answers will vary but should display a coherent sequence. (Sequence)
Support writers at various English proficiency levels.
   Beginning Let students dictate their adventure for someone else to record.
   Intermediate Have students tell partners what they want to say before writing it down.
   Advanced Have students include at least three details for each part of their adventure.

Extend Language *family's, Spain's, Cervantes's, Don Quixote's, Alonso Quixana's, world's*

Answers to page 263:
1. Spain
2. his adventures traveling in the Spanish countryside as a boy; his experiences as a servant, soldier, and prisoner
3. They think he is crazy.
4. because he wants to become a knight
5. courage, loyalty, devotion

Family Link Read aloud the Family Link activity on page 263 before sending copies of the Study Guide home with students. Later, have students share the stories they learned from family members.

Name _____

- **Read** *Cervantes and Don Quixote: Two Adventurers* again.
- Use the book to **answer** the questions below.

Pages	Question	Answer
2–3	**1.** Where and when was Miguel de Cervantes born?	
4–5	**2.** What experiences from his own life did Cervantes use to write *Don Quixote?*	
6–7	**3.** What do other characters in the book think of Don Quixote?	
8–9	**4.** Why does Uncle Alonso want to change his name?	
10–12	**5.** What are some of Don Quixote's good qualities?	

Family Link

Ask family members to share a story about an adventurer that they have read or heard about.

Ancient Cultures and Our Culture

by Elizabeta Lemakos

ELL Reader 6.6.2   Nonfiction

INTRODUCE THE BOOK

Activate Prior Knowledge/Build Background Read the title, and ask students if they have heard of Greece or Rome. Show them where modern Greece and Rome are on a map.

Preview/Use Text Features Preview the reader by talking about the pictures together, naming the labeled items, and reading the captions. Point out the map on page 2, the time lines on pages 3–5, and the *Extend Language* feature on page 8.

Preteach Vocabulary Review the tested vocabulary words that appear in this book: **architecture**, **democracy**, and **empire**. Introduce these key words from the book: **Olympic Games** (p. 2), **trade** (p. 3), and **influence** (p. 9). Discuss these words and add them to a Word Wall.

READ THE BOOK

Choose among these options for reading to support students at all English proficiency levels.

Read Aloud Read the book aloud as students follow along. Pause to verify comprehension and to explain unfamiliar concepts.

Monitored Reading Have students take turns reading aloud. Use the following questions to support comprehension:

- **Pages 2–5** What kind of governments did the Greek city-states have? (Some were democracies; others were ruled by kings or old people.) What is a republic? (a system in which citizens elect officials to represent them)
- **Pages 6–7** What sporting events were included in the first Olympic Games? (chariot racing, javelin throw, wrestling, running, discus, long jump)
- **Pages 8–9** What are some features of Greek architecture? (white columns; high-pointed roofs; carved decorations) What are some features of Roman architecture? (cement, bricks, arches)
- **Pages 10–12** How is the system of government in the United States related to the governments of ancient Greece and

ancient Rome? (It is a combination of a Greek democracy and a Roman republic.)

Reread Have students reread the book with a partner, in small groups, or independently. Have them complete the Study Guide on page 265.

RESPOND

Answers to the Reader's Inside Back Cover:

Talk About It
1. columns; arches; high, pointed roofs (Generalize)
2. In a democracy, all citizens vote on laws. In a republic, citizens elect representatives who make laws for them. (Compare and Contrast)

Write About It
3. Answers will vary but could include: Ancient Greece→early Olympic Games→modern Olympic Games; Ancient Rome→overthrow of king→republic
Support writers at various English proficiency levels.

> **Beginning** Pair students with more-proficient speakers to complete their graphic organizers.
> **Intermediate** Have students brainstorm a list of words they can use when writing about the influence of Greece and Rome on modern culture.
> **Advanced** Have students use their graphic organizers to write a short paragraph telling how one of the ancient cultures influenced aspects of our culture today.

Extend Language *the study of the mind;* Invite students to give other examples of words ending in *-logy*, such as *geology* and *anthropology*.

Answers to page 265:
Answers will vary but could include any of the dates from the time lines on pages 3–5.

Family Link Read aloud the Family Link activity on page 265 before sending copies of the Study Guide home with students. Later, invite students to share what family members say about the Olympic Games.

- **Read** *Ancient Cultures and Our Culture* again.
- Find four important dates in the history of ancient Greece and four important dates in the history of ancient Rome. **Write** the dates and what happened above or below the time line. One has been done for you.
- Next to some of these dates, **draw** pictures to show something about the culture at the time.

Ancient Greece

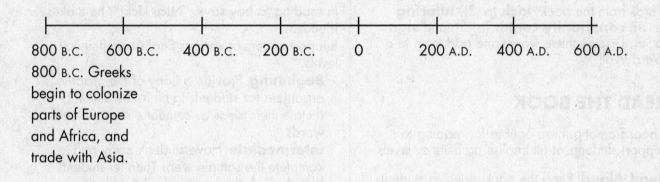

800 B.C.   600 B.C.   400 B.C.   200 B.C.   0   200 A.D.   400 A.D.   600 A.D.

800 B.C. Greeks begin to colonize parts of Europe and Africa, and trade with Asia.

Ancient Rome

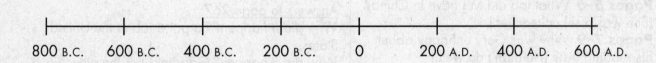

800 B.C.   600 B.C.   400 B.C.   200 B.C.   0   200 A.D.   400 A.D.   600 A.D.

Family Link

Does your family enjoy watching the Olympic Games? Find out what your family members' favorite Olympic sports are.

The Homework Club

by Siu Lee

ELL Reader 6.6.3   Realistic Fiction

INTRODUCE THE BOOK

Activate Prior Knowledge/Build Background Read the title. Ask students if they ever get help with their homework. Ask them if they would enjoy helping another student with a subject that they are good at.

Preview/Use Text Features Preview the reader by talking about the illustrations together and naming the labeled objects. Point out the *Extend Language* features on pages 2 and 6.

Preteach Vocabulary Review the tested vocabulary words that appear in this book: **progress** and **disgraced**. Introduce these key words from the book: **kick** (p. 2), **tutoring** (p. 5), **community center** (p. 5), and **sign** (p. 8). Discuss these words and add them to a Word Wall.

READ THE BOOK

Choose among these options for reading to support students at all English proficiency levels.

Read Aloud Read the book aloud as students follow along. Pause to verify comprehension and to explain unfamiliar concepts.

Monitored Reading Have students take turns reading aloud. Use the following questions to support comprehension:
- **Pages 2–4** Why does Gary do his math homework first? (because math is easy for him)
- **Pages 5–6** What job did Ma have in China? (She was a schoolteacher.)
- **Pages 7–9** Why was Gary unhappy about his reading test? (He didn't do well.)
- **Pages 10–12** How does Gary feel at the end of the book? (He feels better about his reading, happy that his classmates like his mom, and hopeful about his life in the United States.)

Reread Have students reread the book with a partner, in small groups, or independently. Have them complete the Study Guide on page 267.

RESPOND

Answers to the Reader's Inside Back Cover:

Talk About It
1. They try to solve problems with their schoolwork.
2. Gary and Mei will improve in reading. Gary's classmates will improve in math and reading. (Draw Conclusions)

Write About It
3. Possible answers: He gets help with his reading; his classmates think his mother is cool; he realizes even the American kids need help in reading; a boy says, "Nice kick!"; he makes friends.
Support writers at various English proficiency levels.

> **Beginning** Provide a copy of the graphic organizer for students to fill in. Let students dictate their ideas as someone records their words.
> **Intermediate** Have students copy and complete the sample web. Then let students look through the book to find details they can use to complete their webs.
> **Advanced** After completing their webs, have students write a short paragraph explaining how Gary changes in the story.

Extend Language *Hopeless* means without hope. *Hopeful* means full of hope.

Answers to page 267:
Why did it happen? Pa got a job in the United States.
Why did it happen? Gary told her the other children didn't understand the lessons.
Why did it happen? Gary got a low score on his reading test.

Family Link Read aloud the Family Link activity on page 267 before sending copies of the Study Guide home with students. Later, have students share their families' experiences with teaching and learning from others.

- **Read** *The Homework Club* again.
- Use the information in the book to **find out** the cause of each of the effects described below. **Write** the correct cause for each effect.

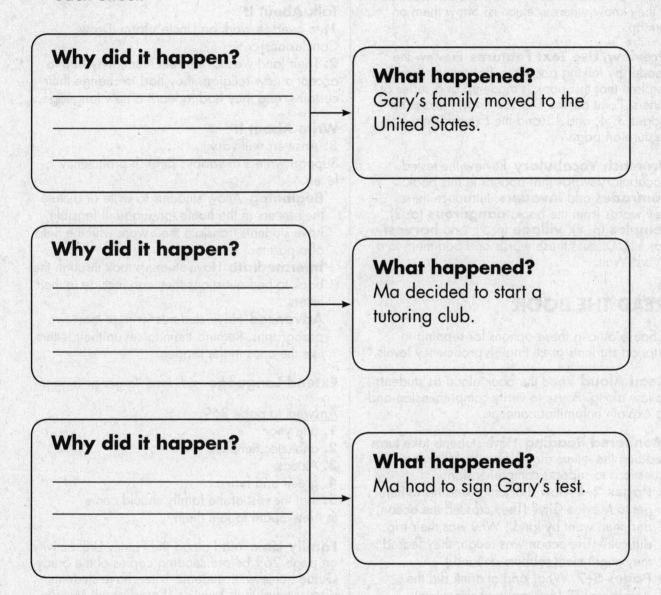

Why did it happen?

_____

_____

_____

What happened?
Gary's family moved to the United States.

Why did it happen?

_____

_____

_____

What happened?
Ma decided to start a tutoring club.

Why did it happen?

_____

_____

_____

What happened?
Ma had to sign Gary's test.

Family Link
Ask family members to tell you about things they have taught others. Find out if they liked sharing what they know. Then ask them to tell you about a person in their lives who has taught them something important.

Letters from New Spain

by Alberto Quintanilla

ELL Reader 6.6.4   Fiction

INTRODUCE THE BOOK

Activate Prior Knowledge/Build Background Read the title, and ask students if they know where Mexico is. Show them on a map.

Preview/Use Text Features Preview the reader by talking about the illustrations together. Explain that this book is made up of a series of letters. Point out the *Did You Know?* boxes on pages 3, 4, and 11 and the *Extend Language* feature on page 7.

Preteach Vocabulary Review the tested vocabulary words that appear in this book: **comrades** and **invaders**. Introduce these key words from the book: **dangerous** (p. 2), **temples** (p. 4), **village** (p. 9), and **harvest** (p. 11). Discuss these words and add them to a Word Wall.

READ THE BOOK

Choose among these options for reading to support students at all English proficiency levels.

Read Aloud Read the book aloud as students follow along. Pause to verify comprehension and to explain unfamiliar concepts.

Monitored Reading Have students take turns reading the letters aloud. Use the following questions to support comprehension:
- **Pages 2–4** How did Tomás and his father get to Mexico City? (They crossed the ocean, and then went by land.) Why was their trip difficult? (The ocean was rough; they feared they might meet robbers on land.)
- **Pages 5–7** What kind of drink did the Aztecs make? (one made of chocolate)
- **Pages 8–12** What kind of fruit were the men harvesting? (tomatoes)

Reread Have students reread the book with a partner, in small groups, or independently. Have them complete the Study Guide on page 269.

RESPOND

Answers to the Reader's Inside Back Cover:

Talk About It
1. to oversee work on Uncle's farm (Draw Conclusions)
2. Their land was taken from them, they had to accept a new religion, they had to change their customs, and they had to learn a new language.

Write About It
3. Answers will vary.
Support writers at various English proficiency levels.
   Beginning Allow students to write or dictate their letters in the home language. If feasible, have students translate their work with the help of a partner.
   Intermediate Have students look through the book to find questions they can include in their letters.
   Advanced Have students write at least two paragraphs. Remind them to set up their letters like the ones in the reader.

Extend Language *old, lose, larger* or *bigger*

Answers to page 269:
1. one year
2. an Aztec temple
3. Aztecs
4. green and fertile
5. that the rest of the family should come to New Spain to join them

Family Link Read aloud the Family Link activity on page 269 before sending copies of the Study Guide home with students. Later, have students discuss what their families shared about Mexico and the Aztecs.

Name _____

- **Read** *Letters from New Spain* again.
- Use the book to **answer** the questions.

Page	Question	Answer
2	**1.** How long does it take for a letter to get from Mexico City to Spain?	
4	**2.** What kind of building was being torn down near Uncle's house?	
7	**3.** Who will work the land at Tomás's farm?	
8	**4.** What is the land like at *Tres Rios*?	
12	**5.** What is the important message that Tomás and his father send to Spain?	

Family Link

Ask family members what they know about Mexico and the Aztecs.
Find out if they have ever visited or seen pictures of any Aztec ruins.

Moving North

by Liza Jones

INTRODUCE THE BOOK

Activate Prior Knowledge/Build Background Read the title, and look at the picture on the cover. Tell students that this is a story about a girl who moves to a big and unfamiliar city with her family.

Preview/Use Text Features Preview the reader by talking about the illustrations together. Explain that this story is told through a girl's diary entries. Point out the map on page 2 and the *Did You Know?* box on page 9.

Preteach Vocabulary Review the tested vocabulary words that appear in this book: **burden**, **sufficient**, and **urban**. Introduce these key words from the book: **moving** (p. 2), **cotton** (p. 3), **apartment** (p. 7), and **blocks** (p. 9). Discuss these words and add them to a Word Wall.

READ THE BOOK

Choose among these options for reading to support students at all English proficiency levels.

Read Aloud Read the book aloud as students follow along. Pause to verify comprehension and to explain unfamiliar concepts.

Monitored Reading Have students take turns reading diary entries aloud. Use the following questions to support comprehension:

- **Pages 2–3** Where does Ellie live at the beginning of the story? (on a farm in Mississippi)
- **Pages 4–5** Why does Ellie's family move to the North? (so Mama and Papa can find better jobs and the children can get a better education)
- **Pages 6–9** Why is it hard for Ellie's family to find an apartment? (Many other people are also looking for apartments.)
- **Pages 10–12** What is the best thing that happens to Ellie on her first day of school? (She makes a friend.)

Reread Have students reread the book with a partner, in small groups, or independently. Have them complete the Study Guide on page 271.

RESPOND

Answers to the Reader's Inside Back Cover:

Talk About It

1. She doesn't want to leave her friends. She doesn't want to wear shoes every day. She doesn't want to play in fenced-in parks. She doesn't like cold weather. She doesn't want to live in a city. (Main Idea and Details)

2. The train station looks like a palace. There are crowds of people from all over the world. The people are "fancy" because they wear suits and hats, scarves, and shiny tops. (Compare and Contrast)

Write About It

3. Diary entries will vary but should include a date and location. They should begin with *Dear Diary,* and end with a signature.

Support writers at various English proficiency levels.

Beginning Show students how to set up a diary entry. Provide the skeleton of a diary entry for students to complete.

Intermediate Have students include at least three sentences in their diary entries.

Advanced Have students include at least two paragraphs in their diary entries.

Extend Language Answers will vary.

Answers to page 271:

Why does it happen? Ellie's parents want to find better jobs.
Why does it happen? They spend days looking.
Why does it happen? She goes to school, makes friends, and learns about the city.

Family Link Read aloud the Family Link activity on page 271 before sending copies of the Study Guide home with students. Later, have students share their families' experiences settling in to a new place.

- **Read** *Moving North* again.
- **Use** the book to find the cause for each of the effects shown.
  Write the correct cause for each effect.

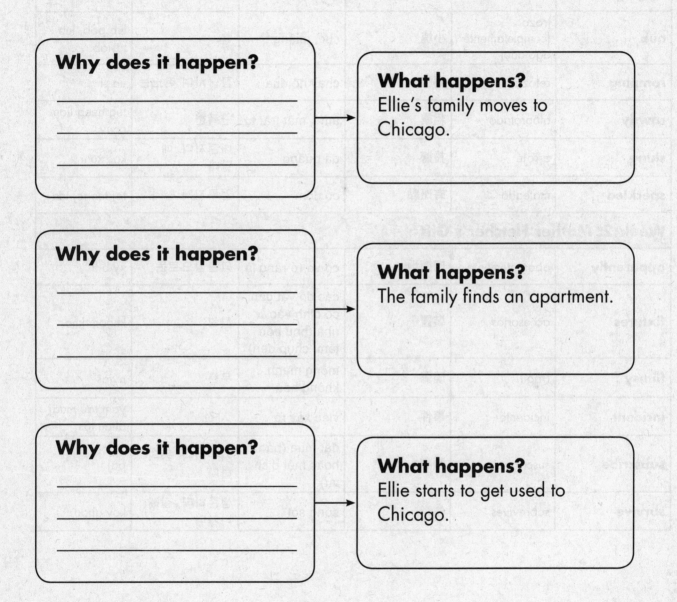

Why does it happen?
_____
_____
_____

What happens?
Ellie's family moves to Chicago.

Why does it happen?
_____
_____
_____

What happens?
The family finds an apartment.

Why does it happen?
_____
_____
_____

What happens?
Ellie starts to get used to Chicago.

Family Link

Talk to your family members about their experiences settling in a new place. Ask them how they found a place to live. Then ask them if they prefer life in a big city or life in the country.

Multilingual Lesson Vocabulary
Unit 1

English	Spanish	Chinese	Vietnamese	Korean	Hmong
Week 1: Old Yeller					
lunging	embestir	刺	lao đến	돌진하는	nphau
nub	trozo (completamente agotado)	小塊	cục, miếng	혹	lub pob, lub ntsiab
romping	retozando	嬉戲	chạy nô đùa	장난치며 뛰노는	ua si
rowdy	alborotado	粗暴	ầm ĩ, mất trật tự	난폭한	tug neeg liam txwv
slung	arrojé	投擲	đã quăng	내던지다, 매달다	kas xum
speckled	moteada	有斑點	có đốm	얼룩지게 하다	tej tee tej tee
Week 2: Mother Fletcher's Gift					
apparently	aparentemente	明顯地	có vẻ rõ ràng là	외관상으로는	xwb li
fixtures	accesorios	裝置	các đồ vật gắn cố định vào nhà (như bồn tắm, chụp đèn)	시설	khoom kho
flimsy	frágil	脆弱	mỏng manh, không bền	무른	nyias
incident	incidente	事件	việc xảy ra	사건	yam tau muaj dhau los
subscribe	suscribir	預訂	đặt mua (báo hoặc một dịch vụ)	기부하다, 동의 하다	paj
survive	sobrevives	生存	sống sót	생존하다, 잘해 나가다	kov dhau

English	Spanish	Chinese	Vietnamese	Korean	Hmong
Week 3: Viva New Jersey					
corridors	pasillos	走廊	hành lang	복도	txoj kev hauv tsev
destination	destino	目的地	nơi đến	목적지	hom phiaj
groping	agarrando a tientas	摸索	dò dẫm	망설이는, 손으로 더듬는	maub, xuas
menacing	amenazador	邪惡	đe dọa	협박하는, 으르는	hawv
mongrel	perro callejero	雜種	chó lai	잡종의	dev liam txwv
persisted	persistió	堅持	khăng khăng	고집하다	rau siab, mob siab
pleas	súplicas	請求	lời khẩn xin, yêu cầu	구실, 변명	thov
Week 4: Saving the Rain Forests					
basin	cuenca	盆地	lưu vực	연못	thaj av cug dej uas dej ntws los rau
charities	organizaciones benéficas	慈善事業	các hội từ thiện	자선	kev siab hlub
equator	ecuador	赤道	xích đạo	적도	txoj kab hauv nruab nrab ntawm lub ntiaj teb
erosion	erosión	侵蝕	sự ăn mòn	부식	av pob
evaporates	evapora	蒸發	bốc hơi	증발하다	yaj
exported	exportados	輸出	xuất khẩu	수출하다	xa ntawm
industrial	industrial	工業	về kỹ nghệ	산업의	tsev ua hauj lwm
recycled	reciclada	回收	tái chế biến	재활용하다	rov nchuav dua tshiab
tropics	trópico	熱帶	vùng nhiệt đới	열대 지방	chaw tshav ntuj kub tshaj nyob rau ntiaj teb, nyob nruab nrab ntawm ob txoj kab uas lub hnub khiav cig

English	Spanish	Chinese	Vietnamese	Korean	Hmong
Week 5: When Crowbar Came					
aggressive	agresiva	進取	hung hăng	공격적인	txheeb heev
detect	detectar	查出	nhận ra	찾아내다	nrhiav tau
dubiously	dudosamente	半信半疑	một cách đáng nghi ngờ	수상하게	tsis paub meej, tsis paub tseeb
frustration	frustración	挫折	sự bực tức	좌절	npau ntaws
imprinted	dejar huella	印記	đã in vào	영향을 주다, 누르다	sau, kos
materialize	aparecer	實現	thành hiện thực	나타나다, 실현하다	ua tseeb
migration	migración	遷移	sự di cư	이동	tsiv tawm
secretive	reservados	遮遮掩掩的	thích giữ bí mật	숨기는	zais (siab)
tolerated	tolerado	容忍	đã chịu đựng	용인하다, 참다	nyiaj

Unit 2

English	Spanish	Chinese	Vietnamese	Korean	Hmong
Week 1: The Universe					
astronomer	astrónomo	天文學家	nhà thiên văn	천문학자	tus neeg mus saum qaum ntuj
collapse	colapsa	崩潰	sụp đổ	무너지다	vau
collide	chocan	碰撞	va vào nhau	충돌하다	sib tsoo
compact	compacto	緊湊的	kết chặt, đặc	촘촘한	tsoo
galaxy	galaxia	星系	ngân hà	은하	cov hnub qub nyob saum qaum ntuj
particle	partícula	微粒	các phân tử	입자	ib yam khoom me me
Week 2: Dinosaur Ghosts: The Mystery of Coelophysis					
fragile	frágiles	易碎	dễ vỡ	깨지기 쉬운	nkig
poisonous	venenosos	有毒的	có chất độc	유독한	muaj taug
prey	presa	犧牲品	con mồi	먹이	tus tsiaj uas lwm tus tsiaj tom tau
specimens	especímenes	標本	các mẫu	견본	ib yam khoom sawv ces rau
sluggish	soñolientos	反應緩慢的	chậm chạp	게으른, 느린	maj mam txav
treacherous	peligroso	詭譎	nguy hiểm, xảo trá	믿을 수 없는	tsis ncaj nees
volcanic	volcánica	火山	về núi lửa	화산의	roob hluav taws
Week 3: A Week in the 1800s					
counselor	consejera	顧問	người cố vấn	지도원	tus pab cuas
identity	identidad	身分	nhân dạng	개성	tus chwj pwm, tus yeeb yam
physical	físico	物理	về thể chất	육체의	ntawm sab cev nqaij daim tawv
surplus	excedente	剩餘	dư thừa	여분의	khoom tshaj
technology	tecnología	技術	kỹ thuật	과학 기술	txuj ci

© Scott Foresman 6

English	Spanish	Chinese	Vietnamese	Korean	Hmong
Week 4: Good-bye to the Moon					
combustion	combustión	燃燒	sự cháy	연소	tawg
dingy	deslucidos	灰溜溜	trông bẩn thỉu	거무스레한, 우중충한	vwm
lunar	lunar	登月	về mặt trăng	달의	lub hli
negotiate	negociar	談判	thương lượng	협상하다	si hais kom los haum
traversed	atravesaba	攀登	đã đi ngang qua	통과하다	mus dhau
waft	aroma	飄動	mùi thoang thoảng	(공중을) 떠돌다	yuj
waning	menguando	減少	đang khuyết dần	(달이) 이운, 작아지는	poob zuj zus
Week 5: Egypt					
abundant	abundantes	豐富	dư dật	풍부한	ntau ntau
artifacts	artefactos	人工製品	các đồ vật do người thời xưa làm ra	공예품	khoom puav pheej
decrees	decretos	法令	các sắc lệnh, chiếu chỉ	법령	txoj cai
eternity	eternidad	永恆	cõi vĩnh hằng	영원	tag ib ntxhim
immortal	inmortales	不朽	bất tử	죽지 않는	dab, tsis tsawj tuag
receded	retrocedían	後退	đã thưa thớt	멀어진, 희미해진, 떨어진	thim
reigned	reinaron	統治	đã thống trị	통치하다	kav

Unit 3

English	Spanish	Chinese	Vietnamese	Korean	Hmong
Week 1: Hatchet					
hatchet	hacha	斧頭	cây rìu	손도끼	rab taus me
ignite	encender	點燃	bốc lửa	불을 붙이다	cig
painstaking	esmerado	刻苦	làm kỹ lưỡng cẩn thận	애쓰는	mob siab
quill	púa	羽毛管	chiếc lông	깃대	tus plaub qaib
registered	se registraran	登記	đã nhớ ra	기록하다	tso npe
smoldered	humearon	悶燒	đã cháy âm ỉ	연기나다	ncho pa
stiffened	(se) entumeció	僵住	bị cứng	굳어진, (바람 따 위가) 세진	txhav
Week 2: When Marian Sang					
application	solicitud	應用	đơn xin	신청, 지원	application
dramatic	dramático	戲劇的	gây ấn tượng mạnh	극적인	tej yam loj
enraged	enfurecidos	觸怒	đã nổi giận	화나게 하다	npau taws
formal	formal	正式	trịnh trọng, theo nghi thức	격식을 차린, 공 식의	raws li txoj cai
momentous	de suma importancia	重大	rất quan trọng	중요한	ib yam tseem ceeb
opera	ópera	歌劇	nhạc opera	오페라	hu nkauj opera
prejudice	los prejuicios	偏見	thành kiến	편견	txoj kev ntxub
privileged	privilegiado	特許	có đặc quyền	특권이 있는	muaj hmoo
recital	recital	吟誦	buổi biểu diễn	독주회, 연주회	hu nkauj
Week 3: Learning to Swim					
customary	habitual	習慣	theo thông lệ	습관적인	raws li siv los
emphasized	enfatizaba	強調	đã nhấn mạnh	강조하다	hais qhia
frantic	frenéticos	狂熱	sợ hãi cuống cuồng	열광하는	txhawj

English	Spanish	Chinese	Vietnamese	Korean	Hmong
stunned	estupefactos	震驚	bị sửng sốt	깜짝 놀란	ceeb
treaded	se mantenían a flote	踩	đã đi, đã bơi đứng	밟은, 지나가는	taug kev

Week 4: Juan Verdades: The Man Who Couldn't Tell a Lie

English	Spanish	Chinese	Vietnamese	Korean	Hmong
confidently	con seguridad	確信地	một cách tin tưởng	자신 있게	muaj peev xwm
dismounted	desmontó	卸下	đã xuống ngựa	내리다	nqis (tsheb)
distressed	angustiado	痛苦的	bị lo buồn	고민하는	nyuaj siab
flourish	crecer con vigor	茂盛	phát đạt	번영하다	tawg paj txi txiv
fulfill	satisfacer	履行	hoàn thành	이행하다	puv npo
permission	permiso	允許	sự cho phép	허가	tso cia
repay	reembolsar	回報	trả lại	돈을 갚다	them rov qab
vigorously	vigorosamente	蒼勁地	một cách sôi nổi	힘차게	siv zog

Week 5: Elizabeth Blackwell: Medical Pioneer

English	Spanish	Chinese	Vietnamese	Korean	Hmong
absurd	absurda	荒謬	buồn cười	불합리한	coj los
behalf	a favor de (de recomendación)	代表	nhân danh, thay mặt	편, 지지	sawv cev
candidate	candidato	候選人	thí sinh	후보자	tus raug xaiv
dean	decano	教務長	trưởng khoa	학장	tus thawj coj nyob tom tsev kawm ntawv
delirious	loca (de alegría)	神智不清	mê sảng	열광적인	zoo siab
diploma	diploma	文憑	bằng cấp	졸업장	ntawv pov thawj kawm tiav
hovers	ronda	翱翔	ở quanh quẩn	서성거리다, 주저하다	yuj ze
obedient	obediente	服從	vâng lời	순응하는	mloog lus
reject	rechazar	拒絕	từ chối	거절하다	tsis txais tos, tsis yuav

Unit 4

English	Spanish	Chinese	Vietnamese	Korean	Hmong
Week 1: Into the Ice					
conquer	conquistar	征服	chinh phục	정복하다	txeeb yeej
destiny	destino	命運	vận mệnh	운명	txoj hmoov
expedition	expedición	遠征	cuộc thám hiểm	탐험	txoj hauv kev
insulated	aislados	絕緣	được cách nhiệt	격리된	nyob twj cuab
isolation	aislamiento	隔離	sự cô lập	고립	nyob ib leeg twm zeej, twj cuab
navigator	navegador	導航員	người lái tàu	탐험가	tus nrhiav kev
verify	verificar	核實	chứng thực	입증하다	kuaj
Week 2: The Chimpanzees I Love					
captive	cautivos	俘虜	bị giam cầm	감금된	raug ntes cia
companionship	compañía	陪伴	tình bạn đồng hành	친구 사이	khub
existence	existencia	存在	sự hiện hữu	존재	muaj (ib zaug)
ordeal	difícil experiencia	考驗	sự thử thách	호된 시련	nyuaj siab
primitive	primitiva	原始	nguyên thủy, thô sơ	원시의	caij ntxov ntxov
sanctuaries	santuarios	聖所	nơi bảo vệ	신성한 곳	ib qhov chaw dawb huv
stimulating	estimulantes	刺激	kích thích	격려가 되는	zoo nyob
Week 3: Black Frontiers					
bondage	esclavitud	奴役	cảnh nô lệ	속박, 노예 신분	raug ua qhev
commissioned	comisionados	委任	được đặt làm	권한을 주다	muaj xiv, muaj cai
earthen	de tierra	土製	bằng đất	흙으로 만든	ua los ntawm av, av ua
encounter	enfrentar	遭遇	đương đầu	마주치다	sib ntsib

English	Spanish	Chinese	Vietnamese	Korean	Hmong
homesteaders	nuevos colonos	擁有農莊的人	những người ở đất do chính phủ cấp	농장 소유자	tsev teb
settlement	asentamiento	居留地	sự định cư	정착	lub zos me

Week 4: Space Cadets

aliens	extraterrestres	外星人	người ở hành tinh khác	외계인	dab saum qaum ntuj
barge	barcaza	駁船	xông, xô mạnh	거룻배	daim ntaub
hospitable	hospitalarios	好客	hiếu khách	환대하는	txais tos
molten	fundido	溶解	nung chảy	용해된	yaj (dej yaj)
ore	mineral	礦石	quặng	광석	pob zeb
refrain	absténgase	制止	kềm chế	삼가다	tswm yus tus kheej
universal	universales	普遍	về vũ trụ	전우주의	thoob nthiaj teb
version	versión	版本	sự thuật lại	변형	yus kev xav, yus kev pom

Week 5: Inventing the Future: A Photobiography of Thomas Alva Edison

converts	convierte	轉化	người đổi sang một điều gì khác	변환시키다	pauv
devise	concebir	構想	sáng chế	고안하다	xav tau
efficiency	eficiencia	效率	sự hiệu quả	능률	ua kom tas sai sai
generated	generaba	引起	đã phát ra	산출하다	ua ntawm
percentage	porcentaje	百分比	tỷ lệ bách phân	백분율	puas xees
proclaimed	proclamaron	宣告	đã tuyên bố	선언하다	lees txais
reproduce	reproducir	再生產	tái tạo	재생하다	rov ua dua
transmitted	transmitía	傳送	đã truyền đi	보내다	xa ntawm

Unit 5

English	Spanish	Chinese	Vietnamese	Korean	Hmong
Week 1: The View from Saturday					
accustomed	acostumbrados	習慣	đã quen	익숙해지다	swm
decline	deterioro	衰落	từ chối	거절하다	tsis lees
former	anterior	前面的	trước đó	이전의	yam dhau los
presence	presencia	存在	sự hiện diện	면전	ziag no
unaccompanied	solo	無伴侶的	không có ai đi cùng	동반하지 않은	tsis muaj khub
Week 2: Harvesting Hope: The Story of Cesar Chavez					
access	acceso	通入	có phương tiện, có cơ hội đến	접근	mus muab tau
authority	autoridad	當局	chính quyền	권위	muaj xiv
lush	exuberante	茂盛的	sum suê	무성한, 번성하는	ntau ntau
obstacle	obstáculo	障礙	chướng ngại vật	장애물	kev nyuaj siab
toll	(había hecho) estragos	損失	thiệt hại	사용료	them choj
torment	tormentos	痛苦	dày vò	괴롭히다	tsim txom
wilt	marchitarse	枯萎	tàn héo	약해지다, 쇠퇴하다	zaus
Week 3: The River That Went to the Sky: A Story from Malawi					
densest	más tupido	最密集	rậm rạp nhất	짙은	tuab tuab
eaves	aleros (techo de árboles)	屋簷	mái hiên	처마	ru tsev uas ntev dhau phab ntsa
expanse	extensión	浩瀚	sự mở rộng	광활한 공간	dav fo, dav heev
moisture	humedad	濕氣	hơi ẩm	습기	noo noo
ventured	aventuraban	冒險	đã đánh liều	위험을 무릅쓰다	ua tej yam txaus ntshai

English	Spanish	Chinese	Vietnamese	Korean	Hmong
Week 4: Gold					
characteristic	característico	典型	đặc tính	특질	zam zuag, chwj pwm
corrode	se corroen	腐蝕	ăn mòn	부식하다	tom hlau
engulfed	sumida	吞噬	đã bao phủ	빨아들이다, 뒤덮다	nyab, nqos
exploit	explotar	開採	bóc lột	개척하다	siv kom tas
extract	extraen	萃取	trích ra	빼내다	tshem tawm
hoard	botín	囤積	tích trữ	저장, 축적	khoom zais tseg cia tau siv yam tom ntej
Week 5: The House of Wisdom					
beacon	faro	烽火台	hải đăng	횃불	daim nqaij npuas nyias nyias
caravans	caravanas	有蓬卡車	đoàn người cùng đi trong sa mạc	여행자 무리	ib pab neeg taug kev tom av suab puam
legacy	legado	遺產	di sản	유물	puav pheej
manuscripts	manuscritos	原稿	các bản thảo	필사본	ntawv sau los ntawm tes
medieval	medieval	中世紀	về thời trung cổ	중세의	puag thaum ub
observatory	observatorio	觀測所	đài thiên văn	관측소, 전망대	lub tsev saib hnub qub
patron	patrón	贊助人	khách hàng, người bảo trợ	후원자	tus fav tuaj

Unit 6

English	Spanish	Chinese	Vietnamese	Korean	Hmong
Week 1: Don Quixote and the Windmills					
lance	lanza	長矛	ngọn giáo	창	ib rab hmuv
misfortune	desventura	不幸	sự không may	불운	tsis muaj hmoo
quests	hazañas	搜尋	các cuộc săn tìm	모험 여행	nrhiav
renewed	renovado	更新	đã tái tân	다시 시작하다, 회복하다	rov pib dua tshiab
renowned	célebre	有名的	lừng danh	유명한	muaj koob nto npe
resound	resonarán	傳頌	vang lên	널리 알려지다, 떨치다	rov nrov dua
squire	escudero	大地主	lính cận vệ	기사의 종자	ib tug txiv neej saib neeg
Week 2: Ancient Greece					
architecture	arquitectura	建築	kiến trúc	건축물	ua vaj ua tsev
democracy	democracia	民主	nền dân chủ	민주주의	kev ywj siab
empire	imperio	帝國	đế quốc	제국	teb chaws loj
ideal	ideal	理想	lý tưởng	이상적인	lub tswv yim
mythology	mitología	神話	thần thoại học	신화	dab neeg
Week 3: The All-American Slurp					
disgraced	deshonramos	恥辱	bị hổ thẹn	비난을 초래하다, 더럽히다	poob ntsej muag
progress	progreso	進展	tiến bộ	진전, 진보	nce ntsiv
promoted	promovido	促進	được lên chức	발전시키다, 장려하다	nce qib
relish	aperitivos	美味	thưởng thức	기호, 흥미	nyiam, qab ros
retreat	retirada	撤退	rút lui	움츠러들다	tim rov qab
revolting	repugnante	反抗	chống lại	불쾌감을 느끼게 하는	ntxeev siab
unison	(al) unísono	一致	đồng thanh	조화	mus ua kev, koom siab

English	Spanish	Chinese	Vietnamese	Korean	Hmong
Week 4: The Aztec News					
benefits	beneficios	好處	các quyền lợi	이득	ntau nqi
campaigns	campañas	競選	các cuộc vận động	(정치적, 사회적)운동	kev sib seem
comrades	camaradas	夥伴	các đồng chí	(같은 정당, 친목 단체 따위의) 당원	phoojywg
enrich	enriquecer	豐富	làm phong phú	부유하게 하다	ua kom nplua nuj ntxiv
foreigners	extranjeros	外國人	người ngoại quốc	외국인	neeg txawv teb chaws
invaders	invasores	侵略者	kẻ xâm lăng	침략자	neeg txeeb teb chaws
Week 5: Where Opportunity Awaits					
burden	carga	負擔	gánh nặng	짐, 부담	teeb meem, kev nyuaj siab
conformed	conformaban	一致	đã tuân theo	따르다	zoo ib yam
leisure	de ocio	休閑	sự nhàn rỗi	여가, 한가한	sij hawm ua si
maintenance	mantenimiento	維護	sự bảo trì	유지	kho
rural	rural	農村	thuộc về vùng quê	시골의	yaj sab
sufficient	suficientes	充足	đủ	충분한	zoo txaus
urban	urbanos	都市	thuộc về đô thị	도시의	hav nroog